CARNEGIE

CARNEGIE

'THE RICHEST MAN IN THE WORLD'

RAYMOND LAMONT-BROWN

SUTTON PUBLISHING

This book was first published in 2005 by
Sutton Publishing Limited · Phoenix Mill
Thrupp · Stroud · Gloucestershire · GL5 2BU

This paperback edition first published in 2006

British Library Cataloguing in Publication Data
A catalogue record for this book is available from the British
Library.

ISBN 0 7509 3371 2

Typeset in 10.5/12.5pt Photina.
Typesetting and origination by
Sutton Publishing Limited.
Printed and bound in Great Britain by
J.H. Haynes & Co. Ltd, Sparkford.

CONTENTS

ACKNOWLEDGEMENTS

This volume has been enhanced by a review of the biographical work done on Andrew Carnegie by three writers in particular. The 'official' biography, *The Life of Andrew Carnegie* (1932), was written by Burton Jesse Hendrick, and remained the key work until the appearance of the biography *Andrew Carnegie* (1970) by Professor Emeritus Joseph Frazier Wall; Wall also wrote a study of Carnegie's Scottish home at *Skibo* (1984). In more recent times Peter Krass's *Carnegie* (2002) has added and expanded biographical research on Carnegie. Funded by Carnegie's daughter Margaret Carnegie Miller, Burton J. Hendrick wrote a biography of Mrs Carnegie, *Louise Whitfield Carnegie* (1950), which was completed after Hendrick's death by Daniel Henderson. In 2000 Linda Thorell Hills, great-granddaughter of Andrew Carnegie, edited the journals of Carnegie's daughter for private circulation. Simon Goodenough produced an important work on Carnegie's trusts and foundations in *The Greatest Good Fortune: Andrew Carnegie's Gift for Today* (1985). To each of these writers I offer my gratitude for a sight of their research.

Much assistance has been given in compiling the book by the following, all of whom receive my indebtedness: Mrs Lorna Owers, Administration Manager, Andrew Carnegie Birthplace Museum; the Earl of Elgin & Kincardine, KT; Mr M. Farmer, Principal, Kilgraston School, Perth; The Carnegie Dunfermline & Hero Fund Trustees, and the Carnegie Trust, both at Dunfermline. Mr Angus McLaren, Club Captain of the Carnegie Club, Skibo, Sutherland, has also rendered important assistance on Carnegie's Scottish 'heaven on earth'. A special thank-you goes to Mr William Thomson, great-grandson of

Andrew Carnegie, for information and advice on the Carnegie family past and present. A particular appreciation is expressed to my wife Dr E. Moira Lamont-Brown, who has acted as companion and helper on my tours of Scotland in search of Carnegie's 'Scottishness'.

Illustrations: Each is identified *in situ* for ownership. Grateful thanks are offered to Laura Whitton of the Picture Library, National Portrait Gallery, London, for tracing and identifying images.

Copyrights: Every effort has been made to trace the copyright holders of works quoted in the text, although the death of authors and reversion of rights often makes this difficult; however, each quote is sourced in the notes. Thanks for granting permission to quote from their copyright works are due to Peter Krass, Linda Thorell Hills and William Smith of Oxford University Press Inc., New York, on behalf of the Joseph Frazier Wall volumes. In 1986 Northeastern University Press (Houghton Mifflin Co.), Boston, produced a new edition of Andrew Carnegie's autobiography. Carnegie's original publisher – Charles Scribner's Sons – is now a part of Simon & Schuster Trade Division, New York.

CHRONOLOGY

1835 25 November. Andrew Carnegie born at Dunfermline, Fife.

1840 Carnegie begins informal education alongside his cousin Dod with uncle George Lauder.

1843 Carnegie attends Robert Martin's Lancaster School, Rolland Street, Dunfermline.

1847 Father William Carnegie's handloom weaving business fails.

1848 17 May. Carnegies leave for America.
6 July. Arrival at New York and journey to Pittsburgh. Andrew Carnegie begins work as bobbin boy.

1849 Carnegie starts work as messenger at O'Reilly Telegraphs.

1850 Carnegie progresses to telegraph operator.

1853 Carnegie becomes personal telegraph operator and private secretary to Thomas A. Scott, Superintendent of the Western Division of the Pennsylvania Railroad.

1855 2 October. Death of father, William Carnegie.

1856 Carnegie purchases stock in the Adams Express Co.

1858 Carnegie signs deal with the Woodruff Sleeping Car Co.

1859 21 November. Carnegie becomes Superintendent of the Western Division of the Pennsylvania Railroad Co.

1861 12 April. American Civil War breaks out; Carnegie organises railroads and telegraph communications on a war footing.

1862 Carnegie and his mother visit Scotland.

1865 26 April. American Civil War ends.
May. Carnegie departs on 'Grand Tour' of Europe.

1866 Returns to America.

1867 April. Carnegie and others organise Keystone Telegraph

Co. Carnegie and his mother move to St Nicholas Hotel, New York.

1870 1 December. Carnegie, Kloman & Phillips manufacture steel.

1871 Carnegie in Europe.

1872 5 November. New company formed to forge steel.

1875 Trip to Dunfermline.

1878 24 October. Carnegie takes trip around the world aboard SS *Belgic*.

1879 Midsummer, back in America.

1880 Carnegie meets Louise Whitfield.

1881 1 April. Carnegie Bros & Co. Ltd formally established.
1 June. Carnegie makes coach trip through Britain.

1884 Coach trip to Europe.
Breaks engagement with Louise Whitfield.
Invests in London *Echo*, and is re-engaged to Louise.

1885 Trip to Britain.

1886 October. Carnegie gravely ill with typhoid fever.
Death of only brother Tom Carnegie.
10 November. Death of mother, Margaret Carnegie.

1887 22 April. Marriage to Louise Whitfield.
Leases Kilgraston House, near Perth.

1888 Leases Cluny Estate, near Kingussie.

1892 1 July. Foundation of Carnegie Steel Co.

1897 30 March. Birth of Carnegie's only child, Margaret.
Carnegie buys the mansion of Skibo and 22,000 acres of Sutherland.

1899 23 June. Foundation stone laid of new part of Skibo.

1900 Carnegie Co. established.

1901 Carnegie and family tour Mediterranean sites.

1902 Christmas Eve. Carnegie purchases the entire Pittencrieff estate, Dunfermline.

1903 3 August. Creation of Carnegie Dunfermline Trust.

1911 Carnegie Corporation of New York founded.

1919 22 April. Margaret Carnegie marries Roswell Miller.
9 August. Carnegie contracts pneumonia.
11 August. Death of Andrew Carnegie.

PREFACE

THE MAKING OF ANDREW CARNEGIE

It's a God's mercy I was born a Scotchman, for I do not see
how I could ever have been contented to be anything else.
The little dour devil, set in her own ways, and getting them,
too, level-headed and shrewed, with an eye to the main
chance always and yet so lovingly weak, so fond, so led away
by song or story, so easily touched to fine issues, so leal
[faithful], so true. Ah! you suit me, Scotia, and proud am I
that I am your son.

Our Coaching Trip, 1882, p. 152

Andrew Carnegie created more millionaires than anyone
before or since. He sold his business for $480 million and
gave away tens of thousands of dollars every day. Newspapers
even ran prize competitions to gather suggestions on how best
he might spend his money. Today his name remains one of the
most famous in the world, and from New York's Carnegie Hall
to the thousands of libraries he endowed, his memorials in
stone outstrip all comers. Born in poverty, he walked with
kings and statesmen and knew the great and good of his days
from Theodore Roosevelt to Rudyard Kipling, from Mark Twain
to Prime Minister William Ewart Gladstone.

But who was Andrew Carnegie? How did he become rich?
Many books have been written about Andrew Carnegie, but for
many he remains a shadowy figure whose money – he was
dubbed 'the richest man in the world' – masks what he was
really like. He was born into poverty, raised in a small two-
roomed Dunfermline cottage and only went to school for four
years in his life, but he challenged penury and advanced

education through the provision of libraries and colleges as no one before him had done. Carnegie was a complex character; of no religious bent he nevertheless endowed thousands of church organs. He was known as 'the King of Steel', but personally he knew little about its actual manufacture. He had no diplomas in management, but succeeded in having hundreds of people working for him. In truth, he never really worked hard in his adult life: instead he travelled and socialised while others made money for him.

Whence did Andrew Carnegie obtain his golden touch, or his restless energy and sleepless ambition? Who influenced his life the most? This book seeks some answers. He admitted that he received his 'brains' from his domineering mother, and said that one of the driving forces of his life and spectacular career was his devotion to her. He even promised never to marry while she was alive. But the basis of Andrew Carnegie's success rested on more than his mother's character, and we go in search of these other folk and events.

In charting the life of Andrew Carnegie from poor Dunfermline weaver's boy, through telegraph operator, railway developer, iron and steel manufacturer, oil magnate, banker and miscellaneous entrepreneur, we seek the real man behind the name. But he laid many false trails. He could be capitalist and socialist in the same breath, republican and democrat in the same sentence. Was he the true philanthropist that his remarkable trusts would suggest, or the robber baron of leftist academe? Was his promotion of 'self-help' a disguise for his own greed? Was he a naive fool, in self-appointedly pursuing international peace and, as has been pointed out, acting as a blinkered 'ambassador extraordinary' for the rapacious Kaiser Wilhelm II before the First World War? Did his competitive spirit only harm the workers he purported to champion? In looking at Andrew Carnegie's life in new areas, and following different slants and angles, some further answers will be sought. As fellow-Scot Sir James Barrie said in his play *What Every Woman Knows*, 'There are few more impressive sights in the world than a Scotsman on the make.'

ONE

THE TREE OF RADICALISM

A word, a look, an accent, may affect the destiny not only of
individuals, but of nations.

Autobiography, 1920

Pattiesmuir lies on the southern edge of what was the
boundary of the old parishes of Dunfermline and
Inverkeithing in the Kingdom of Fife.[1] Today, as when Andrew
Carnegie's forebears lived there, Pattiesmuir – or 'the hamlet of
the muir' – hardly seems a likely centre of revolutionary
thought. Yet two hundred years ago it seethed with secessionism
and radicalism.[2] Once a part of the lands of the Benedictine
Abbey of Dunfermline, Pattiesmuir fell within the policies of the
Earls of Elgin & Kincardine, and it developed in the lee of the hill
that slopes southward to the Firth of Forth.

Writing in 1793, the Presbyterian minister of Inverkeithing,
Andrew Robertson, commented that the folks hereabouts were in
general 'sober, industrious, and attentive'; he saw them as 'kind and
hospitable' and 'much given to company and entertainments in
each others houses'. They were, said the Revd Robertson, 'united in
the same political sentiments and views', but he regretted that,
'Burgh politics, and the election of members of Parliament, had an
unhappy influence upon the morals of the people'. The minister
greatly disapproved of the 'animosity' engendered at election times.[3]

Old Rosyth churchyard contains the unmarked Carnegie
graves[4] and the burial places of the local folk described by the
Revd Robertson, and the whole area, where the King of the
Gypsies once had a palace, was later overshadowed by the
nearby town and naval base of Rosyth established in 1903–9.

Before that no principal highways came directly to Pattiesmuir, although the main route from the Queensferry Passage on the Forth to the north-west was nearby; nevertheless the hamlet enjoyed a vigorous life of its own.

Within this late eighteenth-century weaving society evolved Andrew Carnegie's paternal roots. The Carnegies were a Lowland family and were property owners in Fife; the county was then called Fifeshire (usually with the suffix NB for North Britain). Their surname was derived from a Gaelic place name – *Caither an eige*, 'fort at the gap' – and appears in Fife charters from the late sixteenth century. At that time, one Magister David Carnegie of Kinnaird married Elizabeth Ramsay of Colluthie, in the north Fife parish of Moonzie; his second wife Euphame Wemyss was the mother of David, 1st Earl of Southesk, and John, 1st Earl of Northesk, and of the founders of the principal branches of the Carnegie family in Scotland.[5] Nevertheless the not well-off Carnegies of Pattiesmuir asserted no kindred to their wealthy namesakes, nor would they have wished to, although their rich descendant Andrew Carnegie was a friend of the noble Carnegies.

As far as Andrew Carnegie was concerned, his closest ancestor was his great-grandfather, sometime tenant farmer and weaver James Carnegie, who had moved from his ancestral Kincardineshire to set up home at Pattiesmuir around the year 1760, when the Hanoverian Prince William George Frederick, Prince of Wales, ascended the throne of Great Britain as George III. The new king's Scottish titles included the dukedoms of Rothesay and Edinburgh, and as he got to grips with the reins of government, James Carnegie tackled the problem of earning a living, and married a Fife woman called Charlotte Walker. Records of the Elgin estates show that James Carnegie had the right of 'turf and divet' – that is, the right to build for his own use a sod house at Pattiesmuir from local materials.[6]

Something of a rebel, James Carnegie played a prominent part in the Meal Riots of 1770 and was jailed on a charge of seditious incitement as a result. Nevertheless he earned enough to raise a large family. Customers for his linen came from all classes of society – even Martha, Lady Elgin, wife of the 5th Earl, bought linen from Carnegie.[7]

James's eldest son Andrew followed his father's craft of weaving. Being self-employed and constrained to sell their own wares, the weavers were more mobile than their agricultural neighbours who rarely, if ever, left their home milieux, even in the longest lifetime. So young Andrew – who would be the rich Andrew Carnegie's grandfather – knew Fife well, from the cobbled wynds of Culross to the old ecclesiastical capital of Scotland at St Andrews. And at nearby Limekilns he would encounter romance.

Limekilns, with its then comparatively new Brucehaven Harbour for the burgeoning trade in coal shipments, was the focus of a variety of industries from brewing to soap-making, and was also the home of the seafaring Thom family. Here Andrew Carnegie's grandfather met Elizabeth, daughter of the well-heeled ship owner Captain George Thom and his wife Elizabeth Wilkie. To her father's dismay Elizabeth announced that she would marry the moneyless weaver, and despite the threat of disinheritance marry she did – for love. The Thoms did not attend their daughter's wedding, and Elizabeth was further shunned when her father decided not to give her a vessel from his fleet as a dowry – which he had done when each of his other daughters married. Historian J.B. Mackie tells the story of how Elizabeth attempted a reconciliation with her family by promising that if she gave birth to a boy it would be given her father's name or that of one of her sisters if the baby was a girl. A girl duly arrived and at the baptism Elizabeth's family gathered at Limekilns Secessional Church to hear the child given a Thom family name. To Andrew Carnegie this smacked of bribery, and when the Revd Hadden asked what the child was to be called he declared: 'She is to be called Ann for my aunt of the same name.' Out of the church stormed the Thoms and there were no further inter-family exchanges.[8]

Education had long been held in high esteem in Scotland. After the Reformation had swept away the medieval church, the Scottish Presbyterian movement's 'First Book of Discipline'

(1560) set out a determination for 'one school in every parish'.[9] Furthermore, the eighteenth-century education system that creamed off gifted Scots children had opened up many opportunities for the bright within an atmosphere of educational egalitarianism, but many could still not afford the pennies to buy daily formal education for their children, so self-education was popular among the less well off. Not until the Education (Scotland) Act of 1872 did the state first assume direct responsibility for the education of children. Yet at Pattiesmuir, Andrew Carnegie was already involved in a form of self-education.

At Pattiesmuir is a building which was known as the 'college', where local weavers and agricultural workers met for self-improvement classes in a multitude of subjects from politics and philosophy to economics and theology. Their spiritual father was the working-class hero Robert Burns, whose revelries at the Tarbolton Bachelors' Club in his Ayrshire homeland provided the template for the college. Soon Andrew Carnegie became a self-proclaimed 'professor' of this institution, which actually had as much to do with social drinking as self-education.[10] Local tradition has it that the long-vanished Bull Head Tavern was the main campus of the college. With whatever spare money they had the members subscribed to the *Edinburgh Political & Literary Journal*, which first appeared in 1817 (becoming the *Daily Scotsman* by 1855), and clubbed together for the new Waverley novels produced by Walter Scott from 1814. If there were arguments or running disputes then Grandfather Carnegie was always at their heart. He was very much a man of his time.[11]

For decades Dunfermline was renowned, or abhorred, depending on one's point of view, as the most radical area in Scotland, full of men willing to debate the politics of the day and pursue the philosophies of such men as Rochdale miller turned orator and statesman John Bright, free-trader Richard Cobden and the home-grown Scottish philosopher and historian David Hume. They would gather in groups to subscribe to the London broadsheets and listen to lectures by visiting radicals. It was a hothouse of revolutionary thought in which the Carnegies found a niche.

Andrew and Elizabeth's sixth child William was born on 19 June 1804. He duly became a weaver like his father, but in 1830 he became the first to leave Pattiesmuir for nearby Dunfermline where he could pursue his skills as a damask weaver. Andrew and Elizabeth undoubtedly encouraged their son to move to Dunfermline in an effort to better himself, for in 1826 the Elgin estates factor noted that the Carnegies were unable to pay their rent because they were 'very poor'.[12] At Dunfermline William rented for around £8 per annum,[13] paid on the Scottish quarter days of Candlemas, Old Beltane, Lammas and Old Hallowmans, a portion of a cottage at the junction of Priory Lane and Moodie Street. On the ground floor he set up his loom, living in the small attic room above.

On the heights beyond Priory Lane lies Maygate, where lived the prominent Morrison family. William Carnegie became a welcome guest here, for the head of the family Tom Morrison was a fiery radical. William eventually fell for the charms of Morrison's fourth child Margaret, and in December 1834 they married and set up home together at William's workshop-lodging. William and Margaret were to become the parents of the famous Andrew Carnegie. Thus history assembled the three great early influences on Andrew Carnegie's life: his father William, his mother Margaret (by far the greatest influence) and his grandfather Tom, although in his veins also ran the 'daft' blood of his eccentric, ebullient and exuberant paternal grandfather Andrew. Of the latter Andrew Carnegie would say: 'I think my optimistic nature, my ability to shed trouble and laugh through my life . . . must have been inherited from this delightful old masquerading grandfather whose name I proudly bear.'[14]

To assess these influences properly, it is vital to take a closer look at the main characters involved. William Carnegie was a hard worker, but was far more reticent than his effusive father. Family tradition has it that he was a keen reader and a solitary rambler on the roads and moors around Pattiesmuir. His artistic qualities enabled him to graduate from the plain designs of the weavers' looms to the figured material of damask, which had originally been worked in silk. Dunfermline was the centre of the damask trade.

The manufacture and processing of textiles, particularly wool and linen, appears to have been well established in Dunfermline by the 1400s at the very latest, and the textile industry continued as cottage labour until well into the 1500s. As the centuries passed, textile production became increasingly mechanised and better organised. The development of the damask trade at Dunfermline involved an interesting piece of industrial espionage.

Some time in the early eighteenth century a small damask-weaving manufactory was set up at Drumsheuch in west Edinburgh by craftsmen from the continent. The process by which they worked was secret. So in 1709 a Dunfermline weaver called James Blake set out to discover what he could about the damask process. He decided his best chance lay in impersonating an imbecile. He hung around the homes of the immigrant workers and distracted them with his amusing capers. Gradually Blake was allowed to enter their workshops and there he took note of their machines and practices. Absorbing as much knowledge as he could, he returned to Dunfermline and was able to establish his own damask industry. Thus damask weaving was established at Dunfermline by 1718. The process was revolutionised by the introduction of steam power in 1849, just a year or two after the Carnegie family had left.[15] It should not be forgotten though that coal was mined at Dunfermline as early as 1291, when William de Orbeville, proprietor of Pittencrieff, granted to the Benedictines of Dunfermline the right to extract coal for their use. So steam power was an important innovation.

Politically William Carnegie had been brought up on the Scottish working-class radicalism of his father and his friends, who believed that every man should have a say in who led them politically and religiously, and supported a thorough-going but constitutionally social and political reform. Yet while his father could harangue a crowd, William loathed speaking

6

in public; nevertheless, although slow to anger, William would speak out boldly if his principles were slighted. A regular attender at public meetings, on one occasion William took his young son Andrew to hear John Bright, engendering in Andrew a lifelong respect for oratory.[16]

An anecdote from Andrew Carnegie's autobiography helps to get the measure of William Carnegie. A short while after his son's birth William attended a Sunday service at the Dunfermline Secessionist Presbyterian Church. The minister's sermon that day was on the damnation of infants. His Calvinist rhetoric underlining the sure and certain damnation of children and punishment in the fires of Hell for their sins triggered anger in William's mind. Somewhat out of character he stood up in his pew and said: 'If that be your religion and that your God, I shall seek a better religion and a nobler God.'[17] William Carnegie never returned to the church.

While William Carnegie was fairheaded and reticent, Margaret Morrison his wife was dark and resolute, loyal and determined in all that was personal to her. She proved in marriage to be devoted to the needs of her husband and was a fine Scots wife, 'trig' (neat), 'scrimp' (sparing in economy) and zealous in 'warkin the wark' (carrying out her housewifely duties) as the Lowland tongue described it. Throughout her son Andrew's life she was the single greatest motivational force behind his success in business.

Andrew Carnegie's third great influence was his maternal grandfather Tom Morrison. Unlike the Lowland Carnegies, the Morrisons were of Highland stock, whose clan derived from the ancient Norse inhabitants of the Hebridean island of Lewis. Like other clans, their members were dispersed through feuding. Tom Morrison's immediate family had fetched up in Edinburgh in the mid-eighteenth century as leather workers. Tom was to inherit his father's leather business and married Ann Hodge, the daughter of an Edinburgh merchant. Writing in 1935 John Pattison noted how the Morrisons had a substantial house in Edinburgh with all the refinements of a lower middle-class family.[18] Alas, Tom Morrison made some bad investments; the business was lost, Ann Morrison's marriage portion vanished and they moved to Dunfermline where Tom set up as a shoemaker.

Perhaps embittered by his own failures and shamed by the loss of his position, Tom Morrison took up the spirit of radicalism that was so prominent in early nineteenth-century Dunfermline, becoming part of a company of radicals bent on a programme of grass-roots political (but non-violent) action, which was a precursor of Chartism – a movement which began in 1836 for the expansion of political power to the working classes.

Tom Morrison suffered a bitter blow when his wife died in 1814, but the needs of his family and workbench did not stop him preaching the radical cause in the towns and villages of Fife. Should a representative of the successive Tory Prime Ministers the Earl of Liverpool and George Canning, or perhaps a Whig MP, speak at a political rally in Fife, there would be Tom Morrison heckling and promoting dissension. In those days his pen worked as quickly as his tongue to promote the cause of reform for the working-class masses. Around 1827 Tom Morrison gathered the skilled Dunfermline craftsmen into what was called 'the Political Union', proudly bearing on their banner the motto 'Knowledge, Union and Fraternisation', and thus Tom Morrison and his agitators were part of the pressure that resulted in the passing of the Reform Act of 1832, which initially gave the vote to the middle classes.

Tom Morrison was a friend and devotee of the English essayist and politician William Cobbett, and occasionally contributed copy for *Cobbett's Political Register*, which was begun in 1802 and appeared weekly. Andrew Carnegie was proud of the fact that his grandfather had appeared in the *Register* and had been praised therein by Cobbett; in particular Cobbett said Morrison's thesis on the need for technical education in Scottish schools was 'the very best communication I have ever received in my life'.[19]

Keeping up the political pressure, Tom Morrison wrote and spoke against wealth and privilege. His series of letters attacking Archibald Primrose, Lord Dalmeny, the Liberal MP for Stirling Burghs, as a 'stoolpigeon for landed interests' are considered classics by socialist hagiographers. What Tom Morrison would have thought of his grandson hobnobbing with Lord Dalmeny's son, the Liberal leader Archibald Philip Primrose, 5th Earl of Rosebery, is a matter for speculation. Morrison even started a radical newspaper in Dunfermline; *The Precursor* was to appear monthly at 2*d* from January 1833 but it was too seditious for most printers to risk and the enterprise soon folded. Yet Tom Morrison continued to write for any publication that would publish his rantings. Andrew Carnegie said later: 'I come by my scribbling responsibilities by inheritance – from both sides, for the Carnegies were also readers and thinkers.'[20]

William and Margaret Carnegie, with Tom Morrison, all contributed to the cocktail of genes that would make Andrew Carnegie of Pittsburgh a 'great empire-builder and philanthropist'. Yet he reworked these influences in his own idiosyncratic way, sometimes turning Tom Morrison's opinions about wealth and privilege on their head. Thus Andrew Carnegie's story begins at Dunfermline.

TWO

THE WEAVER'S BOY

A working man is a more useful citizen and ought to be
more respected than an idle prince.

John K. Winkler, *Incredible Carnegie*, 1931

Andrew Carnegie, 'Andra' to his family, was born at
Dunfermline on Wednesday 25 November 1835. It was the
fifth year of the reign of William IV, the 'Sailor King', of the
House of Hanover, and politically the Whigs (Liberals) had just
returned to office with William Lamb, 2nd Viscount Melbourne,
forming his second government as Prime Minister and First
Lord of the Treasury. In those days Scotland remained without
a parliament; from 1707 the 'management' of Scotland was in
the remit of the Home Secretary, by now Lord John Russell.
Andrew Carnegie entered a Scottish society fiercely proud of its
history, culture and individuality, and being 'managed' from
faraway London rankled with such as the Carnegie and the
Morrison relations assembled at his birth.

Andrew Carnegie was eased into the world with the help of his
mother's childhood friend Ailie Ferguson, now Mrs John
Henderson. He first opened his eyes in the little attic room of the
one-storey eighteenth-century red pantiled grey-stone cottage at
the junction of Moodie Street and Priory Lane, Dunfermline. With
its swept dormers, the dwelling was once an end-of-terrace
habitation, and the attic room was the family's main living area.
Today the cottage houses the birthplace museum of Andrew
Carnegie, tracking his career in a 'rags to riches' story, while
adjoining the cottage is architect James Shearer's Memorial Hall
of 1925, endowed by Carnegie's wife Louise to tell the story of

her husband's unique business and charitable career. It is the Scottish focus of all he achieved.[1] As the visitor stands at the corner of Moodie Street, the scenario that Andrew Carnegie first knew is all around; a scenario that embedded itself in his psyche and drove him years later to endow for future generations.

For baby Andrew, Dunfermline was a fine place to be born. Situated in south-west Fife, around 3 miles from the north shore of the Firth of Forth, and at the junction of several important medieval routes, Dunfermline was once the capital of Scotland.[2] Historically it had long held a prominent position, for Carnegie was born in a place which had witnessed the emergence of Scotland's story from the mists of legend. The town's High Street occupies a ridge from which the ground falls away steeply down St Margaret Street and Monastery Street to the ancient abbey precincts below. These two thoroughfares funnel down to Moodie Street with Pittencrieff Park to the west flanked by the Tower Burn and Pittencrieff Glen. Here at the Abbey, the Burn and the Glen Andrew Carnegie spent his earliest days.

High on the eminence above the Moodie Street cottage stand the remains of the Benedictine Abbey of the Holy Trinity, founded as a priory in around 1070 by the saintly Margaret, wife of Malcolm III, King of Scots, soon after her marriage in 1068. It was elevated to the status of an abbey in 1128 by their son David I and functioned as one of Scotland's most prominent ecclesiastical foundations and pilgrimage sites – to the shrine of St Margaret of Scotland – until it was annexed to the Protestant Crown of James VI in 1593. Adjacent to the fratery hall of the abbey lies the shell of the guest house refurbished as the Palace of Dunfermline by the Stuarts; here the royal family often resided and within its walls several monarchs of Scotland were born, the last being Charles I on 19 November 1600. Andrew Carnegie knew every path, wall and hidey-hole of the crumbling site, steeling himself to walk through its threatening shadows when night had fallen.

The history of Dunfermline is hardly separable from the rise of the abbey, without which the former would have remained a lowly place in history. In Pittencrieff Glen, by the abbey precincts, rises Tower Hill, the site of the tower-castle erected by the 'swaggering bully' Malcolm III, Canmore – bynamed 'Bighead' (*c.* 1031–93). Malcolm was changed from a coarse ruffian to a cultured nobleman by his second wife, the Saxon Margaret (d. *c.* 1093), daughter of Edward Atheling, son of Edmund II of England. Here they lived with their eight children. In due time Andrew Carnegie would buy what had been their royal property hereabouts as a gift for the burgh of Dunfermline.

Within the abbey today can be seen the tomb of one of Andrew Carnegie's earliest heroes. The nave of the old abbey is preserved as a national historical monument, but the east end of the abbey was redeveloped as a functioning abbey church. When the site was being cleared in 1818 to make way for the new parish church a skeleton was discovered which experts declared to be that of Robert I, the Bruce. Bruce became Carnegie's paragon, but his tomb was not graced with the fine memorial seen today until 1889, when the Carnegies had long since left Dunfermline. Bruce, though, was somewhat sidelined by the chief champion of Scotland's independence, Sir William Wallace (*c.* 1274–1305), hanged, drawn and quartered for his pains by the English, when the young Andrew Carnegie discovered patriotism.

The original settlement of Dunfermline probably grew up near Malcolm's Tower but was absorbed into a new township around the abbey; it became a Burgh of Regality, dependent upon the abbey from around 1130 until the confirming charter of James VI of 24 May 1588. All this – Malcolm's Tower, Pittencrieff Glen and the surrounding parkland – were within the estate of the Hunt family in Carnegie's time. By the fifteenth century these policies had been in the ownership of the Benedictine abbey, but when they were secularised following the Protestant Reformation they fell to George Seton, 1st Earl of Dunfermline. The estate and Pittencrieff House, a drydashed mansion of around 1635, built for Sir Alexander Clerk, had several owners, but were bought for £31,500 in

1799 by William Hunt.[3] Thereafter the Hunts guarded their property with diligence, but by the 1840s they opened their gates for one day a year in May to allow Dunfermline folk to walk in the gardens. Because of their political affiliations the Hunts barred the Morrison family from visiting Pittencrieff. This angered the young Andrew Carnegie who, as tradition has it, swore that one day he would own Pittencrieff and throw the gates open to all. Buy it he did from the Hunts in 1902 for £45,000 and officially presented it to his native burgh on 21 November 1903; architect Robert S. Lorimer reconstructed the interior as a club and museum between 1908 and 1911. Today, almost as an eternal snub to the Hunt family, Richard Reginald Goulden's 1913–14 statue of Andrew Carnegie in a frock coat is prominently placed in Pittencrieff Park, which is entered through the Louise Carnegie Memorial Gates of 1928.

At the time of Andrew Carnegie's birth, Peter Chalmers, minister of Dunfermline abbey church, tells us the population of Dunfermline was some 11,500 souls, with 5,044 folk of all ages and both sexes employed in the linen weaving trade.[4] As an esteemed craftsman William Carnegie's finished fine weaves were eagerly sought, and he expanded his two looms at Moodie Street to three. This precipitated a move from the cramped cottage premises to a new home in Edgar Street, near Reid's Park, with a bigger living area for his family. Thus Andrew Carnegie's first recollections were of the Edgar Street home.[5] William Carnegie continued to expand his business, acquiring a fourth loom and taking on apprentices to tend them.

For a long time Andrew Carnegie lived the life of an only child in and out of his father's weaving room, fascinated as his busy white-aproned father fired the shuttle from left to right and vigorously pedalled the treadles of the loom. Before the entranced child's eyes the threads trembled, criss-crossed and melded into the fine figured damask. William Carnegie's strong tenor voice often accompanied the shuttle's movement with Scot songs: 'a very good foundation was laid for my love of sweet sounds in the unsurpassed minstrelsy of my native land as sung by my father,' wrote Andrew Carnegie. 'There was scarcely an old Scottish song with which I was not made familiar, both verse and tune.'[6]

A favourite Scots ballad of Andrew Carnegie's which he often recited was Fife's own 'Sir Patrick Spens', which begins:

> The King sits in Dunfermline towne
> Drinking the blude red wine.

Carnegie loved the story of how Sir Patrick was sent from his home at Aberdour, Fife, on a mission by King Alexander III. In the version made famous by Sir Walter Scott the object of the mission was to bring to Scotland Princess Margaret, the Maid of Norway, King Alexander's granddaughter. The mission was a disaster; the company and the Maid were drowned even though:

> Sir Patrick Spens is the best sailor
> That ever sailed the sea.

The metre and flow of the ballad appealed to young Carnegie, who lisped the finale to any who would listen:

> Half ower, half ower to Aberdour
> Full fifty fathoms deep
> There lies the gude Sir Patrick Spens
> Wi' the Scots lords at his feet.[7]

During January 1840 Margaret Carnegie gave birth to a daughter, Ann. The child was sickly and died the following year.[8] With his father busy at his loom, and his mother increasingly engaged for those worrying months with the sickly new baby, Andrew Carnegie was left to his own devices, exploring alone, or with friends, the graveyard and precincts of the old abbey, the mysteries of Pittencrieff Glen and the banks of the Tower Burn. His guide to the formal history of Dunfermline was his maternal uncle George Lauder, who was married to Margaret's eldest sister Seaton and owned a grocer's shop in Dunfermline's High Street. By this time George Lauder was a widower. He was devoted to his young son George, who often joined Andrew Carnegie as a willing listener to his father's tales. The two boys gave each other the nicknames Dod[9] (George) and Naig, and for many years Andrew called Dod 'my brother-cousin'.[10] Dod's father, wrote Andrew Carnegie,

> possessed an extraordinary gift of dealing with children and taught us many things. Among others I remember how he taught us British history by imagining each of the monarchs in a certain place upon the walls of the room performing the act for which he was well known. Thus for me King John sits to this day above the mantelpiece signing the Magna Carta, and Queen Victoria is on the back of the door with her children on her knees.
>
> It may be taken for granted that the omission [of Cromwell's name] which, years after, I found in the Chapter House at Westminster Abbey, was fully supplied in our list of monarchs. A slab in a small chapel at Westminster says that the body of Oliver Cromwell was moved from there. In the list of the monarchs which I learned at my uncle's knee the grand republican monarch appeared writing his message to the Pope in Rome, informing His Holiness that 'if he did not cease persecuting the Protestants the thunder of Great Britain's cannon would be heard in the Vatican'.[11]

Cromwell became a favourite of the two boys, but . . .

> It was from my uncle I learned all that I know of the early history of Scotland – of Wallace and Bruce and Burns, of Blind Harry's history, of Scott, Ramsay, Tannahill, Hogg and Fergusson. I can truly say in the words of Burns that there was then and there created in me a vein of Scottish prejudice (or patriotism) which will cease to exist only with life.[12]

William Carnegie and his relatives the Morrisons played no role in, nor formed any part of, the Presbyterian congregations in Dunfermline within the Church of Scotland or the breakaway Free Church. Yet William was not without a desire for religious refreshment which he eventually found among the Dunfermline Swedenborgians. This group followed the teachings of Emanuel Swedenborg (1688–1772), the Swedish scientist, theologian and mystic. He believed that the universe had a basic spiritual structure and in 1744, after he had a personal vision of Christ, he believed that he had received the call to abandon worldly learning. Thus he spent the rest of his career interpreting the Bible. In essence he believed that the Christian God was the power and life of all living creatures and that the Holy Trinity of old was expressed by the three essential qualities of God – love, wisdom and activity. After his death his followers founded a church in London in 1788 and by 1792 another was organised in Baltimore. This Swedenborgian philosophy appealed to William Carnegie and he took his young son Andrew to their meetings. Margaret Carnegie eschewed joining them; although she did not pursue the active Utilitarianism of the Morrisons, she regularly dipped into the essays and sermons of William Ellery Channing (1780–1842), the Rhode Island-born leader of the Unitarians. Andrew Carnegie said that, while he and his brother were encouraged to attend church and Sunday School, his mother considered the Scriptures 'as unworthy of divine authorship or of acceptance as authoritative guides for the conduct of life'. Her underlying maxim, he said, was the Confucian saying: 'To perform the duties of this life well, troubling not about another, is the prime wisdom.'[13]

Religion thus played little or no part in the early life of young Andrew Carnegie, whose nascent thoughts were moulded by his mother. She did not oppose the 'New Jerusalem' of her husband's religious beliefs, nor the 'Workers Paradise' of her radical relatives, but she regarded life's struggles in practical rather than philosophical terms. Hers was a simple Scottish economic philosophy: 'Hard work brought siller [money], and siller brought meat [i.e. bread].' So

Andrew Carnegie was shown early in his life that the workings of the market-place were what brought a better life in immediate terms.

Andrew Carnegie's formal education did not commence until 1843, when he was 8. Although the majority of his young friends had begun their schooling at 5, young Andrew shied away from the classroom saying he was not ready and his parents indulged him. Years passed without Andrew showing any inclination towards education; a situation which worried his by no means illiterate parents. At length they decided on a course of action. They approached Robert Martin (1806–60), a teacher at the school on neighbouring Rolland Street, to see if he would talk to Andrew about the importance of education. Martin was in charge of a school which taught the form of education promoted by the Quaker Joseph Lancaster (1778–1838); herein older children taught the younger after they had been tutored themselves by the schoolmaster. In this way school fees could be kept down, but the system led to a chaotically large number of children being taught in one room. For any progress to be made firm discipline had to be enforced with a hefty dose of the 'tawse' – a Scots leather strap with tails which was smacked across the hands. Not far away from Dunfermline was the mining village of Lochgelly, which was to become a centre for the making of these straps. Despite all this, Martin – nicknamed 'Snuffy' by his pupils – won the day with Andrew Carnegie, who entered the Rolland Street school soon after the pep talk. Carnegie wrote:

> the school was a perfect delight to me, and if anything occurred which prevented my attendance I was unhappy. This happened every now and then because my morning duty was to bring water from the well at the head of Moodie Street. The supply was scanty and irregular. Sometimes it was not allowed to run until late in the morning and a score of old wives were sitting around, the turn of each having been previously secured through

the night by placing a worthless can in the line. This, as might be expected, led to numerous contentions in which I would not be put down even by these venerable dames. I earned the reputation of being 'an awfu' laddie'. In this way I probably developed the strain of argumentativeness, or perhaps combativeness, which has always remained with me.[14]

Carnegie became 'Martin's pet', a nickname which brought him the 'utmost opprobrium', yet in later years when writing to his old school chums he would sign himself with the nickname.[15] It was through Martin that Andrew Carnegie earned his 'first penny',[16] by the recitation of a poem written by Robert Burns at the height of his inspiration in the mid-1780s. Entitled 'Man was Made to Mourne – A Dirge', it contains the immortal lines:

> Man's inhumanity to man
> Makes countless thousands mourn!

Carnegie recited its eleven stanzas faultlessly for his penny, and retained throughout his life a talent to memorise large chunks of verse which he could declaim at will. It was a trick of memory that he had learned from his uncle Lauder: visualise what is read to fix it in the memory.

Summing up his schooling, Carnegie said: 'I could read, write and cipher, and had begun the study of Algebra and Latin.'[17] But he had also begun to flex his skills for 'business'. 'One of the chief enjoyments of my childhood,' he remembered, 'was the keeping of pigeons and rabbits.' But how could he afford to feed them? He hit upon a plan. Each rabbit was given the name of one of his playmates, who fed the rabbit in return.

I treasure the remembrance of this plan as the earliest evidence of organising power upon the development of which my material success in life was hung – a success not to be attributed to what I have known or done myself, but to the faculty of knowing and choosing others who did know better than myself.[18]

At this time in his childhood Dunfermline was 'paradise' for Carnegie. 'All my recollections of childhood, all I knew of fairyland, clustered around the old Abbey and its curfew bell, which tolled at eight o'clock every evening and was the signal for me to run to bed before it stopped.'[19] As he hurried home from his uncle Lauder's fireside tales he would always avoid the gaslit Maygate and go by the abbey. Often at dusk, when the wind screamed through the old abbey and palace windows high above his head, the spooky story of James VI he had just heard at his uncle's came alive. Once the king had heard a piercing scream from the nurse attending his son, the future Charles I. The nurse was beside herself: 'Your Majesty, an old man came creeping into the room and threw his cloak over the cradle and drew it towards him like he was taking the Prince away.' The king knew well that this was the 'Curse of the Devil'; an old Scots superstition averred that when such an old man crept into a room and engulfed a child with his cloak, that child was doomed to a life of pain and suffering.[20] Carnegie heard such a scream as he passed by, but assured his pals that he was not afraid!

For Scotland in particular the 1840s brought economic depression; unemployment became an increasing blight and strikes began to break out. When the miners in the nearby county of Clackmannan went on strike Carnegie's uncle Tom Morrison became involved in calls for a creeping general strike and the Dunfermline labour force responded, from coal mines to weaving sheds. The burgh became a hotbed of revolutionary intent. The aim was the enactment of the 'People's Charter' of the Chartists. At the time only 10 per cent of the Scots male population had the franchise, and the People's Charter clamoured for six main 'demands': votes for every male; secret ballots; annual parliaments; equality in electoral districts; payment for MPs; and the abolition of property qualifications for MPs. Already the Charter had been voted down in the House of Commons. But when Sir Robert Peel's government threw it out again in 1842 the riots and strikes were renewed. Response to the strike call, though, began to weaken as bellies felt the pangs of hunger and families suffered. Government troops arrived in Dunfermline and Tom Morrison and his agitator colleagues were arrested. Morrison was bailed and his case was never brought to trial, and eventually he was elected to the town council.

Men went back to work. All this was another layer of experience never to be forgotten by Andrew Carnegie, who observed at first hand the workers' agitation going on around him. His hero worship for men like Robert I, the Bruce, and the glories of the Battle of Bannockburn was transferred to his uncle and the Dunfermline men who saw relief in the People's Charter. At 6 or 7 years old Andrew Carnegie enrolled himself as a knight fighting the dragon of privilege, and at 8 he was a republican. In his autobiography he declared: 'As a child I could have slain king, duke or lord, and considered their deaths a service to the state and hence a heroic act.'[21]

Curiously, in these revolutionary times Margaret Carnegie took Andrew and his cousin Dod to a royal Scottish occasion. On Thursday 1 September 1842 Queen Victoria landed at Granton Pier and rode in a barouche to view Edinburgh's sights for the first time. It was quite a spectacle; there had been no royal visit to Scotland since that of the Queen's uncle, George IV, in 1822. In her *Journal* the Queen wrote: 'The impression Edinburgh has made upon us is very great . . . .'[22] Alas, the impression made by the Queen on the two young republicans was not so 'great':

'She's not sae tall as your mither,' said Dod.
'And her dress is nae sae braw [not so fine],' replied Andrew.[23]

In 1843 Margaret Carnegie gave birth to her last child, a boy, named Tom after his maternal grandfather and rebellious uncle. But, economically at least, times were deteriorating. One by one the apprentices left, and William Carnegie's extra looms were disposed of. The Edgar Street premises became too much of an outlay and the family moved back to another cottage on Moodie Street, not far from where they used to live. Here William began work again on his surviving loom, but orders were thin. Margaret supplemented the family finances by selling vegetables and sweetmeats from her front door, and helped her uncle stitch shoes.

If young Andrew Carnegie had not yet fully appreciated poverty, he did now. Years later he remembered:

> I began to learn what poverty meant. Dreadful days came when my father took the last of his webs to the great manufacturer, and I saw my mother anxiously awaiting his return to know whether a new web was to be obtained or that a period of idleness was upon us. It was burnt into my heart that my father, though neither 'abject, mean, nor vile', as Burns has it, had nevertheless to
>
> > 'beg a brother to the earth
> > To give him leave to toil.'
>
> And then there came the resolve that I would cure that when I got to be a man. We were not, however, reduced to anything like poverty compared with many of our neighbours. I do not know to what lengths of privation my mother would not have gone that she might see her two boys wearing large white collars, and trimly dressed.[24]

Slowly the power-looms set up at Dunfermline put many of the handloom weavers out of business and William Carnegie was one of the casualties. The Carnegies now relied on what profit could be made out of the provisions sales and shoe work. It was more and more vital to find a way out of that poverty trap. As he sat at his idle loom, contemplating the sale of their household possessions, William Carnegie sang a new song, offering a clue to Andrew and his brother Tom as to where their future might lie:

> To the West, to the West, to the land of the free,
> Where the mighty Missouri rolls down to the sea;
> Where a man is a man even though he must toil
> And the poorest may gather the fruits of the soil.[25]

Back in 1840 Margaret Carnegie's younger sister Annie, wife of Andrew Aitken, had joined another sister, Kitty, wife of Thomas Hogan, who had earlier emigrated to North America; they settled in Allegheny City at Slabtown, a suburb of Pittsburgh, Pennsylvania. Andrew Carnegie remembered seeing a map of America being set out on their living-room table before his Aunt Aitken had emigrated; were they now to go too?

Aunts Aitken and Hogan had had an anxious time at first in America because of the poor employment prospects; these were the tempestuous years of Democrat John Tyler's presidency. Yet by the winter of 1847 life in Scotland looked pretty bleak for the Carnegies, who were now convinced that their future lay in America. A recent letter from Aunt Aitken had strengthened their resolution:

> Business here is much better now, as most individuals can find employment, although some are out of a job yet, and the wages are considerably reduced. The spring has been a most favourable one . . . and there is no fear of want throughout the length and breadth of the land. This country is far better for the working man than the old one.[26]

The year 1848 might well be described as the Year of Revolution; in February the weak French King Louis Philippe abdicated and fled to England following the republican and socialist revolution in Paris; and violence erupted in Italy, Austria and Germany. Meanwhile in Britain the Chartist Rising led by MP Fergus O'Connor failed and the movement was laughed out of existence. In Dunfermline the Carnegies put up their household goods to public 'roup' (auction), but the struggling local economy meant that the prices they received were low. Even with their meagre savings, they still did not have the amount needed for their passage to America. A loan of £20 from Margaret's childhood friend Ailie Henderson at last allowed the plans to go forward.[27]

The Carnegies' relations were dismayed at their emigration plans. Tom Morrison resolutely refused to help in any way. He considered his sister's plans to be madness. Smarting at the failure of revolution in Britain, he openly called his brother-in-law William a traitor for fleeing the workers' struggle at home. William Carnegie's sister Charlotte Drysdale was less negative and cashed in her insurance money to give them £2 10s. William was tearfully touched: 'If ever I've anything,' he said, 'I'll mind ye.'[28] Margaret Carnegie's brother-in-law George Lauder was unhappy and sceptical about the wisdom of their venture, but he helped make reservations for them aboard the 800-ton *Wiscasset*, a three-masted, square-rigged sailing vessel due to leave Glasgow's Broomielaw pier on 17 May 1848. For the Carnegies the die was finally cast.

THREE

VOYAGE TO AMERICA

Working-men always do reciprocate kindly feeling. If we truly care for others we need not be anxious about their feelings for us. Like draws to like.

Autobiography, 1920

The leaving of Dunfermline was a sad wrench for 13-year-old Andrew Carnegie. Tom Morrison, George Lauder and cousin Dod accompanied the Carnegies the handful of miles on the horse-drawn coal railway omnibus to Charlestown, the model village created in the late eighteenth century by Charles, 5th Earl of Elgin. Tearfully Andrew watched as the old abbey, with the 'talismanic letters' set around its tower roof spelling the name of Robert I, the Bruce, receded and vanished in the distance.

At Charlestown quay, which exported lime to farmers all over Scotland, the Carnegies were ferried by rowing boat to the steamer for Edinburgh anchored in the Forth. 'I canna leave you! I canna leave you!' young Andrew sobbed to his uncle George, who, pressing a sovereign coin into his hand, tried to comfort the boy. Young Andrew was pulled from his embrace and placed into the boat. Thus, under a cloud of sadness the Carnegies left the Firth of Forth they knew so well and via the Union Canal journeyed to Glasgow and the piers of the Broomielaw on the River Clyde. Here they joined the other passengers: weavers, labourers and farmers all eager for a new life away from their beloved but troubled Scotland. That year, 188,233 British emigrants sailed to America to reforge their lives.[1]

Their uncomfortable journey in steerage began on 19 May 1848 as the Maine-built *Wiscasset* breasted the Atlantic out of the Firth of Clyde. Andrew Carnegie remembered the voyage:

> During the seven weeks of the voyage, I came to know the sailors quite well, learned the names of the ropes, and was able to direct the passengers to answer the call of the boatswain, for the ship being undermanned, the aid of the passengers was urgently required. In consequence I was invited by the sailors to participate on Sundays, in the one delicacy of the sailors' mess, plum duff. I left the ship with sincere regret.[2]

What Carnegie did not detail were the horrors of the passage itself. Seasickness was rife and petty theft of belongings was an everyday occurrence, while becalmed days put pressure on the dwindling water and food supplies that the passengers had had to furnish themselves. All feared the outbreak of cholera, and deaths on board added to the deterioration of passenger morale.

Some seven weeks after setting out, the *Wiscasset* docked off Castle Garden, New York Harbour. The Carnegies had arrived in America but immediately had to push on to Pittsburgh. However, there were two familiar faces to greet them at New York. Margaret Carnegie's childhood friend Euphemia Douglas, now Mrs James Sloan, and her weaver husband steered them towards the next leg of their journey. Andrew Carnegie was 'bewildered' at what he saw of New York. While his father haggled with the shipping agents for their onward travel tickets, and over a glass of sarsaparilla in the company of *Wiscasset* sailor Robert Barryman, Andrew Carnegie observed the 'bustle and excitement' of New York.

From New York City they passed into New York State, up the Hudson River to Albany, thence by the Erie Canal to Rochester and Buffalo; via Lake Erie they went to Cleveland, Ohio, and on a portion of the Ohio & Erie Canal, and thence by land to Beaver and finally to Pittsburgh. The last leg of their journey was aboard a paddle steamer from Cincinnati, via Beaver, and here for the first time Andrew Carnegie encountered the American genus of mosquitoes, giving them all a 'horrid' last night aboard.

Here at the junction of the Allegheny and Monogahela rivers was the grimy city with which Andrew Carnegie's name would be immortally linked. In those days the area around Pittsburgh was synonymous with floods, fires and regular visitations of fever. Located in western Pennsylvania, around 110 miles from Lake Erie, the city dated from the eighteenth century and was blessed with rich coal seams, and with salt and iron works; Andrew Carnegie was to earn it the name 'Steel City'. The city had originally been named in honour of William Pitt, Earl of Chatham. His adjutant-general in America Brigadier John Forbes captured Fort Duquesne from the French and on 27 November 1758 informed Chatham that the fort had been renamed in his honour. In Forbes's ranks were many Scots Highlanders who eventually settled in the area, and the Carnegies would mix with their descendants. But what was the city like when Andrew Carnegie arrived in 1848? The city of some 40,000 souls had not yet recovered from the great fire of 10 April 1845, which had caused widespread devastation because few houses were made of brick, and there was still an air of desolation over the commercial heart. Yet if one word summed up Andrew Carnegie's first view of the city, that word was 'bustle'.

Soon after landing the Carnegies made their way to the suburb of Allegheny, where Margaret Carnegie's sisters lived, and received an exuberant welcome. Andrew Aitken had recently died, so Margaret Carnegie's sister Annie lived with her twin Kitty, and Kitty's husband Thomas Hogan. Their dwelling was a frame house at 336 Rebecca Street. The house was the property of Tom Hogan's brother Andrew, and adjoining was a house owned by Annie and rented to Andrew Hogan. Two unoccupied rooms on the second floor of this property were to be the Carnegies' first home in America. As a bonus they were to live rent-free. Annie and Tom could afford a little generosity. Tom had a regular wage as a clerk in a crockery shop, while Annie now ran a small grocery store.[3]

Financially the Carnegies were on their uppers. Their surroundings, though generously given, were squalid. Not for nothing was the suburb of Allegheny better known as Slabtown. The area had developed by 1848 from a fur-trading post to a burgeoning industrial area of 20,000 people; in the eastern enclave dwelt mostly Germans, while in the west the inhabitants included many Scots and Irish. But the area was greatly polluted by the many tanneries and typhus was a daily hazard. Allegheny's population, which exceeded that of Dunfermline in 1848 by some 7,000, thrived on a network of family-run workshops, which mirrored what Dunfermline had once been. Abounding too, was a spirit that reflected that found in Dunfermline: a feeling of self-dependence, individual freedom and a strong work ethic to delight the heart of any Scots Presbyterian. One other emotion was familiar to the Carnegies. Just as workers had gone on strike in Dunfermline, soon after the arrival of the Carnegies in Pittsburgh came the Cotton Mill Riots and Allegheny was rife with industrial discontent which would give the place a history of worker violence.

William Carnegie rented a handloom from Andrew Hogan and set to work immediately, but now he was to produce no fine damasks as he had for the homes of the Scottish middle class, only cheaper napery and ticking. Again, once his products were made, William had to peddle them where he could. Margaret also went to work in their new home binding shoes for neighbourhood cobbler Henry Phipps at $4 a week. She was helped by her son Tom who sat at her side on a stool waxing thread and threading needles. As it turned out, Margaret earned more than her husband.[4] William Carnegie was a skilled craftsman, but for him America was not to be the golden promised land and slowly he became more demoralised.

Andrew Carnegie soon acclimatised to his new surroundings. His first friends were John and Henry Phipps, the sons of his mother's employer. Small for his age and with flaxen hair shading to white, Andrew stood out among the other boys of the neighbourhood. The native Allegheny boys were nicknamed 'Bottom Hoosiers', after the Allegheny river bottom. Andrew's thick Dunfermline accent was incomprehensible to the Hoosiers, who would taunt him with cries of 'Scotchie'. Andrew countered with, 'Aye, I am Scotchie, and I'm prood o' the name.' After a while Andrew was accepted and became a 'Hoosier' himself.[5]

As the summer of 1848 drew on to autumn 13-year-old Andrew Carnegie looked about him for paid employment, his mother ever at his shoulder to advise on work that she considered would be too demeaning. This provoked an incident Andrew Carnegie never forgot. Undoubtedly with good intentions, Thomas Hogan suggested that young Andrew be given a basket full of knick-knacks to sell along the Allegheny quays. His mother was incandescent with rage: 'What? My son a pedlar and go among rough men upon the wharves! I would rather throw him into the Allegheny River. Leave me!'[6] Hogan hastily retreated.

The Scots immigrants of this part of America operated a sort of news network regarding possible employment. The cotton-mill strikes had ended and William Carnegie obtained work at Blackstock's Cotton Mill in Robinson Street, run by a fellow Scot, and brought home word that there was work for Andrew. There the boy could have a job as a bobbin boy at $1.20 a week.

Father and son seized their opportunities, often beginning work before daybreak and returning home in the dark. From the windows of their home in Moodie Street Andrew had often watched the children at Dunfermline set off early in the morning for the mine and mill, and he too now set off for his first job. The millions of dollars he later made, he remarked in his autobiography, never gave him more pleasure than his first week's wages. Soon though, Andrew was to move to John Hay's bobbin factory on Lacock Street for a better wage of $2 a week. His work now included supervising a steam engine and its hungry boiler. He recalled:

It was too much for me. I found myself night after night sitting up in bed trying the steam gauges, fearing at one time that the steam was too low and that the workers above would complain that they had not power enough, and at another time that the steam was too high and that the boiler might burst.[7]

It was a lonely job and involved too much responsibility for a boy of Andrew's age. But he persisted: 'My hopes were high, and I looked every day for some change to take place. What it was to be I knew not, but that it would come I felt certain if I kept on.'[8] He was right.

FOUR

THE INDUSTRIOUS APPRENTICE

Andrew Carnegie believed that if knowledge was made
available to each man, he would find a happy, useful place in
the scheme of things.

Clara Ingram Judson (1879–1963), biographer

Determined not to give up on the hope that a new
opportunity would present itself, Andrew Carnegie was soon
to get his chance. He was approached by John Hay to write some
letters, Hay being 'a poor penman'. Thereafter Carnegie was
employed to prepare the bills sent out to customers; this led, too,
to dealing with current correspondence. The new work was not
taxing and Carnegie fitted it in alongside an added duty of oiling
textile spools, a job he found nauseous because of the smell of
the oil, but he persisted.

As he proceeded with John Hay's bookkeeping, Carnegie
discovered that while the single-entry accounting system he
was using was adequate, bigger firms utilised a double-entry
format. So, along with his new friends William Cowley, Thomas
Miller and John Phipps, he went to William's accountancy
evening class in double-entry at Pittsburgh during the winter
of 1848/9. Another opportunity too was beckoning.

Returning home from work in the early spring of 1850,
Carnegie learned from his uncle Thomas Hogan that his
draughts-playing companion David Brooks, manager of the
Henry O'Reilly Atlantic and Ohio Telegraph Co., was looking
for a competent boy messenger for the telegraph office. Would
Andrew like to be considered? A family council took place. His
father was against the offer: he considered Andrew 'too young

and too small' and feared that the late-night deliveries might take his son into the dangerous haunts of gamblers, whores and drunks. Eventually, though, William Carnegie was outvoted and Andrew Carnegie followed up the vacancy.[1] So one sunny morning Carnegie, dressed in his best (and only) white linen shirt and blue Sunday-best suit and accompanied by his father as far as the office block, walked the 2 miles from Allegheny to Pittsburgh to the telegraph office at Fourth and Wood Street.[2] The interview was short and to the point. Andrew Carnegie got the job, for which he was to be paid $2.50 per week; he considered it 'my first real start in life'.[3] In his delight in starting the job immediately, Andrew Carnegie almost forgot his father waiting outside; suddenly remembering him, he rapidly downed tools to run out and tell him all was well and that he could go home. The other staff in the office, when Carnegie was introduced to them by fellow telegraph boy George McLain, looked askance at the small stature of their new colleague. Would anyone so small be able to carry out the duties of messenger? They were doubtful. No one in the office ever realised how driven Andrew Carnegie was by the need to stave off poverty. He was determined never to sink back into the penury they had endured at Dunfermline.[4]

Carnegie plunged into his new job with enthusiasm, his finely honed memory soaking up business names, company addresses and street locations of the telegraph company's clients. He had told David Brooks at his interview for the job that he did not know Pittsburgh but within weeks he was even able to identify the managers, agents and important employees of the various firms by name, so that he might deliver messages personally and to the right person. This way he could be recognised by those who mattered. He derived great pride from his new company uniform of dark green jacket and knickerbockers, loose breeches gathered at the knee.[5]

After the fire of 10 April 1845 the business area of Pittsburgh was devastated but the city's streets, alleys and sidewalks still teemed with horses and wagons, and a multitude of hawkers, merchants and loafers all contributing to a public din Carnegie had never experienced in Dunfermline. Because of the fire the business premises were scattered but Carnegie soon knew every remaining building intimately, and more importantly he learned which people were the movers and shakers of the city. In particular he made himself known to prominent members of the Pittsburgh bar, such as judges Wilkins, MacCandless, McClure and Shaler; another such was Edwin McMasters Stanton (1814–69), who went on to become Secretary of War in Abraham Lincoln's Republican administration of 1861–5. Carnegie began to whet his appetite for acquaintance with the 'great' and modelled himself on the Pittsburgh businessmen he met on his delivery rounds.[6]

In his new position Andrew Carnegie began to forge new friendships. William Cowley, John Phipps and Thomas Miller were joined by James R. Wilson and James Smith, and together they enter the Carnegie story as 'The Original Six', all bent on bettering themselves.[7] Enjoying rambles together, exploring the environs of Pittsburgh, they regularly met by the White Horse Tavern – where the Pittsburgh borough council assembled – to argue and debate, much as grandfather Carnegie had done at the Pattiesmuir 'college' – although unlike grandfather Carnegie the teetotal six abstained from liquor. Andrew Carnegie's fellow messenger on the eastern section of the telegraph company's area was David McCargo, and the pair were later joined by Robert Pitcairn. Together they shared their duties of office-cleaning and pole-climbing to repair telegraph wires. The work was hard, but there were high spots too. The boys received tips of fruit and cakes from customers who purveyed such delicacies, but they also received cash tips of up to 10 cents a time for messages 'delivered beyond a certain limit'.[8] The cash tips were a cause for friction among the messengers, especially if one recipient was suspected of taking such a job out of turn. So Andrew Carnegie suggested that all the tips should be pooled and divided up equally at the end of each week; the suggestion was agreed and Carnegie acted as treasurer of the fund. 'It was my first essay in financial organisation,' he later noted.[9]

To his fellows, Andrew Carnegie appeared a bit of a prig and a prude; he tended to remove himself from a group telling dirty jokes, and hissily criticised anybody he thought was overindulging in food. As treasurer of the tips pool, he persuaded the local food shops not to extend credit to the messenger boys in anticipation of shared tips. His Scottish sense of morality also caused him to look down on those who smoked or devoured sweetmeats.[10]

Andrew Carnegie savoured his busy employment, sometimes working until after 10pm, but regretted that he had little time and opportunity to advance himself intellectually. At present there was no spare cash for books. But his access to books was to receive a boost when Colonel James Anderson, founder of several free libraries in western Pennsylvania, decided to open his huge library of books to 'working boys' every Saturday. Did young white-collar employees come into this category of borrowers? Carnegie wrote a note to the *Pittsburgh Dispatch* to clarify the matter – 'my first communication to the press'.[11] Colonel Anderson's librarian replied that the library rules meant 'a Working Boy should have a trade' to qualify as a free borrower. Carnegie took up his pen again to argue the point, signing himself 'A Working Boy though without a Trade'. His determination encouraged Colonel Anderson to widen the catchment of library borrowers and Carnegie won plaudits from his special friends who were now exempt from the $2 borrowing fee. Thereafter Andrew Carnegie was never without a new book to hand from Anderson's collection, be it his favourite, Charles Lamb's *Essays of Elia* (1823), or Thomas Babington Macaulay's *Essays* (1843), or the primer on his new homeland, George Bancroft's ten volume *History of the United States* (1834).

While at the telegraph office Carnegie discovered an interest in the works of Shakespeare, by way of the old Pittsburgh Theatre on Fifth Avenue, then under the managership of Mr Foster. In exchange for a free telegraph delivery service for the theatre the telegraph messengers received complimentary tickets. The tragedian Edwin 'Gust' Adams put on a series of Shakespearean plays – and Andrew Carnegie was hooked.

Macbeth, in particular, revived memories of his Dunfermline childhood, for King Duncan's son Malcolm was the Malcolm III of Dunfermline Tower around which Carnegie had played.

During these early American years Dunfermline was not far from Andrew Carnegie's thoughts. In a letter of 22 June 1851 he wrote to his cousin Dod about his posting as telegraph employee and remarked that one day he would return to his birthplace, 'for I can easily manage to save as much money if I behave well.'[12] He kept up a regular correspondence with Dod and his uncle George Lauder, telling them about the family, his father's linen weaving and his discoveries in American history and geography, and waxing lyrical on the construction of the American constitution which he considered a perfect model for aspiring nations. Although Carnegie was idiosyncratic in the subjects he chose to write about, the letters show a developing political and social consciousness. In a letter of 30 May 1852 to his uncle George Lauder he wrote:

I am sure it is far better for me that I came here. If I had been in Dunfermline working at the loom it's very likely I would have been a poor weaver all my days, but here, I can surely do something better than that – if I don't it will be my own fault, for any one can get along in this country. I intend going to night school this fall to learn something more and after that I will try to teach myself some other branches.[13]

He showed an interest in the presidential election of 1852, in which President Millard Fillmore was not nominated by his Whig party to fill the role again. He wrote to his uncle:

You would laugh to see how low [the politicians] have to bow to their sovereigns [*sic*] the People. The 2 most prominent candidates I am sorry to say are warriors one [Maj] Gen [Winfield] Scott Comm-in-Chief USA. He is a Whig; the Whigs here go for Protection against foreign labor, are in favour of a National Bank & are conservative. The Democrats go for Free Trade and no Chartered Bank. I take great interest in politics here and think when I am a man I would like to dabble a little in them. I would be a democrat or rather a free-soil-Democrat, free soilers got that name from their hatred of Slavery and slave labor. Slavery I hope will soon be abolished in this Country . . . There is much excitement here upon the subject of Temperance. The State of Maine passed a law prohibiting the manufacture or sale except for medical purposes of all intoxicating liquors; several states have passed similar laws and of course the Rum sellers are trying all they can to protect their rights to sell what they please. That is a step in advance of [Britain] at any rate.[14]

The election was won by New Hampshire lawyer Franklin Pierce, who dismayed Carnegie by enforcing the Fugitive Slave Act.

In Pittsburgh Carnegie was reunited with the Swedenborgians who had founded a society there. Aunt Anne Aitken was a keen Swedenborgian and Andrew Carnegie found an interest in music participation through the oratorios attached to their hymn book. His developing interest caused him to join the Swedenborgian choir under Mr Koethen, although Carnegie admitted that he was 'denied much of a voice', but his enthusiasm for the music forgave any 'discords'.[15] He also browsed in the Swedenborgian library and wrote for their tract *Dewdrop*. Significantly for his future pacifism, he wrote an article denouncing the Crimean War, which had broken out in 1854 with its first engagement at the Battle of Alma on 20 September.[16]

Andrew Carnegie had served as a telegraph messenger for some twelve months when office manager Colonel John P. Glass recruited him to 'watch' the downstairs office in his absence. These duties became more frequent as Glass pursued other interests, and Carnegie quickly learned various other aspects of the telegraphic business. In the process he encountered some hostility from the other telegraphic boys, which reminded him of being taunted as 'Martin's pet' during his childhood. One of his future character traits became apparent at this time, too – a meddlesome approach to the work and affairs of others. Another bone of contention with his office peers was that they considered Carnegie to be mean; he never socialised with his fellow workers, preferring to save every penny. However, gradually the Carnegies amassed enough dollars to repay the £20 Ailie Ferguson Henderson had advanced for their 1848 passage; the debt once idemnified, 'that was a day we celebrated'.[17]

Then came a moment of panic. One pay day Colonel Glass failed to pay Andrew Carnegie's wages. Was he to get the sack? Relief came when Glass revealed that Carnegie was to receive a pay rise for his satisfactory extra office work, his salary rising from $11.25 to $13.50 per month. Carnegie was triumphant: 'No subsequent success, or recognition of any kind, ever thrilled me as this did.'[18] On his return home he handed his mother the $11.25 she was expecting and he gave no indication that he had had a rise. He wanted to savour the moment. With his brother he fantasised, as they retired to bed that night, that one day they would go into business together as 'Carnegie Brothers'. Next morning he told his proud mother of the rise, enjoying his moment of theatricality.

In 1852 Andrew Carnegie began to learn the art of telegraphy, its operation and language. Before the telegraph operators came into the office each morning the messenger boys had to clean the floors. Carnegie's innate sense of opportunism caused him to try sending and receiving messages on the unattended machines. On one occasion he ventured to take down a message without permission; tentatively he told David Brooks what he had done and instead of receiving the expected reprimand he was complimented on his actions but warned to be careful. His cheek paid off and he was allowed to relieve the regular telegraph operators from time to time. The system of receiving messages was complicated; they came through on a roll of paper tape, printed with the dots and dashes of the Morse alphabet (later called Morse Code) invented in 1832 by Samuel Morse, and then they had to be translated by the operator. Carnegie heard that operators elsewhere were taking messages by *listening* to the transmission of the Morse Code letters instead of reading them off the tape. Despite being mocked by his fellows, Carnegie learned to receive messages this way, which proved much quicker. Soon he was given a trial as a relief operator at Greensburg, some 30 miles from Pittsburgh. At Greensburg Andrew Carnegie observed the foundation work being carried out for the Pennsylvania Railroad, little realising that this venture would be his next great opportunity.

Having carried out his duties at Greensburg to his employers' satisfaction, Andrew Carnegie was promoted to assistant operator on David Brooks's recommendation to the General Superintendent of the line, the Fife-born James D. Reid. Reid commented: 'I liked the boy's looks, and it was very easy to see that though he was little he was full of spirit.'[19] Carnegie's pay was increased to $25 a month and he considered himself 'performing a man's part'.[20]

Carnegie's skills were soon to be further exploited. At that time international news entered America via the Cape Race receiving station, south of St John's in Newfoundland, and from this the press built up their foreign news columns. The local papers employed one man to translate these wired despatches, and the Pittsburgh agent now offered Carnegie a dollar a day to prepare multiple copies of the despatches for the papers. This way Carnegie added $30 a month to the household budget, enabling the family to purchase the house Margaret Carnegie desired.[21] This was the house recently vacated by the Hogan relatives who had moved to East Liverpool, Ohio. The purchase price was $550. The Carnegies were now property owners – a situation that would never have been possible for them in Dunfermline.

As Andrew Carnegie prospered and became the financial bedrock for the family, his father continued to struggle; he was hardly better off than he had been in Dunfermline. He peddled his webs where he could but had little financial return. He became noticeably more despondent. On one occasion, when Carnegie was working on despatches at the Steubenville office, after a flood on the Ohio River had destroyed lines with Wheeling, he met his father on his way to Wheeling and Cincinnati to sell tablecloths. William Carnegie was to travel by riverboat and Andrew was shaken by the fact that his father could not afford a cabin and was to spend the night on deck. He attempted to comfort his father by saying, 'Well, father, it will not be long before mother and you shall ride in your own carriage.' Much touched, the usually undemonstrative William Carnegie replied: 'Andra, I am proud of you.'[22]

The pubescent Andrew Carnegie seems to have had little interest in girls. Certainly his autobiography of 1920 and his other anecdotal writings offer no clues to any romantic leaning or girls' names. Yet biographer Joseph Frazier Wall recounts a curious tale from the 1850s. Quoting a letter from Carl Engel to Robert M. Lester dated 24 April 1935 (and now in the Carnegie Corporation of New York files), he recounts how Andrew Carnegie was paid 25 cents, from time to time, by the Athertons to take their daughter Miss Lou Atherton to evening parties and escort her home again.[23] Was Carnegie obsessed with staying one step ahead of poverty, suppressing any developing sexuality and giving all things a price tag? Possibly, but the dominance of his mother in his thoughts may also have put a dampener on any developing romance.

Andrew Carnegie said that two societies in particular were a 'decided influence' over his early life in America. The first was Pittsburgh's premier club, the Webster Literary Society, where regular discussions took place on literature past and present, and the second was the Debating Society set up by the 'Original Six'; members met at Henry Phipp's workroom after the journeymen shoemakers had finished work for the day. In these two societies, Carnegie said, he learned the art of public speaking, for which he propounded two rules: 'Make yourself perfectly at home before your audience, and simply talk *to* them, not *at* them. Do not try to be somebody else, be yourself and *talk*, never "orate" until you can't help it.'[24]

The 'Six' clubbed together to buy copies of the *New York Weekly Tribune*, the Whig-turned-Republican newspaper founded by Horace Greeley in 1841. A letter to the *Tribune* from Carnegie on the slavery issue 'enhanced his local standing' in Pittsburgh.[25] In debate and in print Andrew Carnegie still spouted the Dunfermline radicalism of his birthplace, but his 'early political allegiance' began to shift and his outlook was decidedly more American; something else was changing too, as his rich Dunfermline brogue was tempered by Americanisms.[26] Public speaking and success at work helped Carnegie's growing confidence. Secure in the fact that his family was earning the $300 per annum he once calculated that they needed for a comfortable life, Andrew Carnegie was psychologically ready for the next twist fate had in store for him.

FIVE

THE WHITE-HAIRED SCOTCH DEVIL

The rising man must do something exceptional, and beyond the range of his special department. HE MUST ATTRACT ATTENTION.

Speech at Curry Commercial College, 23 June 1885

A ndrew Carnegie was ready for a change. He had had enough of office life. Sudden judgements and resolutions like this were to be a hallmark of Andrew Carnegie's advancement and prosperity. This time the change came through a man called Thomas A. Scott. In the early 1850s the railroads around Pittsburgh were still developing but there was a direct link between Pittsburgh and Philadelphia, and the O'Reilly Telegraph Co. anticipated increased business on the east coast with the new links.

Thomas A. Scott was one of the most notable pioneers of mid-nineteenth-century America. Like financier and steamship owner Cornelius Vanderbilt (1794–1877), Scott is hailed as a prime developer of public transport in America. He had worked his way up from farm boy at Blair County, Pennsylvania, to astute businessman. In many ways he shared certain character traits with Andrew Carnegie – both became resolute leaders, workaholics and commercial visionaries – and already Scott was a key figure in Pennsylvania railroad circles. He realised that the movement of trains would be greatly enhanced if the railroad had its own telegraph system. As usual, Scott was keen to embrace modern ideas that would expand his network.

Towards this end Scott needed a telegraph operator to run his new independent wire; as this job would only be part-time,

Scott was also looking for a clerk-cum-personal secretary. A regular visitor to the O'Reilly Co., he knew of Carnegie's reputation as a telegraph office operator. Could Carnegie be tempted to move? People shook their heads. They did not know what was going on in Carnegie's head. John P. Glass offered Carnegie a salary of $400 a year if he would stay, but Carnegie was taking the long view. To him railways were the coming thing and thus offered greater prospects. A direct employment offer was made to him by the Pennsylvania Railroad Co. which he immediately accepted, taking up his new employment on 1 February 1853 at a salary of $35 per month.

All this news was put in a letter to his uncle George Lauder dated 14 March 1853: 'I am liking [the job],' he wrote, 'far better than the old one. Instead of having to stay every night till 10 or 11 o'clock I am done every night at six . . . .' Carnegie went on to say that his father was trying to sell some $70 worth of cloth and that his mother was buying new things for the house but that things 'are double the price they are in Scotland'. He was still keeping up a keen interest in what was happening in Britain, and asked for his uncle's comments on the new Tory coalition administration led by Prime Minister George Hamilton-Gordon, Earl of Aberdeen (1784–1860), and puzzled over the expansion of the French Navy of Napoleon III's Second Empire; and he looked forward to the day when the United Kingdom and United States would unite 'against Despotism'.[1]

Carnegie entered a new world of brakemen and firemen, ex-riverboat workers and railroad operatives, and found the 'coarse men' he met a cultural shock that he was not ready for.[2] In those days the railway employed ex-mariners, disillusioned gold hunters, illiterate new immigrants and a general hotchpotch of undisciplined humanity alongside the more diligent workers like Carnegie. For the rest of his life he would abhor foul language, sexual innuendo, chewing and smoking tobacco and drinking alcohol, all of which he now encountered in abundance. Yet around him there were some 'respectable citizens', and to his delight his friends David McCargo and Robert Pitcairn also found work with the Pennsylvania Railroad Co.

Although his formal education had been patchy, Carnegie was now absorbing a new style of enlightenment which would provide an important basis for the future. Each facet of his employment introduced him to current business practices and to the activities of all the companies on the railroad's books. Carnegie shared an office with Scott and became so indispensable that up and down the Pennsylvania's lines he was known as 'Scott's Andy'. This gave him inordinate pleasure, particularly when one day he was so addressed by the President of the Pennsylvania Railway, J. Edgar Thomson.

New lines were being laid through the mountains, and the village of Altoona developed as an important construction and maintenance depot. Here Andrew Carnegie nearly met his nemesis. One day he had collected the monthly payrolls and cheques from Altoona and was travelling back to Pittsburgh. As he preferred to ride in the engine cab, he had a rough journey and after a particularly hard jolt he reached into his coat where he had placed the payrolls to find that they had gone. Panic-stricken he asked for the train to be stopped. As it slowly reversed back up the line Carnegie spotted where the package had fallen. Greatly relieved, he retrieved it and climbed back on the train. He had one further problem: both the driver and the fireman had witnessed his carelessness. Would they report him? Luckily they did not, and Carnegie's career was saved.[3]

Now aged 18, Andrew Carnegie had already laid the foundations of his lifelong character traits. His employers and colleagues noticed his quickness of decision, his assertiveness and absolute confidence in himself, and his willingness to accept responsibility, and the audacity, self-reliance, ruthlessness and opportunism he displayed in carrying out his duties. Anecdotes abound about all these Carnegie traits. His opportunistic nature came to the fore again on another occasion. Just as he had taken liberties in David Brook's telegraph office, he was to do the same in Thomas A. Scott's. One day he arrived at the office to find that a serious accident had taken place on the Eastern Division line. This was not unusual: the log for 1853 had clocked up around 150 such accidents.[4] Freight and passenger trains were disrupted and Scott himself could not be found to give orders for unsnarling the rail traffic. Carnegie had issued countless orders in Scott's name and with his authority, and now he did so again but this time *without* authority. The trains were ordered to proceed.

Carnegie had taken an enormous risk. When he found out what had happened, Scott neither praised nor censured Carnegie for his actions but later that day he spoke about it to one of his colleagues:

'Do you know what that little white-haired Scotch devil of mine did today?'

'No.'

'I'm damned if he didn't run every train on the division in my name without the slightest authority.'

'And did he do it all right?'

'Oh, yes, all right.'[5]

His luck often made Carnegie smug, but after this incident he mused: 'The great aim of every boy should be to do something beyond the sphere of his duties – something which attracts the attention of those over him.'[6] Carnegie's risk-taking again paid off: Scott obtained permission from Mr Lombaert, General Superintendent of the Pennsylvania Railway, for Carnegie to be in charge of the Eastern Division during his absence. Told that permission was granted, Carnegie declared it 'the coveted opportunity of my life'.[7]

Another incident at this time nearly scuppered Carnegie for good with the railway. Thomas A. Scott was away from the office and so was not available to deal with a disciplinary matter. An accident happened which was entirely due to the negligence of a railway ballast crew. In such serious matters it was company policy to hold a 'court martial'. Confident in the role that Scott had given him, Carnegie held his own court martial into the incident.[8] Having identified the culprits, he sacked one and suspended two others for four weeks without pay. It put him in bad odour with the workforce, foreshadowing Carnegie's poor labour relations at another time and another place. He had certainly exceeded his authority; Scott knew it, but took no further action and let Carnegie's decision stand.

Then there was the occasion of the letter. Among the businessmen of Pittsburgh there had been some criticism of the Pennsylvania Railroad. As a consequence Robert M. Riddel's *Pittsburgh Journal* had published an anonymous letter in support of the railroad. Who had written it? Colonel Niles A. Stokes, lawyer for the railway, telegraphed Thomas A. Scott to ascertain who had written it . . . in his opinion some congratulation was due. Scott duly investigated and Carnegie admitted that he was the author. Scott was 'incredulous' and Carnegie smugly noted, 'The pen was getting to be a weapon with me.'[9] Very soon after this, an invitation came for Carnegie to spend one Sunday with Stokes at Greensburg. Carnegie leapt at the opportunity and recalled:

The grandure [*sic*] of Mr Stokes's home impressed me, but the one feature of it that eclipsed all else was a marble mantel in his library. In the centre of the arch, carved in marble, was an open book with the inscription:

> He that cannot reason is a fool,
> He that will not a bigot,
> He that dare not a slave.

These noble words thrilled me. I said to myself, 'Some day, some day, I'll have a library . . . and these words shall grace the mantel as here.'[10]

In future years the 'noble words' of the quotation which had 'thrilled' him graced the mantel of his library at Skibo Castle.

Andrew Carnegie prospered and his salary was advanced to $40, drawn in two $20 gold coins. They were, he said, 'the prettiest works of art in the world'.[11] His euphoria at his advancement was tempered by the decline of his father. In these early American years William Carnegie had contributed little or nothing to the family purse. Much of his woven material lay stacked in the house unsold. He also endured extended weeks of ill health. Despite everything, he had still not come to terms with life in America. Unlike his elder son, William Carnegie was not interested in American history or politics, and even when he became eligible for American citizenship he showed little interest. It was only because of Andrew's nagging that on 20 November 1854 he presented himself to the Court of General Sessions for Allegheny County where the clerk received his declaration of intent. William would have to wait two years before the naturalisation would become lawful after taking a final oath. This never happened for William Carnegie died on 2 October 1855. The fact that his father had presented himself to the Court of General Sessions at all was lodged in Andrew Carnegie's mind and he felt that this amounted to William becoming an American citizen; as he was considered a minor at the time, then he too was a citizen of America. Technically, however, Andrew Carnegie was never an American citizen; although his future enemies taunted him with this fact, his wealth and position meant that no one ever openly challenged his claim to American citizenship.

Andrew Carnegie greatly mourned his father's passing. He said: 'My father was one of the most lovable of men, beloved of his companions, deeply religious, although non-sectarian and non-theological, not much of a man of the world, but a man all over for heaven.'[12] Despite his grief, Andrew Carnegie took on the greater burden of organising the family's daily life and ensuring that the loan for the house on Rebecca Street was paid off. His mother continued her shoe-binding and his 12-year-old brother Tom progressed to secondary education.

Carnegie's life was a round of work, socialising with his close friends, writing to his cousin Dod at Dunfermline and hoovering up information about local commerce. One event of national importance was interesting him too: the rise of the Republican party, which held an important meeting at Pittsburgh on 22 February 1856. In the late eighteenth century the evolution of the French revolutionary republic and the execution of Louis XIV had brought the development of political parties in America into fine focus, and by 1795–6 the Republicans had become a force to be reckoned with, supporting policies based on 'liberty and humanity'. Since Andrew Jackson's presidency of 1828, America had been governed by a succession of Democrat and Whig administrations. Carnegie was excited about what the Republicans had to say about anti-slavery and the promotion of land reform. Somehow land ownership and the exploitation of wealth for personal prosperity and common good was slowly being distanced from the radical socialist atmosphere of his childhood Dunfermline. Although he was not yet old enough to vote, Carnegie considered himself a member of the Republican party and gave voice to their policies.

Carnegie was soon about to undertake his first real venture into capitalism. Thomas A. Scott asked him if he had $500 to spare for a particular investment in a package delivery company which traded with the Pennsylvania Railroad.[13] The shares had suddenly come on the market when their owner Mrs Ann Patrick had need to raise cash.[14] Carnegie did not have that kind of money but he was not going to let that confound his chances of hitching up to Scott's financial wagon. He discussed the matter with his mother, and they decided a loan would have to be taken out. Carnegie agreed to the deal and was overjoyed when Scott himself loaned him the $500 (plus the premium of $110) on 17 May 1856, payable by November. Thus Carnegie made his first investment: ten shares in the stock of the Adams Express Co. were his and would pay him a monthly return. His first dividend cheque of $10, drawn on the Gold Exchange Bank of New York, would be emblazoned on his memory for ever:

I shall remember that cheque as long as I live, and that . . . signature of 'J.C. Babcock, Cashier'. It gave me the first penny of revenue from capital – something that I had not worked for with the sweat of my brow. 'Eureka!' I cried. 'Here's the goose that lays the golden eggs.'[15]

All did not go smoothly. Carnegie was unable to pay off the loan by November 1856, and had to borrow what was owed at an 8 per cent rate of interest, higher than his return. With his mother's agreement the house at Rebecca Street supported the loan, and by 1858 the debt was cleared. More significantly Carnegie had shown a willingness to undertake a complicated loans return to support a financial risk. This lesson would make him rich.

By the autumn of 1856 the now-widowed Thomas A. Scott succeeded Herman Lombaert as General Superintendent of the Pennsylvania Railway. He thus relocated to Altoona and Andrew Carnegie accompanied him as secretary, working at the Altoona office at a new salary of $50 per month. Until Scott acquired a permanent home for his children, both he and Carnegie lived at the Altoona railway hotel: 'He seemed anxious always to have me near him,' noted Carnegie.[16]

Scott inherited a troubled office. There had already been strikes among the freight men, and now the maintenance men threatened a walkout in the important depot at Altoona. J. Edgar Thomson was bent on cutting costs for the Pennsylvania Railroad and proposed a wage reduction of 10–25 per cent on a range of manual jobs. When the cuts became effective on 1 November 1857, the railwaymen rebelled.

In his autobiography Carnegie offers a curious story about how he helped to break the impending strike. It seems that one night he was walking back to the hotel in Altoona when he 'became aware that a man was following me'. Eventually the man approached him. Explaining that Carnegie had once found the man a job as a blacksmith at Pittsburgh and that he would like to return the favour, he said that papers had been circulated to the maintenance men urging them to strike the following Monday. He listed the names of the strike leaders and supporters. Carnegie immediately informed Scott. Next morning Scott ordered the posting of notices in the maintenance shops naming the men Carnegie had been told about and detailing their dismissal. With satisfaction Carnegie noted 'the threatened strike was broken'.[17]

These were changed days for Andrew Carnegie; here was the young revolutionary from Dunfermline who had cheered on the weavers' strikes almost glorying in the role of strike-breaker. Would not the Morrisons be turning in their graves? Certainly Carnegie put any such thoughts out of his mind, remarking:

> It counts many times more to a kindness to a poor working-man than to a millionaire, who may be able some day to repay the favour. How true Wordsworth's lines:
>
> > That best portion of a good man's life –
> > His little, nameless, unremembered acts
> > Of kindness and of love.[18]

The self-satisfaction he derived from his role as a strike-breaker caused Andrew Carnegie to become more cocky and dogmatic in his attitude. He augmented his 5ft 3in stature and his baby-faced demeanour with grave clothes, weighty boots and a capacious overcoat. But now he was learning to combine his arrogance with charm and to project his personality better at work and social gatherings.

As the spring of 1857 passed, Carnegie was able to bring his family from Pittsburgh to Altoona. They sold their house at Slabtown for $1500.[19] At Carnegie's insistence, despite his mother's reluctance, a servant was hired. Soon a cook was also added to the household, but Carnegie acknowledged that his mother never took to having strangers in the house. 'She had cooked [for] and served her boys,' he said, 'washed their clothes and mended them, made their beds, cleaned their home. Who dare rob her of those motherly privileges!'[20]

Free at last from the pollution of Pittsburgh, the Carnegies enjoyed the rural setting of Altoona and Carnegie took up horse-riding. He bought a fiery horse called 'Dash' and thundered about the countryside with an incautiousness that made friends and neighbours gasp. Because he only occasionally saw his old friends McCargo, Miller and Pitcairn, Carnegie lived a rather lonely existence in Altoona. Soon, though, gossips were linking his name to that of an eligible female.

Rebecca Stewart came to Altoona to act as hostess and child-carer for her widowed uncle Thomas A. Scott. At the time Rebecca was around 25 and Carnegie 23, and both were lacking in company:

> [Rebecca] played the part of the elder sister to me to perfection, especially when Mr Scott was called to Philadelphia or elsewhere. We were much together, often driving in the afternoons through the woods. The intimacy did not cease for many years, and re-reading some of her letters in 1906 I realised more than ever my indebtedness to her. . . . It was to her I looked up in those days as the perfect lady.[21]

Did he fancy Rebecca? We can't be sure as at this time 'matrimony [was] something not seriously entertained'.[22] Certainly Carnegie was more impressed with wealth than a pretty face; decades later his friend Thomas Miller reminded him of 'the awe you felt – or was it exultation? – when I took dinner with you at Scott's and "Beck" Stewart was our hostess? She went out for some service, and you hastily took up a cream pitcher and said "Real silver, Tom!"'[23] But with or without Rebecca, Carnegie was soon to have another chance encounter that was to spur his career ever onwards.

SIX

WAR CLOUDS AND A SILVER LINING

Carnegie . . . was the most genial of despots, bending men to
his will by an unfailing charm.

Burton J. Hendrick, biographer, 1932

Sitting in Auchnagar, the little bungalow that he built in
Sutherland, Carnegie began to write his memoirs in 1914.
His memory was sharp, but his tendency to romanticise parts
of his life grew stronger. A good example of this was in his
recollection of the events of 1858 and his encounter with
Theodore T. Woodruff.

According to Carnegie he was travelling one day in a
Pennsylvania Railroad observation car, watching the
scenery, when a man of rustic aspect came and sat beside
him. The man carried 'a small green bag' and said that the
brakeman had pointed out Carnegie as an employee of the
railway company.[1] The man produced from his bag a model
of a new-style railway carriage with a section of a sleeping-
car. 'Its importance flashed upon me.' Carnegie said that he
would take the matter up with Thomas A. Scott with a view
to the railway company developing the idea.

Thus Carnegie gave the impression that Woodruff was an
unknown inventor that he cultivated and so brought to the
world the concept of the sleeping-car. Nothing could be further
from the truth. Woodruff had begun his business life as a
wagon maker with a flair for innovation and invention. He
became master builder for the Terre Haute, Alton & St Louis
Railroad and in 1856 secured patents for his sleeping-car. In
time he established T.T. Woodruff & Co. (later called the Central

Transport Co.), and himself pursued a deal with the Pennsylvania Railroad.

Always keen to pursue new ideas for the Pennsylvania Railroad, J. Edgar Thomson had introduced various innovations from carriage heating to gas lighting, so he jumped at Woodruff's idea and placed an order for four sleeping-cars. Woodruff needed finance to meet his swelling order book, and both Thomson and Scott became investors. Again luck fell Carnegie's way. Another investor was needed, and Carnegie was given 'an eighth interest in the venture'.[2] His initial investment was $217.50, raised by means of a bank loan.[3] The returns would be vast and Carnegie later said of the investment that 'the first considerable sum I made was from this source',[4] and 'Blessed be the man who invented sleep'.[5]

Carnegie's version of his first meeting with Woodruff appeared in his *Triumphant Democracy* in 1886. Woodruff was incandescent. The concept of sleeping berths on long-distance trains was not new, and was certainly not pioneered by Carnegie. Some lines ran freight cars with bunks built into their sides. The first sleeping-cars were cramped, cold, noisy, insanitary and unsafe, and no woman ever travelled in them. Woodruff's invention was different; the day carriages could be quickly converted to night sleeping carriages which were both hygienic and safe, and Woodruff had successfully sold, and operated, such systems to other railway companies long before he had anything to do with the Pennsylvania Railroad, with whom the first contract was signed on 15 September 1858.

Why did Carnegie lie? In a letter dated 12 June 1886 Woodruff said that it was 'arrogance' that 'spurred [Carnegie] to make the statements'.[6] Carnegie did not reply publicly to Woodruff, who, still angry, published his version in *Philadelphia Sunday*. Carnegie eventually wrote a disingenuous reply to Woodruff, in which he avoided all mention of Woodruff's assertions. Within two years Carnegie's initial investment of $217.50 was bringing him annual dividends of $5,000.[7] In future he could afford to be cavalier with his accounts of his life.

During the autumn of 1859 Thomas A. Scott announced that William B. Foster, the vice-president of the Pennsylvania Railroad, had died suddenly. It seemed likely that J. Edgar Thomson would ask Scott to take over Foster's position, with Enoch Lewis replacing Scott. Where would that leave Carnegie? He was disturbed that he would no longer be within Scott's immediate orbit. But would he consider the job of manager of the Pittsburgh (Western) Division of the railroad, in place of Enoch Lewis?

Fully confident that, like his Dunfermline heroes William Wallace and Robert Bruce, he 'could manage anything', Carnegie accepted.[8] Scott then asked: 'What salary do you think you should have?' Offended, Carnegie replied: 'Salary, what do I care for salary? I do not want the salary. I want the position.'[9] Despite his show of indifference to money, which was probably genuine enough if his *Autobiography* is to be believed, Carnegie was set a new salary of $1,500 a year rising to $1,800 for satisfactory progress. An agreement appointing him to the position of Superintendent of the Western Division was signed on 1 December 1859. What mattered most to Carnegie though, was that orders could now be sent out bearing his signature or initials rather than Scott's.

In accordance with his promotion the Carnegies soon returned to Pittsburgh, renting a house on Hancock Street (later 8th Street) near the Pennsylvania Railroad section. Immediately they missed the fresh air of Altoona. Carnegie wrote:

> Any accurate description of Pittsburgh at that time would be set down as a piece of the grossest exaggeration. The smoke permeated and penetrated everything. If you placed your hand on the balustrade of the stair it came away black; if you washed your face and hands they were as dirty as ever in an hour. The soot gathered in the hair and irritated the skin, and for a time after our return from the mountain atmosphere of Altoona, life was more or less miserable.[10]

Pittsburgh was now the sixteenth largest city in the USA, with glassworks and rolling mills creating extra jobs. It swarmed with immigrants seeking work in the streets leading down to the paddle-steamer wharves. The Carnegies felt stifled. Relief was at hand, though, in the person of Rebecca Stewart's brother David, a Pennsylvania Railroad freight agent. Why didn't the Carnegies come to his residential neighbourhood of Homewood, in the East Liberty Valley, some 15 miles north-east of the city? The Carnegies convened a family conference and duly purchased there 'a modest tawny coloured, two-storey framed house, embowered in Norway spruce trees'.[11]

The Carnegies launched themselves into a new society of well-heeled neighbours, and Benjamin and John Vandervort particularly became their firm friends. As Carnegie rubbed shoulders with such men as the octogenarian former US Minister to Russia the Hon. Judge William Wilkins, whose brother-in-law was George W. Dallas, Vice-President of the USA under President James K. Polk, he perfected his social graces and conversational skills on a new range of topics of the day; there were Vandervort musical evenings, skating parties, theatre visits and squirrel hunts, and games in Wilkins's parlour. One subject that became taboo was politics. Judge Wilkins and his wife Matilda were ardent Democrats and racists. The fact that negroes were even admitted to the military academy at West Point dismayed Mrs Wilkins. On one occasion the abolitionist Carnegie could not hold his tongue and addressed her directly: 'Mrs Wilkins, there is something even worse than that. I understand that some [negroes] have been admitted to Heaven.' There was a pregnant silence, and with a fluttering of her fan Mrs Wilkins replied: 'That is a different matter, Mr Carnegie.'[12]

Around this time Andrew Carnegie met at the Wilkins' house one Leila Addison, the daughter of a prominent Pittsburgh physician, originally an emigrant from Edinburgh. The Addisons were well-heeled literary folk and Leila had been a pupil of Thomas Carlyle when the famous man was living at 21 Comely Bank, Edinburgh, before his move away from the city in 1828.

From Leila, Carnegie said he learned to enjoy the English classes and how to be better spoken and better dressed; he also acquired better table manners and 'better behaviour'.[13] Although there was no romance – Leila was probably too old for him – Carnegie was always appreciative of her influence and much later secured some lucrative investments for her.

In addition to altering his manners and dress, Andrew Carnegie also did something about his youthful appearance. At 5ft 3in and of baby-faced mien, Carnegie was often treated with disrespect by those employees who did not know him. Quoting a letter from George Alexander to Thomas Miller of 12 May 1903, biographer Joseph Frazier Wall notes that Carnegie was once seized by a large Irish railway worker who shoved him aside saying: 'Get out of my way, you brat of a boy. You're eternally in the way of the men who are trying to do their job.'[14] The Irishman was greatly abashed when he found out that the 'brat' he had dismissed so rudely was his boss. Nevertheless, in an attempt to look older Carnegie grew a curious fringe-beard; alas, it did not have the desired effect and he still looked vulnerably youthful.

Carnegie was anxious to stand on his own feet. No longer did he have the crutch and protection of being 'Mr Scott's Andy'. His attempts to be more assertive and in command of his job made him more officious, interfering and workaholic. Of this he remarked:

At one time for eight days I was constantly upon the line, day and night, at one wreck or obstruction after another. I was probably the most inconsiderate superintendent that ever was entrusted with the management of a great property, for never knowing fatigue myself, being kept up by a sense of responsibility probably, I overworked the men and was not careful enough in considering the limits of human endurance. I have always been able to sleep at any time. Snatches of half an hour at intervals during the night in a dirty freight car were sufficient.[15]

He also began to fill jobs around him with people he could trust. He appointed his American friends David McCargo as superintendent of the telegraph department and George Alexander, whom he had met when living in Rebecca Street, as conductor. His cousin Marie Hogan became a freight station telegraph operator and his brother Tom became his secretary. Carnegie regularly boasted in company that he was the first man in America to employ a woman as a telegraph operator, yet this was to be a shrewd move as women would soon take on prominent new roles following the coming disaster that would push 620,000 men into the jaws of death.

Ever since the party had been formed (in its modern sense) in 1854, Carnegie had been a staunch Republican. The Dunfermline socialist rebel had, by his 25th birthday, become a devout capitalist, and the Republican party appealed to him. A strange mixture of political philosophy formed in Carnegie's mind; his socialist idealism gleaned at Dunfermline had been interlarded with American business opportunism to evolve a new political animal. The Tory and Liberal landed aristocracy of Scotland and England, which a youthful Carnegie had learned to hate, had been replaced in his new home and his conscience by the slaver–planter aristocracy of the southern United States.

To challenge Democrat President James Buchanan, a former Minister to Great Britain, the Republicans chose as their candidate a man who greatly interested Carnegie. Abraham Lincoln, born at Hardin County, Kentucky, on 12 February 1809, had grown up in ignorance and poverty in the wilderness of the frontier, and had risen through self-education to be a surveyor, a postmaster, a member of the Illinois Legislature, a lawyer and a member of Congress. He was just the kind of man Carnegie admired. Now in possession of the US franchise, Carnegie cast his vote for Lincoln in 1860; Lincoln was inaugurated as President on 4 March 1861 and almost immediately had to get to grips with a growing crisis.

Almost from the birth of the American Republic on 4 July 1776, rivalry and sectional differences had separated the North and South. By 1860 slavery and secession divided America into two hostile camps whose differences could ultimately be solved only by war. Lincoln had fought his election from an anti-slavery standpoint; he had triumphed in the North, but in ten states of the South he received not a single vote. On 20 December 1860 the South Carolina Legislature at Charleston decided to secede from the Union, to be followed by other states. In the early hours of 12 April 1861 the first shots of the Civil War were fired by the new Southern Confederacy batteries at Charleston, under Brigadier General P.G.T. Beauregard, against the brick bastion of Fort Sumter, a Federal (Northern) offshore garrison defended by Major Robert Anderson. After nearly 3,400 missiles had rained down on Fort Sumter during a 34-hour cannonade, Major Anderson surrendered on 14 April 1861. Four years of vicious slaughter had begun.[16]

On the evening of the attack on Fort Sumter the telegraph clacked the war message to Pittsburgh. The city's militia contingents were organised and a military camp set up near the Allegheny River. Pennsylvania was to live up to its nickname of the Keystone State, through its stalwart contribution to the Union war effort. Out of a population of 2.8 million whites and 56,373 free blacks in 1860, Pennsylvania contributed 315,017 white and 8,612 black soldiers to the Union armies. It ranked second only to New York in total population and men under arms. Pennsylvania witnessed more military action than any other Northern state, and the largest battle of the entire war was fought on its acres at Gettysburg, on 1–3 July 1863, between Major-General George G. Meade's Army of the Potomac and Confederate General Robert E. Lee's Army of Northern Virginia. Lincoln's inspired address at the dedication of a national cemetery at Gettysburg on 19 November 1863 brilliantly captured the enduring meaning of the war. But all this still lay in the future. Carnegie realised that the railroads would play a vital part in the coming conflict. By 1860 Pennsylvania had nearly 2,500 miles of the 30,000 miles of track completed in America, and the whole east coast had rail links from Portland,

Maine and the Canadian border in the North, to Jacksonville in Florida in the South. In 1862 President Lincoln was able to authorise the construction of the Union Pacific Railway, running west from Omaha, Nebraska, and the Central Pacific and running east from San Francisco.

As the war clouds darkened Carnegie was in no doubt about his personal position. He was a patriot, yet he hated the concept of war and despised militarism; nevertheless he looked upon it as 'justifiable'. As a schoolboy in Dunfermline, Carnegie had been awarded a penny prize for a Burns recitation by visiting statesman John Morley (1838–1923, later Viscount Morley of Blackburn), and later he would be a friend and correspondent of Morley's, but now Carnegie echoed Morley's attitude to the American Civil War:

> An end has been brought to the only war in modern times as to which we can be sure, first, that no skill or patience of diplomacy could have averted it, and second, that preservation of the American Union and abolition of negro slavery were two vast triumphs of good by which even the inferno of war was justified.[17]

The war would make Carnegie, along with the likes of the Rockefellers, the Vanderbilts and the Harrimans, a representative figure of the age. But in 1861 what was he to do? He was ready to 'support the flag'. Soon after the Confederate success at Fort Sumter, Thomas A. Scott was contacted by Lincoln's Secretary or War, Simon Cameron, and requested to journey to Washington to work for the War Department as a transport administrator. Scott was relieved by both the Pennsylvania Railroad Co. and from his post as new aide to Governor Andrew Gregg Curtain at Harrisburgh. Without much delay, and with the agreement of railroad president J. Edgar Thomson, Scott summoned Carnegie to Washington 'to act as his assistant of the military railroads and telegraphs'.[18] He was also to set up a force of railwaymen on war alert.

Communications between Washington and Baltimore, where Union troops were assembling, had been threatened with several inflammatory events, including a riot in Baltimore when a pro-secessionist mob attacked the 6th Massachusetts Regiment. Washington itself was being threatened as the armies of the Confederacy were advancing through Southern states. The northern regiments were desperately needed in the federal capital, as Maryland became increasingly hostile. Carnegie's first job was to facilitate the passage of Major-General Benjamin F. Butler's troops to the south. The severed line at Annapolis Junction was repaired, and a train bearing General Butler, his staff and members of the 8th Massachusetts Regiment plus their impedimenta set off with Carnegie riding on the lead engine. Even before they sighted their destination a problem developed. Carnegie recounted:

Some distance from Washington I noticed that the telegraph wires had been pinned to the ground by wooden stakes. I stopped the engine and ran forward to release them, but I did not notice that the wires had been pulled to one side before staking. When released, in their spring upwards, they struck me in the face, knocked me over, and cut a gash in my cheek which bled profusely.[19]

Looking back later, Carnegie boasted that he 'entered the city of Washington with the first troops', and added that he was 'among the first' to 'shed blood for my country'.[20]

The capital was duly secured, and Maryland, despite its divided allegiances, stayed in the Union. At Scott's instruction Carnegie now set about organising the telegraph communications and railroad south to Virginia; the Union target there was Richmond. Carnegie summoned the best telegraphers he knew, with the help of his old friend David McCargo, now superintendent at Altoona.

By July 1861 Carnegie had made his headquarters at Alexandria in Virginia, a key area for repelling any attack on Washington. Virginia had been the first state in the Upper South to leave the Union, and after Carnegie's move Richmond and Virginia were often in the cockpit of national drama. One-fifth of the Confederacy's railroad mileage was in Virginia and the state ranked first in wealth, population and (white) manpower as well as having massive mineral and munitions potential.

Carnegie was at Alexandria during the First Battle of Manassas (known as Bull Run to the Union forces), on 21 July 1861. For the Union Brigadier-General Irvin McDowell organised the largest army ever assembled in North America, some 35,000 strong. Their immediate goal was Manassas Junction, a village of important military and railway significance. Carnegie's maps showed that the railroads leading to and from Washington, the Virginia Piedmont and the Shenandoah Valley all joined up here. The whole was defended by Confederate Brigadier-General Pierre Gustave T. Beauregard and 22,000 ill-trained citizen-soldiers camped behind the meandering stream known as Bull Run. They were to be joined by 12,000 more rail-transported soldiers from Brigadier-General Joseph E. Johnston's 1st Brigade Virginians led by Brigadier-General Thomas J. Jackson. Carnegie saw at first hand the crucial importance of railroads in war.

The tide of battle ebbed and flowed. At length Beauregard won the day at a cost of some 5,000 casualties on both sides. Based at Burke's Station, some 5 miles from the battlefield, Carnegie rushed to gather all the railway stock he could find to ferry out the 2,700 Union wounded. He himself emerged unscathed on the last train out of Alexandria, except for a bout of 'thermic fever' contracted by too much work out in the Virginian sun. Thereafter he always avoided open sunny areas.[21] Yet he was always proud to have been part of the Union defeat, which he believed was 'a blessing in disguise'.[22] It certainly stirred the Union to better efforts. He said, 'I believed it was my duty to be on the field.'[23]

The railroad men of Carnegie's division also emerged unscathed and his telegraphic team were all accounted for. On his return to Washington, Carnegie was engaged in setting up a ferry to Alexandria and extending the Baltimore & Ohio

Railroad track in Washington across the Potomac River, with the rebuilding of the Long Bridge across its width. The whole was accomplished in seven days.[24]

After the events at Manassas/Bull Run Thomas A. Scott was appointed Assistant Secretary of War and asked Carnegie to stay in Washington as his assistant. From time to time Abraham Lincoln would visit Scott's office, and it was here that Carnegie first met and conversed with him. Now aged 52, President Lincoln was of striking appearance, just as George P.A. Healy had portrayed him, and Carnegie left this personal assessment of him:

He was certainly one of the most homely men I ever saw when his features were in repose; but when excited or telling a story, intellect shone through his eyes and illuminated his face to a degree which I have seldom or never seen in any other. His manners were perfect because natural; and he had a kind word for everybody, even the youngest boy in the office. His attentions were not graduated. They were the same to all, as deferential in talking to the messenger boy as to Secretary [of State, William Henry] Seward. His charm lay in the total absence of manner. It was not so much perhaps what he said as the way in which he said it that never failed to win one. I have often regretted that I did not note down carefully at the time some of his curious sayings, for he said even common things in an original way. I never met a great man who so thoroughly made himself one with all men as Mr Lincoln . . . He was the most perfect democrat, revealing in every word and act the equality of men.[25]

Carnegie was to be involved emotionally in another aspect of the war, with the added fear that he would be classed as an enemy alien. On 8 November 1861 Captain Charles Wilkes of the Union warship *San Jacinto* ordered the seizure of two Confederate envoys, erstwhile Southern senators James M. Mason and John Slidell, travelling from Havana, Cuba, on the unarmed British mail-steamer *Trent* bound for Southampton. Their mission was to plead the Confederate cause in Britain and France. Wilkes acted entirely on his own initiative. However, his seizure of two lawfully travelling passengers on a neutral vessel travelling between two neutral ports, although approved in general by the Union interests, was a clear breach of international law which the mission of the envoys could not justify. Carnegie realised that the vast majority of public opinion in Britain was pro-Confederacy; even his relatives back in Dunfermline were sympathetic to the South. Carnegie was bewildered by their stance. How could the radicals of Dunfermline, in particular, support the slave-owners of the South? Scotland's response was both economic and emotional; the Union was blockading the southern markets for imported goods and the Scots tended to favour the underdog in conflicts. Nevertheless, Carnegie was deeply disturbed; his prosperity and future progress could be destroyed if Britain went to war, and he might not even be welcome back in Dumfermline if he had to flee.

Thomas A. Scott, as Assistant Secretary of War, was privy to Lincoln's Cabinet talks on the matter, so Carnegie was in the position of knowing what was happening. He privately emphasised to Scott that Britain would fight for the neutrality of her ships. Like many Americans past and present, Scott knew little about foreign affairs and favoured the Lincoln line of defying Britain. Carnegie kept on that this policy would mean war.[26]

Britain sent troops to Canada and the Liberal government of Henry Temple, Viscount Palmerston, prepared a bellicose note of protest. The wording of the note was modified by the Prince Consort – constitutional protocol required that the note be sent to Queen Victoria – but pressure was put on Lincoln's administration because the French supported the British stance. At length Secretary of State William Henry Seward persuaded Lincoln that the British would go to war; Lincoln and his administration backed down, releasing Mason and Slidell from prison in Boston. Carnegie breathed a sigh of relief: his life and career were safe. British opinion, though, remained embittered.

By early September 1861 Carnegie was back in Pittsburgh putting into practice the rail improvements necessitated by the war. He worked, too, on crew roster administration to encourage more efficient working practices and brought in a range of reduced passenger fares on new lines. Carnegie's ideas were very much in tune with the current spirit in Pittsburgh, whose entrepreneurs were keen to make capital out of the war. The military machine demanded ever more iron products, and more goods were being transported by rail. Herein Carnegie forged a set of commercial systems that would create his own road to success: to make work more efficient, to discount charges and to reduce overall costs. Meanwhile another developing industry caught his eye.

Oil was being drilled in increasing quantities north of Pittsburgh at Oil Creek, a tributary of the Allegheny River, and Pittsburgh's businessmen were beginning to see rich opportunities. One of the investors in the Titusville oil fields near Oil Creek was Carnegie, who bought 1,000 shares for $11,000 in the Columbus Oil Co., founded by one of his Homewood neighbours, William Coleman. In his first year Carnegie clocked up a dividend return of some $17,868.[27] By this time Carnegie was physically and mentally exhausted, for he had driven himself hard these past months. What he needed was a breath of Scottish air.

SEVEN

BRIDGING GAPS

Andrew Carnegie belonged to that great race of nation builders who have made the development of America the wonder of the world.

Elihu Root (1845–1937), US Secretary of War

Carnegie consulted his physician. Out in all weathers, in rail yard and oil field, he had not eaten properly nor slept well for months. He had not given himself enough time to recuperate from his sunstroke and he was debilitated. He told the doctor that he had not had a holiday for fourteen years. Diagnosing the symptoms of exhaustion, the physician advised rest and recreation; overwork would kill him, the doctor warned. Carnegie listened, thought and realised for the first time that he could afford a lavish holiday. All he needed now was some time. An application was made for leave to the president of the Pennsylvania Railway J. Edgar Thomson. On 26 May 1862 Carnegie received the required sanction and he wrote that evening a euphoric letter to his cousin Dod:

Ten minutes ago I received glorious news. The dream of a dozen years is at last on the very threshold of realisation. Yes I am to visit Scotland, see and talk with you all again! – Uncles, Aunts and Cousins, my schoolfellows and companions of my childhood – all are to be greeted again. The past is to be recalled. I shall once more wander through Woodmill Braes, see a hundred other spots that have haunted me for years till Dunfermline and its neighbourhood has grown to be a kind of 'Promised Land' to me. And all this is six short weeks from now. I can scarcely believe my senses and yet I'm sure I have just been notified that our Company grants me three months leave of absence to date from July first. Hurrah! Three cheers for this! There is nothing on earth I would ask in preference to what has just been given me. The exuberance of my joy I find is tempered by a deep feeling of thankfulness for the privilege vouchsafed. . . .

I shall miss one I longed much to see, my only school teacher, Mr Martin. Would he were now alive. Surely Aunt Charlotte will be to the fore when I arrive. . . .

We will make a bee line for Dunfermline. I won't turn my head to look at anything until I see Bruce's Monument [i.e. the tower memorial to Robert Bruce at Dunfermline Abbey]. I remember that was the last thing I saw of Dunfermline and I cried bitterly when I could see it no more. I intend to remain in Dunfermline until I'm glutted with all it can give and then I will take a run over the Continent as far as the Rhine perhaps. Can't you go along? You must at least arrange to go through Scotland with me sure. We must spout Roderick Dhu [a character in Sir Walter Scott's *The Lady of the Lake*, 1810] on his own ground. I haven't forgotten my part, get to work at yours. I count upon Uncle giving us a good part of his time. If any of the friends intend visiting London I would like them to postpone and we will be of the party. Uncle Tom and Aunt Morrison always intended visiting Yankeeland; they had better come over with us. We have everything now to render such a visit desirable; besides I want to show Uncle Tom what the 'great Glorious and Free' is. But of this more when we meet. Four weeks and I'm afloat, six and I'm in 'Dunfarlin Town'. Whew! that's about enough to make one jolly, isn't it? I confess I'm clean daft about it. I fancy I look like an ardent lover who has just obtained a flattering 'yes'. I'm wreathed in smiles and couldn't be cross if I should try my very best. . . .

And now My Dear Dod good night. Tell all our friends we expect to meet them soon; that we look forward to that long wished for day with an intensity of desire felt only by exiles from home, and with feelings of the warmest friendship for all connected with us in dear old Scotland. Good bye. Let's pray for the early meeting of Dod and Naig. Truly your affectionate Cousin. . . .[1]

On 28 June 1862 the Carnegie party set off. Carnegie and his mother were joined by his old friend Thomas N. Miller, now a railway executive. Brother Tom was left behind to take care of family business; he was disappointed and disgruntled. First-class passages were booked aboard the Inman Line passenger steamship *Aetna* for the two-week Atlantic crossing.

From Liverpool they travelled to Scotland by the LNER railway to Edinburgh. From South Queensferry they crossed the Firth of Forth on the line of saintly Queen Margaret's royal ferry to North Queensferry, and thence to Dunfermline. It was an emotional return for the Carnegies; Margaret was tearfully triumphant as she caught her first glimpse of the abbey tower; her American gamble had paid off and they had exchanged poverty for prosperity. 'For myself,' said Carnegie, 'I felt as if I could throw myself upon the sacred soil and kiss it.'[2]

Carnegie visited all his old haunts with great eagerness. His birthplace in Moodie Street, his Rolland Street school, the old well, the abbey, the glen, the royal palace were all the same . . . yet there was something different:

The High Street, which I had considered not a bad Broadway, uncle's shop, which I had compared with some New York establishments, the little mounds about the town, to which he had run on Sundays to play, the distances, the height of the houses, all had shrunk. Here was a city of the Lilliputians. I could almost touch the eaves of the house in which I was born, and the sea – to walk to which on a Saturday had been a considerable feat – was only three miles distant. The rocks at the seashore, among which I have gathered wilks [whelks] seemed to have vanished, and a tame flat shoal remained. The schoolhouse, around which had centred many of my schoolboy recollections – my only Alma Mater – and the playground, upon which mimic battles had been fought and races run, had shrunk to ridiculously small dimensions. The fine residences, Broomhall, Fordell and especially the conservatories at Donibristle, fell one after the other into the pretty insignificant.[3] What I felt on a later occasion on a visit to Japan, with its small toy houses, was something like a repetition of the impression my old home made upon me.[4]

Even the people had changed. Although the old women still sat at their doors in mutches (close-fitting caps) and black dresses, where were the weavers of old, with their webs over their shoulders? And there was a silence too; no clacking of looms. A lot of the poverty seemed to have gone; working folk had better dwellings, the middle classes were building new houses at Abbey Parks and there were new industrial sites like St Leonard's Works in Bothwell Street (demolished in 1984). Carnegie's head buzzed with the changes. And then there were the friends and relations. The Morrisons and the Lauders clamoured for news; Aggie Gibson, a childhood sweetheart, was greeted with delight; Ailie Ferguson Henderson, who had loaned them the £20 needed to emigrate, was embraced. And cousin Dod, now a civil engineer, lapped up the details of Andrew's new life in America; should he up sticks and go too? And Aunt Charlotte Drysdale – who had also criticised them for going to America – was in her element. She regaled the company with reminiscences of Carnegie's childhood when she had nursed him. In her enthusiasm she turned to her nephew and said: 'Oh, you will just be coming back here some day and *keep a shop in the High Street*.'[5] She also added more embarrassing tales of how Carnegie had screamed as an infant if he were not fed with two spoons one after the other.[6] As he walked through his childhood haunts one particular thought formed in Carnegie's mind. Much as he loved his native land and birthplace, he could never have prospered here. There was in his relatives a deadening lack of ambition and limitation of thought; if he stayed here longer than a holiday his drive would be inhibited.

Despite the delights of family reunions and old haunts revisited, conversations with friends and relations soon turned sombre for Carnegie. Dunfermline was suffering because of the war in America. Linen exports had declined, and local opinions were largely against Abraham Lincoln and the Union cause. Carnegie was depressed by the Dunfermline folks' attitude, yet he found one supporter in Uncle George Lauder. Still a comparatively young man, George Lauder followed every phase of the war, charting its progress carefully on maps marked with battles from the early conflicts at Fort Sumter, and Wilson's Creek, Missouri (10 August 1861), to the more recent Pea Ridge, Arkansas (7–8 March 1862), and Glorita Pass, New Mexico (26–8 March 1862). He particularly revelled in Carnegie's personal story about the fight at Bull Run.

Uncle George went further in his support. He handed over to Carnegie what amounted to the whole of his savings to invest in US Federal Bonds. 'Invest this for me as you think best,' he said to his nephew, 'but if you put it into United States bonds it will add to my pleasure, for then I can feel that, in the hour of her danger, I have never lost faith in the Republic.'[7] The bonds were a risk, the Bank of England regarding them as 'untrustworthy'. Later Carnegie made this assess-ment: 'Three times the value of [Uncle Lauder's] gold was remitted, and double the value of his patriotic investment since, has rewarded his faith in the triumph of democracy.'[8]

During Carnegie's absence, Uncle Tom Morrison's influence had grown in Dunfermline and Fife in general. He was now one of Dunfermline's six town councillors but the fire of his radicalism still burned bright. After the Reform Bill of 1832 Dunfermline was in the constituency of Stirling Burghs. The sitting Member of Parliament, (Sir) James Caird of Baldoon, an agriculturalist who had toured Canada and the United States in 1858–9, was more than familiar with Morrison's opinion. Indeed, Morrison remained a thorn in the side of local and national politicians until his death, still in municipal harness, in 1879. Carnegie and his uncle had many a walk by Woodmill Braes reminiscing and discussing a wide range of topics; in particular they compared notes on oratory. Carnegie revelled in the speeches he gave to the various societies of which he was a member and constantly sought ways to improve his public speaking style. He told his uncle:

> I think that when, in making a speech, one feels himself lifted as it were, and swept by enthusiasm into the expression of some burning truth, he feels words whose eloquence surprises himself, he throws it forth, and, panting for breath, hears the roar of his fellow men in thunder of assent, the precious moment which tells him that the audience is his own, but one soul in it and that his; I think this the supreme moment of life.[9]

Although Morrison had opposed the Carnegie emigration, he now accepted his nephew's success with pride.

Carnegie had intended that his trip to Dunfermline would be followed by several weeks touring Britain, France and Germany. Alas, he fell ill at Dunfermline; still debilitated by the episode of sunstroke in America, his wanderings around damp south-west Fife brought on a severe chill which led to coryza and an unresolved pneumonia. He was cared for during a period of six weeks at his Uncle George's flat above the grocer's shop in the High Street. He noted, 'Scottish medicine was as stern as Scottish theology . . . and I was bled.'[10] Following the blood-letting his condition worsened, putting his Dunfermline family in a panic. At the physician's suggestion, rented accommodation was taken at nearby Loch Leven in Kinross, where a slow recovery was made. Eventually Carnegie felt well enough to visit some sights in Edinburgh and Glasgow before returning to America.

Recuperating after the tiresome sea voyage to the United States in the autumn of 1862, Carnegie prepared himself to return to work. The weeks at sea had given him time to reflect on his Dunfermline trip and on his future. Carnegie was 28 years old and had an earned and unearned income that was remarkable for the time. For instance, a statement found in his papers for 1863 showed an income of $47,860.67.[11] His investments in transport, iron bridges and various stocks made a substantial foundation for his future wealth. He now made a review of his work practices. After his hard work as a boy, Carnegie planned to devote half his time to play. He saw his future role as an ideas man; he would supply the inspiration and driving energy for projects, but would employ others to supply the drudgery of putting ideas to work. He believed that the future secret of his success would be found in his Scottish upbringing and 'genes'. There was one mistake though, that he was determined not to make, and this he set down in a letter to his cousin Dod: 'Isn't it strange how little ambition most of our Scottish acquaintances have to become independent *and then enjoy the luxuries which wealth can (and should) procure?'*[12] He also gave Dod an insight into his future plans:

> For my part, I am determined to expand as my means do and ultimately to own a noble place in the country, cultivate the rarest flowers, the best breeds of cattle, own a magnificent lot of horses and be distinguished for taking the deepest interest in all those about my place. The position most to be envied, outside the ring of great men, I think is that of a British gentleman who labours diligently to educate and improve the condition of his dependents and who takes an independent part in National politics, always labouring to correct some ancient abuse – to curtail the privileges of the few and increase those of the many.[13]

Carnegie returned to work in high spirits, but Pittsburgh was in a state of alarm. Union Army intelligence showed that the Confederate General Robert E. Lee was aiming to capture Pittsburgh. The city began to fortify and some 6,800 volunteers put the place in a state of readiness. Carnegie helped with the transportation of soldiers and goods by rail until he had satisfied the quotas set by Major-General Brooks, commander of the Monogahela region south of Pittsburgh. There was now to be enacted the best-known military engagement in American history. General Lee and his Army of Northern Virginia moved north to Gettysburg. Here over the three days of 1 July to 3 July 1863 battle raged. Lee's army of 75,000 faced the 83,300 troops of the Union under Major-General George G. Meade. Finally Lee began to retreat on 4 July. His drive north had failed, and he told his men: 'It is I who have lost this fight, and you must help me out of it the best way you can.' Although Lee lost 28,100 men at Gettysburg (against 23,000 Union casualties), Meade did not follow up his victory with more slaughter, and the pressure was taken off Pittsburgh.

The Civil War had driven up the price of iron to more than $103 per ton, and it was now in short supply. Consequently the railway system was suffering from a lack of maintenance and repairs. Added to this there had been a run on locomotives, dozens of which had been destroyed in the conflict. Carnegie was to make a killing in both areas.

Carnegie decided to invest in the iron business to the tune of $10,000, and in 1864 formed with others the Superior Rail Mill and Blast Furnaces. In 1866, together with Thomas N. Miller, a colleague in the Sun City Forge Co., another of Carnegie's interests, they set up the Pittsburgh Locomotive Works. Again Carnegie saw an opportunity to invest in track infrastructure, having observed how the traditional American wooden bridges were very vulnerable in war. Thus with bridge designer H.J. Linville, engineer John L. Piper and his partner Aaron Shiffler, he formed the Piper & Shiffler Company to build iron bridges. Carnegie involved Thomas A. Scott in the venture as co-founder, with each of the principals contributing $1,250; the company was merged into the Keystone Bridge Co. in 1863. A major contract was bridging the Ohio River at Steubenville, with a cast-iron bridge of 300ft span; this would be the first of many important contracts which gave rise to the Carnegie motto: 'If you want a contract, be on the spot when it is let.'[14]

If he had not consciously realised it before, Carnegie had

developed into a capitalist, a term that would have sent shock waves through his radical relatives' nerves, and there was another socialist hate-word to add to Carnegie's latest category of achievements, namely exploitation; in future years Carnegie detractors would castigate him for exploiting the war needs for his own ends. One day his old telegraph office friend Tom David called to see him. In conversation about how well he was doing Carnegie mimed exultation with his arms and exclaimed, 'Oh! I'm rich, I'm rich.' By this time he had personal capital deposits in the region of $50,000 and interests in more companies than any colleague realised. In terms of the old Scots proverb which Carnegie often recited, he was successful in 'gathering gear', 'gear' being the Scots term for possessions, money or property.[15]

The day after General Lee began his retreat from the disaster at Gettysburg, another key defeat loomed for the South. Vicksburg in Mississippi was one of the two remaining strongholds in Confederate hands (the other was Port Hudson, Louisiana). Of Vicksburg Abraham Lincoln said, 'the war can never be brought to a close until that key is in our pocket.' Vicksburg was also an important east–west railway junction. Some 77,000 Union troops under Major-General Ulysses S. Grant and Acting Rear Admiral David D. Porter were assembled at Vicksburg to face 62,000 Confederates under General Joseph K. Johnston and Lieutenant-General John J. Pemberton. After a 47-day siege of Vicksburg, the white flag was raised by the Confederates on 4 July 1863 and closure was brought to one of the most important chapters of the Civil War; as the Confederate General Stephen D. Lee remarked, Vicksburg was 'a staggering blow from which the Confederacy never rallied'.

The summer of 1864 saw Union Major-General William T. Sherman embark his army on the Western & Atlantic Railroad bound for Atlanta. On 27 June he successfully defeated Confederate General Joseph E. Johnston's Army of Tennessee at the battle of Kennesaw Mountain; within a few months he would raise the US flag over Atlanta. Further north Lieutenant-General Jubal A. Early was the only Confederate general to win a major battle north of the Potomac; he triumphed against Major-General Lewis Wallace at Monocacy, Maryland, on 9 July 1864. While these and other battles were raging, Carnegie received a shock.

His efforts to increase his wealth and his work for the US government had put from his mind the notion that he might be eligible for military service. When he received his letter to this effect, he was aghast. It was ridiculous: how could he be drafted? He was doing very important transportation and construction work for the war effort. All that he considered far more important than toting a rifle through the cornfields of Maryland, or chasing rebels across Tennessee. And what was more, had he not already shed blood for his new country? The telegraph wire incident? But his enquiries only emphasised his eligibility for draft.

According to the US Conscription Act of 1863 Carnegie could dodge the draft by paying a fee to the government, or by negotiating with another man to fill his draft position. To sort out the details for him he employed draft agent H.M. Butler, who supplied an Irish immigrant called John Lindew to take Carnegie's place. The draft dodge cost Carnegie $850 in agent's fees. In exchange he received a Certificate of Non-Liability valid until 19 July 1867.[16] It was not an episode he would bring to public notice in his autobiographical writings.

More changes were in the wind for Carnegie. Rumours were circulating that he would soon be offered the post of Assistant General Superintendent, ranking just below Enoch Lewis. At 29, this would be his route to a vice-presidency of the Pennsylvania Railroad. Did he want to emulate his patron Thomas A. Scott? At length J. Edgar Thomson did offer Carnegie the position, and the dilemma had to be faced.

Carnegie had reached a crossroads. He decided he didn't need promotion in the railroad as his investment dividends brought him more than his working salary and he had a notion of returning to Scotland, maybe to act as American Consul at Glasgow. Towards this end he asked Thomas A. Scott to mediate with Abraham Lincoln's

Secretary of State, Simon Cameron, to get him the job. Cameron did not oblige.[17] Nevertheless, Carnegie was adamant he was getting out of railroads in order to follow his determination 'to make a fortune' – something he could not do 'honestly' in transportation.[18]

A little short of two weeks before General Lee surrendered the Confederate Army to General Grant at Appomattox Court House, Virginia, Carnegie sat down and wrote his letter of resignation:

PENNSYLVANIA RAILROAD COMPANY
SUPERINTENDENT'S OFFICE
PITTSBURGH, MARCH 28 1865
TO THE OFFICERS AND EMPLOYEES OF THE PITTSBURGH DIVISION:

Gentlemen:

I cannot allow my connection with you to cease without some expression of the deep regret felt at parting.

Twelve years of pleasant intercourse have served to inspire feelings of personal regard for those who have so faithfully laboured with me in the service of the Company. The coming change is painful only as I reflect that in consequence thereof I am not to be in the future, as in the past, intimately associated with you and with many others in the various departments, who have through business intercourse, become my personal friends. I assure you although the official relations hitherto existing between us must soon close, I can never fail to feel and evince the liveliest interest in the welfare of such as have been identified with the Pittsburgh Division in times past, and who are, I trust, for many years to come to contribute to the success of the Pennsylvania Railroad Company, and share in its justly deserved prosperity.

Thanking you most sincerely for the uniform kindness shown toward me, for your zealous efforts made at all times to meet my wishes, and asking for my successor similar support at your hands, I bid you all farewell.[19]

Carnegie's rather pompous letter was not the end of his railroad interests. His investments kept him a keen follower of the postwar railroads, bridge-building and telegraphic industries. What a step he had taken. The poor boy from Dunfermline, desperate for a job, had now jettisoned a position with greater prospects. Wealth had boosted Carnegie's confidence and there was now greater chance of gallivanting.

EIGHT

EUROPEAN INTERLUDE

No business man is worth his salt . . . who does not have his affairs so expertly organised that he cannot drop them at a moment's notice and leave for parts unknown.

Burton J. Hendrick, *The Life of Andrew Carnegie*, vol. I, p. 138

Carnegie was getting itchy feet again. For two years he had juggled his financial interests which had now mutated into two distinct balance sheet groupings. There were the businesses like the Keystone Bridge Co., the Pittsburgh Locomotive Works, the Superior Rail Mill and the Union Iron Mills, which demanded Carnegie's direct attention and relevant intervention, and company interests like banks, insurance concerns, Adams Express, Columbian Oil and Woodruff Sleeping Cars that were run by others.

As Carnegie assessed his financial sheets, America jogged along after the shock assassination of Abraham Lincoln on 14 April 1865 at Ford's Theatre, Washington, by actor John Wilkes Booth. His death removed the only man who could have reconciled North and South, and the country had a new president in Lincoln's Vice-President Andrew Johnson (1808–75). As Johnson settled into his struggles with the radicals in his own party, Carnegie set out for Europe in May 1865, with share revenue flooding into his pockets.

Inspiration for the journey came from a book by American travel writer James Bayard Taylor entitled *Views Afoot: or, Europe Seen with Knapsack and Staff* (1846). But there was another underlying motive for Carnegie to undertake the five-month tour. He wanted to round off his 'mind and character' and achieve the 'desirable expansion of his soul' through travel.[1] His arrangements for the voyage made, Carnegie left his interests principally in the hands of a quartet of trusted colleagues: Andrew Kloman, of the iron-working firm of Kloman & Co., who had brought Carnegie into the iron manufacturing business; John Piper of the bridge builders Piper & Shiffler Co., in which Carnegie had made a key investment; his old friend Tom Miller; and his much put-upon young brother Tom. This group of individuals underlined another of Carnegie's secrets of success: put into roles of responsibility people who are more accomplished at the job than you are yourself.

This time Carnegie's travelling companions were Henry Phipps and John W. 'Vandy' Vandervort; it would cost them some $3,000, earned from oil revenues.[2] They sailed from New York in May 1865 aboard the *Scotia*, bound for Liverpool, and thence travelled directly to Dunfermline. A sojourn with the Lauders and Morrisons was a happy time. Carnegie honed his sentimentality for Scotland and was overcome by a sense of 'coming home'; he wrote to his mother and brother: '[At Dunfermline] we have a local history extending to the third generation, and many a one speaks kindly of our ancestors.'[3]

The party now retraced their steps to Liverpool where they met up with a distant cousin of Henry Phipps, John Franks, who joined them for the rest of the tour. They crossed France, Germany, the Netherlands, Switzerland and Italy, sojourning at London, Paris, Antwerp, Amsterdam, Dresden, Vienna, Naples and Pompeii, soaking up art galleries and theatres, opera and architecture, scenery and volcanoes, much as eighteenth-century aristocrats had done on the Grand Tour. Carnegie recalled how they 'climbed every spire, slept on mountain-tops, and carried our luggage in knapsacks upon our backs'.[4]

John Franks put together a sort of journal of the continental tour in correspondence to his sister. He reported that Carnegie was 'exuberantly joyous' throughout the trip.[5] Other important letter extracts offer a rare glimpse of Carnegie at 30. Franks explained:

He is full of liveliness, fun and frolic. His French is to carry us through when Vandy's German is no longer required. I had to acknowledge my obligation to him no later than yesterday, when, wishing my portmanteau forwarded by rail and the German porter being so stupid as not to understand my good English, Andy kindly stepped forward to the rescue with 'Voulez vous forward the baggage to Mayence?' It is, I expect, needless to tell you that in time I found my Portmanteau at its destination . . .

Visited the theatre one evening to witness the performance of 'The [sic] Biche au Bois' [*The Hind of the Forest*] by Parisian Actors. This was by Andy's desire, who, having seen it in Paris, was in raptures with it. Another evening a visit to the Theatre Royal to witness and hear the opera 'La Traviata' . . .

Located in comfortable quarters on the Unter den Linden, seated in my sumptuously furnished bedroom, my friends seated on the velvet cushioned sofa and chairs, busily writing at a large round table in the centre of the room, we are all occupied in our usual Sunday avocation of established lines of communication to our respective homes. Harry is writing to his sister, Vandy to his brother, and Andy is engaged in communicating his constant experiences to the editor of the Pittsburgh 'Commercial'. Behold us then in my room which presents, if not a 'lettery' at any rate a truly 'littery' appearance. What with Andy's confident assumption of the French language, which he displays at every possible opportunity, to our great amusement, and what with the arguments we have upon most questions, social, political, etc., Andy brimming first upon one side, then upon the other, with admirable impartiality, and possibly to keep the balance even, it must be confessed, that upon the whole we make up a tolerably lively party . . .

[Prague] On Friday last, we were up shortly after six and at half past seven were on our way to Brunn. A beautiful bright day made our journey cheerful, which was further enlivened by discussion of various subjects. Andy's opinion and judgements, Vandy's general abstinence from discussion, for which he was taken to task by Andy, Harry's precipitate conclusions, then running onto politics and art. It was afterward varied by readings from [Lord Byron's] 'Childe Harold' . . . Andy is so overflowing that it is extremely difficult to keep him within reasonable bounds, to restrain him within the limits of moderately orderly behaviour – he is so continually mischievous . . .[6]

Carnegie was particularly ebullient when they visited the Doge's Palace in Venice; having placed his friends in poses among the Doge's antique furniture, he declaimed a speech from *Othello* for effect.

Franks was to offer a further interesting comment illustrating that business was never far from Carnegie's thoughts: 'The boys are elated by glorious news in letters of continued advance in prices, of stocks advancing, of their mills working double turns, of large orders pouring in, of new patents obtained and of still greater success looming in the future.'[7]

Carnegie deemed the visit to Europe the most 'instructive' he had ever undertaken: 'Up to this time I had known nothing of painting, or sculpture, but it was not long before I could classify the works of great painters . . . My visit to Europe also gave me my first great treat in music . . . Handel . . . at the Crystal Palace in London . . . I had never, up to that time . . . felt the power and majesty of music in such high degree.' Even the choir of Pope Pius IX at Rome cut across his natural Scottish anti-Catholic bias to offer him 'a grand climax to the whole'.[8]

Although Carnegie walked through the streets of Paris with wonderment, admiring the remodelling of the boulevards under the direction of Baron George Eugene Haussman (1809–91), the France of Napoleon III did not impress him as a whole, while Prussia, under its seventh king, Wilhelm I (the first German Emperor in 1871), was more to his liking. He wrote to his mother and brother:

In France, all seems dead. The soil is miserably farmed, and one is at a loss to account for the leading position which the Gauls have attained. I am one of those who hold that they cannot maintain it long – that they must give way to the German element which, you know, is Anglo-Saxon and therefore has the right 'blend'.[9]

Four years after Carnegie's trip Napoleon III declared war on Prussia, leading to the capitulation of Paris on 28 January 1871. Carnegie had sensed the impending Gallic doom, but in this letter home he also foreshadowed his own attraction towards Germany which would lead to his future support for Kaiser Wilhelm II.

Back home, though, all was not happy. Carnegie's brother Tom was feeling the pressure of tending to his brother's business, and the mail from Europe regularly brought a flurry of letters urging Tom to undertake a whole range of tasks. Now 22, Tom's early education was more firmly based than Carnegie's, and he had a more relaxed nature. Where Carnegie was melancholy by nature, Tom was cheerful, and where Carnegie was solemn, Tom was bright, and although his brother was 'protective', Tom never forgot the childhood bullying. The stress brought about by Carnegie's letters was continually rising and Tom took to the bottle. Finally he could stand it no more and sent Carnegie a letter of complaint. In a condescending reply Carnegie attempted to assuage his brother's ire:

It is a heavy load for a youngster to carry, but if you succeed, it will be a lasting benefit to you. Talk to mother freely; I always found her ideas pretty near the right thing. She's a safe counsellor, safer than I, probably, who have made money too easily and gained distance by carrying full sail, to be much of an advisor when storms are about, or sail should be taken in.[10]

Carnegie showed little real understanding of his brother's predicament or his feelings, but continued his trip with a resolve to search for more moneymaking ideas in Europe. Victorian London particularly pleased him. The underground railway was progressing from its first operation in 1863, and as novelist Sir Walter Besant was to remark in *South London* (1899), houses 'sprang up as if in a single night: streets in a month, churches and chapels in a quarter'. London was the focus of 'national thought and industry', and as he viewed all that was going on from pavement and cab Carnegie was enchanted by the 'World City'. 'I am quite taken with London,' he wrote to his mother, 'and would like to spend a year or two there.'[11]

As he sought out new ideas and business concepts Carnegie was particularly interested in steel replacing iron for railways; at that time his own company was finding that iron rails were too brittle for high-speed main line trains. A new process strengthening iron rails with steel had been invented by one Thomas Dodd, who evolved 'dodderised rails' which were stronger than the ones used by the Pennsylvania Railroad. So along with cousin Dod, Carnegie investigated the matter further with a view to investing in the idea. He took steps to win an exclusive contract for supplying such rails to the American market. With his persuasive business acumen at full blast, Carnegie talked Dodd and his colleagues into a satisfactory deal. All this was undertaken while his travelling companions spent three weeks in Switzerland. Carnegie joined his friends at Mayence, but followed up his steel researches at the Iron Works in Prussia and the cast-iron plant at Magdeburg, and looked into the manufacturing of 'dodderised' material at Ruhwart on the Rhine.

Carnegie arrived back in America during the spring of 1866 raring to get back into business, although his commercial interests had rarely been far from his thoughts in Europe. He launched afresh into his bridge-building, telegraph and sleeping-car interests, but the manufacture of iron would increasingly grab more of his attention. His companies were very much tied to the production of iron and this was one of the reasons why he had founded the Cyclops Iron Co. with

Thomas Miller back in 1864; this had been merged in 1865 with the rival company of Kloman & Phipps to form the Union Iron Mills. However, at the time of his return the Union Iron Mills were not doing well; orders were not coming in via the feeder companies like the Keystone Bridge Co., and internal management rivalries made meetings sticky. In essence Thomas Miller could not stand Henry Phipps and meetings regularly boiled over until Carnegie bought out Miller's share of the company, which was renamed as Carnegie, Kloman & Co.

Meanwhile Carnegie's negotiations for an extended exclusive contract for the 'dodderised' rails were not proceeding smoothly. Thomas Dodd had travelled to the United States and set up the American Steeled Rail Co., and had granted rights to other American companies. The exclusivity that Carnegie thought he had won was not valid, and he endeavoured to clarify the position. Carnegie did much to promote the Dodd process to keep his interests high. Alas, the rails did not stand up to the American weather conditions. J. Edgar Thomson advised that the Pennsylvania Railroad had no further trust in them. For a while Carnegie pressed on with the Dodd process but at last he had to withdraw his efforts. In true Carnegie fashion he kept his name clean by blaming Dodd for the failure.

Back in Britain the London-based engineer James Livesey, who was acting as Carnegie's agent with the Dodd company, wrote about the 'Webb process' he had discovered for economically priced hard-wearing rails. Negotiations for this process also failed, as the product proved dubious. Carnegie began to look elsewhere.

NINE

NEW YORK AND THE WOLVES OF WALL STREET

> As a businessman . . . Carnegie was the most driven and
> competitive, the most obsessive and compulsive, the most
> independent and daring. He was so convinced of his own
> rightness – on business, politics and philanthropy – that he
> couldn't conceive of being wrong. He was intoxicated by his
> own holiness.
>
> Peter Krass, biographer, 2002

Iron-manufacturer William Coleman was one of the
Carnegies' Homewood neighbours at Pittsburgh and a co-
investor in oil. During the late summer of 1867 his daughter
Lucy married Tom Carnegie and the Homewood house became
their new home. Carnegie took this event as a time to reassess
his position: 'My field appeared to be to direct the general
policy of the companies and negotiate the important
contracts.'[1] Tom and Henry Phipps 'had full grasp of the
business at Pittsburgh', so Carnegie decided to move with his
mother to the centre of all the 'important enterprises' at New
York. They took up residence at the plush 600-room St
Nicholas Hotel, Manhattan, in the autumn of 1867. In due
course the owners of the St Nicholas opened the Windsor Hotel
and the Carnegies were residents there until 1887.[2] In
personal relationships Carnegie's mother was still the core
figure of his life: 'we would be happy anywhere as long as we
were together'.[3] Carnegie opened an office at 19 Broad Street
(later moved to 57 Broadway) and employed a full-time
personal secretary in Gardner McCandless.

New York in those days was hardly better than Pittsburgh;

indeed, Carnegie's biographer Burton J. Hendrick describes it as 'crude, provincial and dirty'.[4] It had a population of less than one million, 50 per cent of whom were immigrants, and 'an unwashed proletariat' lived in a shanty town bordering the 843-acre Central Park. Public transport was still primitive, ranging from 'rickety horse carts' to ferries, and in winter sleighs still jingled their way up Broadway. The Carnegies, though, were distanced from the drunken stage-drivers and the rooting pigs of Central Park, cocooned in one of the finest of America's hotels amid Carrara stairways and 'pendant chandeliers of iridescent crystal'. Carnegie could well afford it; an inventory of his current income dated December 1868 revealed that he had an annual return of $56,110 from bridge building, transport, oil, telegraphy and banking.[5] This was a time too, when Carnegie was expanding his interest in steel manufacture.

Following the failure of the Dodd and Webb iron projects, both of which Carnegie had been reluctant to drop, by 1868 he was investing in and promoting Bessemer steel. This process had been invented by (later Sir) Henry Bessemer (1813–98). An entrepreneur in the manufacture of metal processes – he invented a type-composing machine as early as *c.* 1838 – Bessemer described his steel process at a meeting of the British Association for the Advancement of Science at Cheltenham in 1856. His process involved the manufacture of steel from melted pig-iron through which air under pressure (or steam) was blown with the object of abstracting carbon. In 1859 he established a steelworks at Sheffield, where he specialised in making guns and the manufacture of steel rails. Bessemer steel was introduced to America by Alexander L. Holley and by 1866 Carnegie had started to make Bessemer steel in his reformed Freedom Iron & Steel Co.

Another important document relevant to the time of his move to New York was found in his papers, which speaks volumes about his sense of achievement and his plans for the future. In the form of a letter to himself Carnegie wrote this at the St Nicholas Hotel in December 1868:

Thirty-three and an income of $50,000 per annum! By this time two years I can arrange all my business as to secure at least $50,000 per annum. Beyond this never earn – make no effort to increase fortune, but spend the surplus each year for benevolent purposes. Cast aside business forever, except for others.

Settle at Oxford and get a thorough education, making the acquaintance of literary men – this will take three years' active work – pay especial attention to speaking in public. Settle then in London and purchase a controlling interest in some newspaper or live review and give the general management of it attention, taking a part in public matters, especially those connected with education and improvement of the poorer classes.

Man must have an idol – the amassing of wealth is one of the worst species of idolatry – no idol more debasing than the worship of money. Whatever I engage in I must push inordinately; therefore should I be careful to choose that life which will be the most elevating in its character. To continue much longer overwhelmed by business cares and with most of my thoughts wholly upon the way to make more money in the shortest time, must degrade me beyond hope of permanent recovery. I will resign business at thirty-five, but during the ensuing two years I wish to spend the afternoons receiving instruction and in reading systematically.[6]

In contemplating what he thought would be an ideal existence, Carnegie's letter exhibits a mindset that harped back to his childhood. He emphasised self-improvement to supplement the poor education he had as a child. He wanted to perfect the art of public speaking to emulate his uncle Tom Morrison, whose public utterances had been so much a part of his childhood memories, as well as to get over the main thrust of what he wanted to say. He was keen too, to own a newspaper, like his uncle Tom's *The Precursor*.

Not long ago he was boasting that he was rich, now he was condemning the amassing of money. In 1868 Carnegie started to change his views on money and began to be apprehensive about its power. How could he avoid its perils? By giving it away. But not in a socialistic way like the state handing out welfare willy-nilly; having been poor himself, Carnegie believed he could analyse the needs of the poor and satisfy those needs with donations.

This letter was simply a statement of intent; he never did go to Oxford, instead pursuing a course of self-improvement culled from omnivorous reading. He joined the Nineteenth-Century Club, then under the directorship of Mr and Mrs Courtland Palmer, which met as a 'salon' to discuss topics of the day. As the membership grew, public rooms were taken and Carnegie absorbed the techniques of the orators who addressed the meetings.[7] He befriended and cultivated all he could. He took up a study of the politics, commerce, social problems and opportunities of the United States and Britain, while working out how he might stimulate educational opportunities and better the social conditions of the less fortunate. Thus from 1868 he laid down new avenues for his life.

Philosophically and intellectually Carnegie was filling his days but there was one vacuum in his life: he lacked a romantic companion. Clearly his mother was a domineering woman; her fight with poverty had made her so. She had always run her son's domestic affairs with efficiency, but now they were ensconced in a luxury hotel, she had more time to indulge her son, often bullying him to take paths she chose for him. Whatever sexuality Carnegie had he seems to have suppressed it. Whatever love he felt was channelled towards his mother; the women he came close to had been treated in a platonic way. Although his Scottish soul was not encased in fundamental Presbyterianism, he was repulsed by the carnality expressed in the verses of his poetic hero Robert Burns. For Carnegie romance was abstract and not sexual.

There was also another revulsion growing in Carnegie. He was aghast at the web of political improbity and commercial dishonesty of the wolves of Wall Street and the New York legislature. New York was a great money-pot for investors in speculative ventures out West and in money-for-nothing deals. In his autobiographical writings Carnegie made his position clear:

I was surprised to find how very different was the state of affairs in New York. There were few even of the business men who had not their ventures in Wall Street to a greater or less extent. I was besieged with inquiries from all quarters in regard to the various railway enterprises with which I was connected. Offers were made to me by persons who were willing to furnish capital for investment and allow me to manage it – the supposition being that from the inside view which I was able to obtain I could invest for them successfully. Invitations were extended to me to join parties who intended quietly to buy up the control of certain properties. In fact the whole speculative field was laid out before me in its most seductive guise.

All these allurements I declined . . . I never bought or sold a share of stock speculatively in my life . . . I have adhered to the rule never to purchase what I did not pay for, and never to sell what I did not own.[8]

Insider dealing was not for Carnegie, but between indulging himself with horse-riding in Central Park and savouring such cultural delights as the newly opened American Museum of Natural History (1869), he did nurture his investments. 'My first important enterprise after settling in New York was undertaking to build a bridge across the Mississippi at Keokuk.'[9] The 2,300ft-long bridge with a 380ft span was built by the Keokuk & Hamilton Bridge Co., with Carnegie picking up a large parcel of stock investment. Carnegie was not only responsible for building the bridge, but he would be involved in selling iron for the construction and he would also run trains over it. A key player in this was Carnegie's Keystone Bridge Co., soon to have a further engorged order book.

The Keokuk venture led Carnegie to branch out further into a new project to promote designer Colonel James B. Ead's bridge over the Mississippi at St Louis. 'This,' he said, 'was connected with my first large financial transaction.'[10] Again Carnegie secured contracts for the Keystone Bridge Co. and the Pennsylvania Railroad, while his next task was to raise $4 million in mortgage bonds for the project. These negotiations would prove to be a greater moneyspinner for Carnegie than the actual bridge building. With the backing of his Pennsylvania colleagues Thomson and Scott, he approached the chairman of the St Louis Bridge Co. committee, Dr William Taussig, for the commission to raise the funds. He duly won the commission – which would bring him a return of $50,000 if successful.[11] Armed with his letters of authority, in March 1869 Carnegie set off for London to enlist the help of the American financier Junius Spencer Morgan (1813–90), now based at 22 Broad Street, London.

Carnegie made his presentation and Morgan was interested, although his lawyers baulked at some of the details of Carnegie's prospectus. Wiring the principals in the United States, Carnegie made the necessary changes and Morgan agreed the deal, 'This was my first negotiations with the banks of Europe,' Carnegie noted.[12] Work went ahead and the bridge was opened in 1874.

While Morgan was mulling over the deal, Carnegie paid another visit to Scotland. He spent three weeks at Dunfermline and saw his first 'considerable gift' come to fruition. This was to result in the town's first public baths, eventually opened in 1877. Years before, at the instance of his uncle George Lauder, Carnegie had given a subscription to the fund for architect John T. Rochead's monument on Abbey Craig, Stirling, to patriot William Wallace, the foundation stone of which was laid on 24 June 1861. Carnegie's mother had been particularly proud to see her son's name on the list of subscribers; years later Margaret Carnegie presented a bust of Sir William Wallace to be displayed in the monument's Hall of Heroes.[13] Carnegie viewed the monument before he returned to London and Morgan's acceptance.

The American sleeping-car business, in which Carnegie had

a continuing interest, was steadily expanding. A key player in the field was cabinet-maker turned sleeping-car inventor George Mortimer Pullman (1831–97). At this time Pullman was keen to run his cars on the almost completed transcontinental line operated by the Union Pacific Railroad (East) and the Central Pacific Railroad (West). To do so would be a great coup and several parties were intent on securing such a deal, including Carnegie.

After carefully considering his options, Carnegie decided that his best bet would be to enter into a formal partnership with Pullman, linking the latter's interests with the Central Transportation Co. (i.e. the T.T. Woodruff Co.). In the summer of 1869 Carnegie found out that Pullman was in New York and was about to discuss matters with the Union Pacific Vice-President Thomas C. Durant at the St Nicholas Hotel – a meeting to which Carnegie, as an interested party, had been invited. He seems to have engineered an accidental meeting with Pullman on the Carrara stairway of the hotel. 'Good evening, Mr Pullman!' Carnegie beamed, charm at full throttle. 'Here we are together, and are we not making a nice couple of fools of ourselves?' Guardedly Pullman asked: 'What do you mean?' Carnegie quickly explained that by competing against each other for the Union Pacific contract they were queering each other's pitch. Pullman stopped on the stairs: 'Well, what do you propose to do about it?' 'Unite', said Carnegie. And then he suggested that the company be called The Pullman Palace Car Co. Carnegie had hit his target.[14]

Vanity won the day and a merger was agreed. Carnegie now set about the difficult task of winning over the reluctant executives of the Central Transportation Co. Several of the board believed that Pullman had used their design patents fraudulently in producing his cars. At length a compensation deal was agreed and by 1871 the Union Pacific Railroad had three new directors in Thomas A. Scott, G.M. Pullman and Andrew Carnegie. 'Until compelled to sell my shares during the financial panic of 1873, I was, I believe, the largest shareholder in the Pullman Company.'[15] Thus Carnegie, by 'accidentally' bumping into Pullman on the St Nicholas staircase, associated his name and company with one of the most historic of public services.

Carnegie was never far away from what he called 'educative influences' and two people he particularly cultivated were Professor and Madame Vincenzo Botta. Anne Botta presided over a 'salon' at their house at Murray Hill, and for decades 'she wielded a broad, if unobtrusive, influence in the artistic and literary life of New York'.[16] Here Carnegie met the literati of the day from both sides of the Atlantic. Botta was Professor of Italian Literature at New York University and was a specialist in the works of Dante; Anne was a poet and her chatter about such men as Edgar Allan Poe, Ralph Waldo Emerson and Washington Irving, who had all formerly graced her drawing room, was a delight for Carnegie, taking his thoughts away from railway carriages and pig-iron. The Bottas looked upon Carnegie as one of their 'discoveries', but he learned more from them than they ever did from him.[17]

There was some cross-fertilisation between the Botta soirées and the Nineteenth-Century Club organised by the Palmers. Anne Botta had sponsored Carnegie for the club's membership and Carnegie was thrust deep into the club's enthusiasm for the philosophical theories of the French thinker Auguste Comte (1798–1857). Generally accepted as the founding father of 'sociology' – the study of the structure and function of human society – Comte promoted his own 'positivism' and 'sociocracy', wherein scientists would monitor the progress of humanity for the common good. At Anne Botta's in particular, Carnegie learned of the works of Herbert Spencer (1820–1903), the English railway engineer turned philosopher. Carnegie studied closely Spencer's *First Principles* (1862) and *Education* (1861), and incorporated many of Spencer's ideas into his own life – especially the theory of the 'survival of the fittest' (*Principles of Biology*, 1864–7) and the notion that 'education has for a chief object the formation of character' (*Social Statics*, 1850). Anne Botta, although twice Carnegie's age, became an important female influence in his life at that time, becoming one of his 'maternal tutors', able to give him an intellectual direction that his dominant mother could not.[18] With the help of the Bottas Carnegie was able to balance his dealings with the wolves of Wall Street with his socialising with the likes of Charles Kingsley, James Anthony Froude and Matthew Arnold, all of whom would figure in his future life.

In these early days of the 1870s Carnegie was actively wheeler-dealing his sleeping-car, oil, iron, telegraphy, bridge-building and railway interests, interlarding these with negotiating bonds, stock and shares. To these he added land speculation ventures with his friends the McCandlesses and coal mining with Robert Pitcairn. His income was now in excess of $100,000 per annum. Not everything went smoothly. In March 1872 Carnegie, Scott and Thomson were voted off the Union Pacific board because the other board members believed that the three had promoted insider dealing – selling shares in the company that they had bought at privileged prices, and making a substantial profit. In his usual manner Carnegie later professed his total innocence of underhand dealing, blaming Scott for selling the shares; in fact Carnegie was as guilty as the others.

As the autumn of 1872 approached, America was still in distress, licking its battle-inflicted wounds. The country was now led by one of the nation's greatest military heroes, the Republican Ulysses S. Grant (1822–85), but although he had been a masterful leader on the battlefield he proved ingenuous in the White House. Even though he had brought the Civil War to a close he was not the right man to bind the nation's wounds. However, the passage of the Amnesty Bill in 1872 restored civil rights to most Southerners and at this point Carnegie considered it time to reassess his interests once again.

In his mind Carnegie was formulating a new dictum: 'Put all good eggs in one basket and then watch the basket.'[19] He would later explain to enquirers that this meant that no man in manufacturing in particular achieved 'pre-eminence in money-making' by being 'interested in many concerns'. Out of this he believed that for the future 'steel was king' so with careful planning he extended his already established steel interests into his proverbial basket. His visit to the Bessemer works at Sheffield in 1872 put paid to any doubts he might have had that steel was the future.

On 5 November 1872 the steel firm of Carnegie, McCandless & Co. was founded, with Tom Carnegie, Harry Phipps, Andrew Kloman and a few others as partners. Carnegie held $250,000 of the $700,000 company equity. Their mill was established at Braddock's Field, some 12 miles outside Pittsburgh, to a design by steel plant genius Alexander Holley.

Problems arose in 1873 when financial panic gave birth to the United States' first economic depression which would last until 1879. Financial trouble in Europe made things worse as foreign investors pulled out of American securities. Pressure was put on all parties involved as banks failed and money became tight. One financial casualty of the depression was Thomas A. Scott, Carnegie's old mentor. He made several requests for Carnegie to help him out from his reserves, and even asked J. Edgar Thomson to speak to Carnegie on his behalf. But Carnegie declined to assist, his excuse being that there were too many people already dependent on him for financial protection, from his family to his steel partners. This refusal, said Carnegie, 'gave more pain than all the financial trials to which I had been subjected up to that time'.[20] Many believed – rightly – that Carnegie had betrayed his old friend, who had given him vital support when he was starting out.

As the financial problems took their toll on both Scott (who died in 1881) and Thomson (who died in 1874), Carnegie began to suffer from nervous debilitation, but he never allowed circumstances to alter his focus on his targets. Employment in New York reached 25 per cent and soup kitchens flourished. One by one the wolves of Wall Street were growing leaner. Another blow fell when his steel partner Andrew Kloman overstretched himself with investments which he kept secret from his partners. Carnegie made sure that Kloman was declared bankrupt, later buying out Kloman's shares. Nevertheless Carnegie also suffered financial difficulties as certain of his bonds failed, particularly the Davenport & St Paul Railroad stock, which left him with lawsuits to settle. These would rumble on for years, but in 1874 Carnegie, McCandless & Co. was dissolved and reorganised as the Edgar Thomson Steel Co.

New management structures were effected, with Carnegie interfering at every level to secure his own candidates in prime positions. Certainly his most successful appointment was Captain William Jones, late of the Cambria iron works in Johnstown, as general superintendent, ably backed by general manager William P. Shinn.[21] On 1 September 1875 the first steel rolled off the line at the Edgar Thomson Steel Co., where Holley's genius had produced the largest steel mill in the world with every aspect of modern technology reflected. It was a tough job to win orders in the depression, and Carnegie worked hard to raise capital, to which end a trip to London in 1874 was helpful.

Carnegie enjoyed consorting with America's steel magnates like Samuel Felton at Pennsylvania Steel and Joseph Wharton of Bethlehem Steel. Several of these steel 'aristocrats' looked upon Carnegie as a jumped-up jackanapes, especially when he bombastically boasted that the Edgar Thomson Steel Co. would outshine them all. Back in 1866 the 'aristocrats' had formed the Pennsylvania Steel Association, later renamed the Bessemer Steel Association. Their intent was to purchase, administer and allocate for large fees steel patents in America. By 1877 Carnegie had enough influence to become one of their number, although he grumbled at the royalties he had to pay for the privilege.

Weathering market, employee, partner and financial difficulties, by 1878 Carnegie had seen the Edgar Thomson Steel Co. grow to a capital stock of $1,250,000, Carnegie's $741,000-worth making him the majority partner.[22] As many of the wolves of Wall Street and others were being ruined by the depression, Carnegie became 'the richest man of his time'.[23]

On 12 July 1877 Carnegie received 'the greatest honour' of his life when he was accorded the freedom of Dunfermline. He glowed with pride that his name was thus associated with Sir Walter Scott, whom his parents remembered sketching in the grounds of Dunfermline Abbey during one of his visits to Fife.[24] In all, Carnegie was to beat William Ewart Gladstone's record of fourteen municipal freedoms.[25] And once again Carnegie's feet itched to travel.

TEN

ROUND THE WORLD

> It is therefore only a matter of time when the Chinese will drive
> every other race to the wall. No race can possibly stand against
> them . . .
>
> Andrew Carnegie, December 1878

During mid-October 1878 Carnegie left the management of the Edgar Thomson Steel Co. in the hands – he thought capable – of William P. Shinn. He was now bound for the greatest tour of his life, this time to the Orient. Settling his mother with brother Tom at Pittsburgh, Carnegie packed his bags – including a 13-volume pigskin-bound *Works of William Shakespeare* a gift from his mother to while away the long hours at sea – and met up with John 'Vandy' Vandervort on the first leg of the journey to San Francisco. This was the realisation of an undertaking they had made on their Grand Tour, while at the foot of Mount Vesuvius, that they would tour 'around the Ball'. This was no modern package tour with each booking made in advance; Carnegie was entering lands of which he had little or no knowledge, to meet people whose languages and writings were a mystery to him. But it would be the commencement of a new epoch of his life away from the luxuries of his New York habitat and the fussings of his mother.

They set sail on 24 October 1878 aboard the SS *Belgic* and on 15 November they reached Japan's main island of Honshu. For Carnegie it was a complete culture shock. They based themselves in Tokyo, which had been the capital of Japan only since 1868. Here they were introduced to the bustling metropolis, the imperial capital of Emperor Meiji (r. 1867–1912) who had seized the reins of government from the Shoguns (generalissimos) who had ruled Japan for centuries. Carnegie was able to observe how the emperor was beginning to raise the status of his nation from an obscure, insular and little-known country to a first-class power. Even so he observed much that had not changed from Japan's medieval past, from the *tera* (temples) to the *chamise* (tea-houses), while the modern warships at Yokohama – part of Emperor Meiji's developing fleet – depressed Carnegie as a symbol of Japan's developing militarism.

Traditional dress was being replaced by Western costume, but as the *jinrikshas* (man-powered carriages) weaved in and out of the traffic Carnegie saw their women passengers sporting the fashions, hairstyles and make-up of an ancient era – and he was not impressed: 'How women can be induced to make such disgusting frights of themselves I cannot conceive.'[1] Despite the great changes being wrought by Emperor Meiji, Carnegie was not enamoured of Japanese culture: 'the odour of the toyshop pervades in everything, even their temples'.[2]

From Japan Carnegie and Vandervort sailed on 27 November 1878 to Shanghai, via Nagasaki. The port of Nagasaki was a complete contrast to Tokyo. Here Westerners had set up shop from the days when the first Portuguese merchant ships arrived in 1571, to spew out guns, goods and Christianity. The steep streets, the vistas, the gardens impressed Carnegie, who caught the magic of the place that would inspire Giacomo Puccini to site his opera *Madame Butterfly* (1904) in the city.

Setting up base at the Astor House in the American Settlement at the treaty port of Shanghai, in the fertile delta of the Chang Jiang River, Carnegie and Vandervort obtained their first view of China. They were to spend nine days in the port, before taking a mail steamer to the British Crown Colony of Hong Kong for Christmas Day. Carnegie voiced his opinion of China as the year came to a close. For him China outshone Japan, for the Dragon Empire had forged a depth of civilisation that impressed him and he liked the fact that it was the scholars who held pride of place in society. He believed that the rapid Westernisation of Japanese society would lead it to disaster, but not so for the Chinese:

> Here in Asia the survival of the fittest is being fought out. . . . In this struggle we have no hesitation in backing the Heathen Chinese against the field. Permanent occupation by any western race is of course out of the question. An Englishman would inevitably cease to be an Englishman in a few, a very few, generations, and it is therefore only a question of time when the Chinese will drive every other race to the wall. No race can possibly stand against them anywhere in the East.[3]

From Hong Kong they travelled across the South China Sea to Saigon (modern Ho Chi Minh City) and thence to Singapore, part of the British colony of the Straits Settlements, which Sir Stamford Raffles of the British East India Company had leased from the Sultan of Johor. Apart from the heat making their bulky clothes uncomfortable, Carnegie was unimpressed by what he saw in this part of South East Asia.

An English mail steamer from Singapore on 14 January 1879 carried them across the Indian Ocean to Ceylon (Sri Lanka), a British possession since 1796. Coffee plantations had been widely devastated by disease in the 1870s and Ceylon tea was now the great export commodity. As Carnegie sipped the flavoured brew, which had been a luxury in his Dunfermline childhood, he reflected more on the Buddhism he had first encountered in Japan and which had marched alongside the national religion of Shintoism. In Ceylon too, he absorbed the concept of making happy discoveries by accident – serendipity. The Arab traders had called Ceylon 'Serendip', a name which English author Horace Walpole adapted for the adjective in 1754.

A three-day journey by mail steamer along the Coromandel coast brought them to Madras, once a centre for the British East India Company as Fort George, with the oldest town charter in India (1688) and the oldest English church (1678). From here they sailed across the Bay of Bengal to the port of Calcutta.

Here, in the capital city of West Bengal, they saw British India in all its magnificence, now two years into its role as the imperial capital after the proclamation of Queen Victoria as Empress of India. Trade in cotton, silks, indigo and opium interested Carnegie, though he found India's public bathing and open-air cremation of the dead disturbing.

A train journey to Benares (Varanasi), the ancient and holy Hindu city, on 6 February introduced the travellers to the real culture of the Ganges, with its bathing ghats and cremations, and the mazes of narrow city streets and hundreds of temples. They moved on to the Mogul city of Agra, with its Red Fort and most famous neighbour the white marble Taj Mahal, the mausoleum of 1630–48 built to honour and inter Mumtaz-i-Mahal, wife of Shah Jahan, the great patron of Indian engineering and architecture. Up to this point Carnegie's favourite monument was that to Sir Walter Scott in Princes Street Gardens, Edinburgh, but the Taj Mahal now pushed it into second place. At last he caught the great spirit of the country, and although he considered that India could never outstrip China in cultural or economic potential, he believed that the development of Christianity in India would be to its great advantage, with one directive god supplanting a whole pantheon. He felt too, that India would ultimately rebel against her imperial rulers, although he had glowing words to say about the British administration:

> The more I see of the thoroughness of the English Government in the East – its attention to the minutest details, the exceptional ability of its officials as evinced in the excellence of the courts, jails, hospitals, dispensaries, schools, roads, railways, canals, etc, – the more I am amazed.[4]

Ten days after arriving at Agra they journeyed on to Delhi on the Yumuna River, not yet proclaimed the capital of India by the British (this did not take place until 1911). Thence they went to Bombay (Mumbai), the Gateway to India since the opening of the Suez Canal in 1869. Carnegie described Bombay as the 'Rome of India', and settled back in its relaxed atmosphere to catch up with his correspondence. It was not all good news. He opened a letter from W.P. Shinn dated 1 December 1878 informing him of the death of David McCandless, chairman of the Edgar Thomson Steel Company. Carnegie was deeply upset. His friendship with the McCandless family had dated from his first days at Allegheny; indeed, his father William, his aunt Annie Aitken and David McCandless had together founded the first Swedenborgian church and McCandless had opened many doors for Carnegie. He grieved that he had not been able to say a final goodbye to his old friend. On 22 February 1879 Carnegie wrote to William P. Shinn one of the most heartfelt letters that he ever composed:

> It does seem too hard to bear, but we must bite the lip & go forward I suppose assuming indifference – but I am sure none of us can ever efface from our memories the images of our dear, generous, gentle & unselfish friend – To the day I die I shall never be able to think of him without a stinging pain at the heart – His death robs my life of one of its chief pleasures, but it must be borne, only let us take from his loss one lesson as the best tribute to his memory. Let us try to be as kind and devoted to each other as he was to us. He was a model for all of us to follow. One thing more we can do – attend to his affairs & get them right that Mrs McCandless & Helen may be provided for – I know you will all be looking after this & you know how anxious I shall be to cooperate with you.[5]

The next stop on the world tour was Egypt and the mosques and bustling streets of Cairo, under the country's new ruler Khedive Tawfiq of the dynasty of Muhammad Ali. The usual tourist round was enjoyed, with Carnegie being hauled rather unceremoniously up the Great Pyramid of Khufu, King of Memphis. After two weeks in Egypt a four-day cruise brought them to Sicily, Naples, Rome and Florence, and thence by other means to Paris and London. As he left the Orient behind, Carnegie began to distil his thoughts about what he had seen there; it would become important to him shortly. But first, on their arrival in London, Carnegie was joined by his mother and four weeks were spent visiting friends and family in Scotland. They sailed for home on 14 June 1879 arriving at New York on the 24th – the world tour had taken eight months.

In his luggage Carnegie had placed 'several pads suitable for penciling' and had jotted in them each day throughout the trip.[6] It had not been his intention to write a book, but rather a sort of informal publication to circulate to friends and colleagues. In due course his notes were produced; the publishers Charles Scribner's Sons saw mention of the notes in a newspaper and made a bid for them for the wider commercial market. The book of the tour was published in 1884 as *Round the World*, and Carnegie was delighted: 'I was at last "an author".'[7] The volume sold around 5,000 copies in nine editions[8] and rekindled the idea of a writing career in Carnegie's mind.

The voyage, reflected Carnegie, 'quite changed my intellectual outlook'.[9] He delved more into Herbert Spencer's works on evolution, contrasting the various races he had seen in the East. He also studied the works of Charles Darwin, the English naturalist whose book *The Origin of Species* had appeared in 1859, to be followed by several titles on orchids and other plants and works on human and animal emotions. Carnegie's readings of Confucius, Buddhism and Zoroastrianism, he said, gave him 'a philosophy at last'.[10] His world tour had shown him that no culture had all the answers regarding the true religion and philosophy. He found himself quoting Matthew Arnold:

> Children of men! the unseen Power, whose eye
> For ever doth accompany mankind
> Hath looked on no religion scornfully
> That men did ever find.

Which has not taught weak wills how much they can?
Which has not fall'n in the dry heart like rain?
Which has not cried to sunk, self-weary man,
Thou must be born again.[11]

Carnegie also relived his experiences in the East by dipping into
the poet Sir Edwin Arnold's work on Buddhism, *The Light of Asia*
(1879).

However, during his trip to the world's most populous
nations, and even though he was with Vandervort, Carnegie
felt alone. At 44 he could look forward to a solitary life;
Margaret Carnegie was almost 70 and he began to realise that
he required a supplementary emotional rock, someone who
would eventually replace her. He resolved to look about him.

ELEVEN

ROMANCE AND THE CHARIOTEER

*What Benares is to the Hindoo, Mecca to the Mohammedan,
Jerusalem to the Christian, all that Dunfermline is to me!*
                                        Andrew Carnegie, July 1881

Carnegie enjoyed horse-riding; he looked taller in the saddle, and always cut a dash in his tailored suits while out riding in New York's Central Park among the well-to-do. It also offered him a welcome respite from the multitude of business projects now administered from his new office at 19 Broad Street. By 1 January 1880 Carnegie and his mother were well ensconced in their new accommodation at the Windsor Hotel on Fifth Avenue. Junketing was an important part of Carnegie's life, mixing business with pleasure on both sides of the Atlantic. When New York and Pittsburgh sweltered in the summer heat, Carnegie and his mother decamped to Cresson in the Allegheny mountains to the gothic residence they dubbed Braemar Cottage. Here they invited a whole range of visitors – putting them up at the Mountain Inn – during their usual vacations from June to October. Margaret Carnegie was happy here as she had more of her son's attention; her other son Tom was busy rearing a family of nine and had little time, or inclination, to indulge his mother.

Carnegie enjoyed a widespread acquaintanceship with the good and the great of New York. Some could not stand his arrogance and apparent self-centredness and returned his tipped hat salutes in the park with frostiness, while others appreciated his ebullience and enthusiasm for life. Despite his flirtations with the pretty girls he met riding in the park,

Margaret Carnegie was solidly sure that her son would not stray from her affections or her domination. After all, did he not believe that he owed his success to her? The emotional umbilical cord was strong, but as 1879 gave way to 1880 a threat to her dominance began to loom. As was the custom he had established for New Year's Day, Carnegie strolled out to visit friends – but this was a walk that would alter the whole course of his life. On this occasion he was joined as usual by fellow Scots Alexander and Agnes King, whose prosperity had derived from the thread industry; together they visited the home of the Kings' friends, the Whitfields of West 48th Street.

John W. Whitfield, a wholesaler of fine material, had died two years earlier leaving an ailing widow and three children. Carnegie had been introduced to the Whitfields by the Kings as far back as 1870, and was charmed to see that the eldest daughter Louise was no longer a schoolgirl. She had blossomed into a well-educated, confident young woman of 22 who now ran her mother's household. Louise Whitfield was not one of the New York society beauties; she was taller than Carnegie, and her portrait by Sarah MacKnight of the 1880s shows her with dark hair and eyes and a strong face. Soon Louise was to join Carnegie, with Alex King as chaperon, on his rides in Central Park; a short while later Carnegie received Mrs Whitfield's permission to ride out *à deux* with her daughter. Louise looked back on this occasion as a turning point in her life: 'After my first ride, I decided, whatever the future might hold in store, that would remain the greatest experience of my life.'[1] Her diaries now became full of Carnegie and horse-riding: 'Went riding with Mr Carnegie. Glorious time! . . . In afternoon Mr Carnegie came and took me horseback riding. Splendid time!'[2] Similarly Carnegie wrote:

> We were both very fond of riding. Other young women were on my list. I had fine horses and often rode in the Park and around New York with one or other of the circle. In the end the others all faded into ordinary beings. Miss Whitfield remained alone as the perfect one beyond any I had met.[3]

Carnegie was certainly smitten but he was no Lothario; his courting, if he ever thought of it as that, was peripatetic because of his business commitments and was largely conducted on horseback. Nevertheless he began to include Louise in family outings and recruited his mother as chaperone. Margaret Carnegie was not discomfited; her hold on her son was absolute . . . or so she thought. Theatre trips *en famille* became somewhat regular and a romance was certainly blooming.[4] But Carnegie's 'gypsy spirit' was at work again and the hills of Scotland were calling him.

For a while he had been contemplating a coach trip around Britain, and thought it would be a great idea for Louise to come too. Mrs Whitfield was not sure that it was 'proper'; stirred up by her son's passion Margaret Carnegie went to discuss the matter with Mrs Whitfield, her demeanour making it clear that she thought that it would be 'improper'. Louise, who had already been informally invited by Carnegie, was saddened by the decision that she should not go, but attended the farewell dinner at the Windsor Hotel for Carnegie's travelling party – whom he called the Gay Charioteers – but wished she hadn't. She wrote in her diary: 'Was very sorry I went, but did not know how to get out of it . . . I must learn to be satisfied with what I have and not long for more.'[5]

When he had travelled around Britain back in 1865 with his cousin Dod and 'Vandy' Vandervort, Carnegie had vowed that 'when my "ships come in" I should drive a party of my dearest friends from Brighton to Inverness'.[6] He saw his new adventure as an 'air castle' and 'idyllic', just as had been described in his reading of Scots novelist William Black's, *The Strange Adventures of a Phaeton* (1872); Carnegie was to meet Black at Brighton, having discussed the book at dinner a week before the trip with President James A. Garfield at the home of Senator James G. Blair, Secretary of State. (On 19 September Garfield was to be fatally shot by a crazed office-seeker as he waited for a train at the Washington depot.)

Carnegie and his party set off for Liverpool on 1 June 1881, aboard the Cunard liner SS *Bothnia*. The party included

Margaret Carnegie, Jeannie Johns, Alice French, Mr and Mrs David McCargo, Mr and Mrs Alex King, Benjamin F. Vandervort, Harry Phipps Jr and Gardner McCandless. They arrived at Liverpool on Saturday 11 June and departed straight away for London's Westminster Hotel to spend five days sightseeing in the capital. At the House of Commons they were hosted by Sir Charles Wentworth Dilke (1842–1911), then Under-Secretary to the Foreign Office in Gladstone's Liberal government, and heard John Bright (1811–89), Chancellor of the Duchy of Lancaster, address the House; Carnegie remembered Bright speaking at Dunfermline in 1842 when Carnegie was just 7 years old. He glowed with pride when the statesman remembered the occasion. At Stafford House (now Lancaster House) in St James's they were entertained by George Granville, Marquis of Stafford.

On 16 June they set off for Brighton and the Grand Hotel, an entourage of 'coach, horses and servants' having preceded them.[7] Next morning they set off on their 831-mile trip to Inverness, in a shiny black and red coach drawn by four horses, with Perry the coachman and Joe the footman both wearing smart silver and blue uniforms. A series of complicated arrangements ensured that their luggage preceded them for their convenience, and hotel accommodation was booked ahead by telegraph.

Over the Weald of Sussex and via various watering stops they went to Guildford (The White Lion), and then put up at the Castle Hotel, Windsor, during 18–20 June. 'Windsor is nothing unless royal,' observed Carnegie, although Queen Victoria was elsewhere; nonetheless they did see Albert Edward, Prince of Wales and W.E. Gladstone at a Windsor church service. Carnegie was shocked to see how 'careworn' Gladstone looked. Margaret Carnegie celebrated her 71st birthday at Windsor on 19 June and partied with great vigour. They found the service at St George's Chapel impressive, but Carnegie remarked that the castle was not, adding 'as royalty itself, [the castle] should be [viewed] at a safe distance'.[8]

At Windsor they were joined for dinner by Sidney Gilchrist-

Thomas, an amateur chemist with an interest in metallurgy. His invention, the 'Thomas Basic Process', allowed phosphorus to be removed from iron ore, a boon to Bessemer steel production. Shortly before the tour Carnegie had sold the US franchise on the Thomas patent for $250,000, creaming off $50,000 in commission for himself.[9] Gilchrist-Thomas had collaborated with his cousin on the process, and Carnegie remarked: 'These young men have done more for England's greatness than all her kings and queens and aristocracy put together.'[10] At the dinner, where Gilchrist-Thomas was joined by his family, all were invited by Carnegie to join them on the trip to Scotland. Gilchrist-Thomas declined, and his sister Lilian left this comment on Margaret Carnegie: '[Carnegie's] devotion to his mother, a trenchant old lady who called a spade a spade with racy Scottish wit, was delightful to see.'[11]

From Windsor they detoured to Stoke Poges in Buckinghamshire so that Carnegie – who generally avoided graveyards – could view the grave of the poet Thomas Gray, whose poem 'Elegy Written in a Country Church-Yard' (1751) was one of his favourites. In his twopenny jotter Carnegie recorded these lines from Gray's tomb:

> One morn I missed him on the accustomed hill,
> Along the heath, and near his favourite tree;
> Another came, nor yet beside the rill,
> Nor up the lawn, nor at the wood was he.

Much moved, the party lunched by the Thames at the Old Swan Inn, picnicking under the trees. This was followed by a row on the river and then it was on to Reading and the Queen's Hotel, and thence to Oxford. Their route across the Isis and up the High Street brought them to the Claremont Hotel, but as the university term was to begin the next day they had to be accommodated in nearby houses. A comprehensive tour of the principal colleges, the Sheldonian Theatre and the martyrs' monument (to the Protestant martyrs Bishop Hugh Latimer and Bishop Nicholas Ridley, burned at the stake opposite Balliol College on 16 October 1555) filled their day, yet Carnegie still found time on 21 June to write to Louise – who had never left his thoughts. He urged her to write to him care of his agents J.S. Morgan & Co. at London.

Then it was on to Banbury Cross and Blenheim Palace, Woodstock. At the palace, given by a grateful nation to John Churchill, 1st Duke of Marlborough (1650–1722), Carnegie vented his spleen on the likes of John Churchill and the Duke of Wellington as Britain's 'most successful murderers' and ridiculing the nation's penchant for honouring 'butchers'.[12] He calmed down when he viewed Blenheim's gardens and library, but began to seethe again as his coach clattered down the drive and he recalled 'the bad [British] men who did the dirty work of miserable kings . . . no man should be born to honours, but that these should be reserved for those who merit them. . . . The days of rank are numbered.'[13] His republican blood had ceased to boil by the time he settled down at Banbury's White Lion Hotel, where he enjoyed a long talk on railways with the constituency's Liberal MP (later Sir) Bernhard Samuelson, a Manchester engineer and ironmaster at Middlesbrough.

A visit to Wroxton Abbey brought them to Edgehill in Warwickshire, where King Charles I's Royalist Army was defeated by the Parliamentarians led by Robert Devereux, Earl of Essex, on 23 October 1642. As he mounted the elevation above the battlefield, Carnegie's republican heart swelled with pride at Charles's rout.

Warwick and Leamington gave way to the old market town of Stratford-upon-Avon, where the party stayed at the Red Horse Inn. A visit to Shakespeare's birthplace on Henley Street and his grave in the parish church by the Avon was a must, with Carnegie reflecting on his first encounters with Shakespeare's genius as he stood 'beside the ashes' of the great man.

By 24 June they were at a rain-soaked Coventry, to walk in the footsteps of Mary Ann Evans, who won fame as the writer George Eliot and lived here from 1841 to 1849. They were now entering the heartlands of the industrial Midlands, dubbed the 'Black Country' – a name derived from the concentration of mines and factories stretching approximately from Castle Bromwich in the east to Wolverhampton in the north-west. After his jottings on daffodils, pretty dells, streams and thatched farms, Carnegie now recorded the industrial scene:

> We see the Black Country now, rows of little dingy houses beyond, with tall smoky chimneys vomiting smoke, mills and blast furnaces . . . and such dirty, careworn children, hard-driven men, and squalid women. . . . How can people be got to live such terrible lives as they seem condemned to here? Why do they not all run away to the green fields beyond. . . . But do not let us forget that it is just Pittsburgh over again.[14]

This was a somewhat hypocritical comment since Carnegie's own workers toiled in similar slum conditions.

Then they went on to Birmingham, where a free concert of organ music at the Public Hall raised their spirits ahead of a six-day stay at Wolverhampton – described as 'one vast iron-working, coal-mining establishment'.[15] A garden party at the Mayor's, a tour of the free library, theatricals at Clifton House and assorted junketings set them in a good mood to travel to the cathedral city of Lichfield on 1 July. A stopover at The Swan and a feast of medieval architecture saw them off to Dovedale in Derbyshire, where Izaac Walton had fished the River Dove, his enthusiasm eventually producing his *The Compleat Angler* (1653). Carnegie wrote down his own thoughts on fishing. Thence by way of several aristocratic homes they went to Chatsworth and the Edensor Hotel, and admired the model village erected by the Duke of Devonshire. Refreshed by the country air at Buxton spa they prepared for the bustle of Manchester and the formality of the Queen's Hotel; they made a rapid review of the 'principal streets' of the city. Chorley (Anderton Hall) and Preston (The Victoria) gave way to two days at Lancaster and the County Hotel. Here they joined the crowds to cheer along the procession of the newly elected High Sheriff of Lancashire. Next they travelled through the Lake District via Kendal (The Kings Arms), Grasmere (The Prince of Wales), Keswick (The Keswick) and Penrith (The Crown), and along the way Carnegie was interested to see the number of American flags on display at various hotels. Highlights of the visit were rowing on the lakes and a visit to William Wordsworth's grave at Grasmere, although Carnegie dismissed the Lakeland Poets as inferior to 'our own' Walter Scott. By 15 July they were at Carlisle (the County and Station Hotel) and Carnegie and his mother were eager to take the next step: 'Do any people love their country as passionately as the Scotch?,' asked Carnegie. 'Tomorrow we are to enter that land of lands.'[16]

That Saturday, 16 July 1881, when they crossed the border into Scotland, Carnegie was in lyrical mood and quoted Lord Byron's lines from 'Hours of Idleness' (1807):

Away, ye gay landscapes, ye gardens of roses
In you let the minions of luxury rove;
Restore me the rocks where the snowflake reposes,
Though still they are sacred to freedom and love:
Yet, Caledonia, beloved are thy mountains,
Round their white summits though elements war;
Though cataracts foam 'stead of smooth flowing fountains,
I sigh for the valley of dark Loch na Garr.

Carnegie's gushing sentiment for Scotland was poured into his twopenny jotters: 'It's a God's mercy I was born a Scotchman, for I do not see how I could ever have been contented to be anything else.'[17] A small boy was rewarded with a shilling (5p) for guiding them round the romantic blacksmith's shop at Gretna Green, where couples still flocked to the site for 'irregular marriages'; at nearby Gretna Hall Richard Brinsley Sheridan had married Maria Grant in 1835 . . . twice! After lunch at Annan the party rested for two days at Dumfries (The Commercial), with Carnegie seeking out relics of the burgh's worthies and making a pilgrimage to the grave of Robert Burns at St Michael's churchyard.

The road to Sanquhar and the Queensberry Hotel led them to Drumlanrig Castle, the seat of the Dukes of Buccleuch on the River Nith. Carnegie was overcome once more and declaimed more from 'Hours of Idleness':

> England! thy beauties are tame and domestic
> To one who has roamed on the mountains afar.
> Oh, for the crags that are wild and majestic!
> The steep frowning glories of dark Loch na Garr.

At Old Cumnock (The Dumfries Arms) the party and their coach were immortalised by the local photographer, and then they moved on to Douglas (The Douglas Arms), Lanarkshire. Here Carnegie explored the tombs of the Douglas family at the Church of St Bridge, pausing at the vault of his hero Robert I's friend the loyal Sir James of Douglas, killed in battle with the Moors in Spain on his way to the Holy Land with the heart of Bruce in a reliquary in accordance with the dead king's wishes. Epitaphs became the main topic of conversation with the party and Carnegie jotted down a classical Scottish example:

> Here lies David Elginbrod,
> Ha'e mercy on his soul, O God!
> As he'd a-had, had he been God
> And ye'd been David Elginbrod.

In hilarious mood they made for Edinburgh on 20 July, to stay in the capital for six days. From their base at The Royal Hotel in Princes Street the party split up to explore Edinburgh in pursuit of their separate interests. Carnegie went down to Leith to witness the official opening of the new Edinburgh Dock. He was eager to cross the Forth to Dunfermline, but then received a telegram from Dunfermline's town clerk Mr Simpson asking him to delay his visit by one day, as arrangements for his reception were not quite ready. His anticipation rising by the hour, Carnegie spent the evening with Queen Victoria's limner (painter) in Scotland, Sir Joseph

Noel Paton, described by Carnegie as 'Dunfermline's most distinguished son'.[18]

Carnegie was beside himself with joy as the ferry took them to North Queensferry and Fife, and he searched his memory for a quote from Sir Walter Scott's 'Marmion' (1808) to celebrate the voyage:

> But northward far, with purer blaze,
> On Ochil mountains fell the rays,
> And as each heathy top they kissed,
> It gleamed a purple amethyst.
> Yonder the shores of Fife you saw,
> Here Preston Bay, and Berwick Law;
> And broad between them rolled,
> The gallant Firth the eye might note,
> Whose islands on its bosom float,
> Like emeralds chased in gold.

They were met at the shore by Uncle George Lauder and assorted relations. As rainclouds threatened their planned picnic at ruined Rosyth Castle they went instead to a Rosyth inn to be greeted by a flustered landlady. Carnegie lapped up her Fife accent: 'I'm a' alane! There's naebody in the house! They're a' awa' to Dunfermline! There'll be great goings on there the day.' Lunch was partaken without the landlady guessing that her guest was the cause of the 'great goings on' at Dunfermline.[19]

With his emotions barely under control Carnegie sat on the outside top of the coach as it breasted the top of the Ferry Hills and Dunfermline came into view: 'What Benares is to the Hindoo [*sic*], Mecca to the Mohammedan, Jerusalem to the Christian, all that Dunfermline is to me!'[20] In mid-afternoon the coach rolled up St Leonard's Street and at the top of Bothwell Street encountered the huge civic and civil party assembled to welcome Carnegie amid bunting, brass bands, pipers and banners announcing 'Welcome Carnegie, Generous Son'. A mile-long procession formed up behind the Provost, councillors and magistrates, and Carnegie was led up Netherton and into steep Moodie Street, halting at the cottage where he had been born. Inside the carriage Margaret Carnegie wept with pride.

An important part of the visit was the laying of the foundation stone of Dunfermline Free Library (now the Central Library) in Abbey Street by Margaret Carnegie, who was given this honour at the request of her son. Her tears suppressed, her neat black silk dress making her stand out proudly, Margaret Carnegie 'spread the mortar with a silver trowel, gave the [stone] three mystic taps and announced in a firm voice that carried to the edge of the throng: "I pronounce this memorial stone duly laid, and may God bless the undertaking".'[21] Completed on 27 July 1881 to the design of James Campbell Walker this was Carnegie's first major library gift; extensions were added to it during 1914–21. While formulating his architectural plans Walker had asked Carnegie for his coat of arms to display on the building; Carnegie had none, but suggested that a rising sun shedding its rays should be placed above the entrance; the motto would be taken from Genesis 1:3 – 'Let there be Light'.

Provost Walls accompanied Carnegie on a tour of the adjacent abbey grounds with a top hat salute to the American flag flying on the Abbey Tower. As the abbey bell pealed in his honour – stirring memories of the curfew bell of his childhood – Carnegie broke down in tears. On their special half-day holiday for the event the cheering Dunfermline townsfolk pursued Carnegie wherever he went and the *Dunfermline & West Fife Journal* declared: 'The demonstration may be said to be unparalleled in the history of Dunfermline.'

A celebration dinner followed the stone-laying with Provost Wall offering fulsome praise to the guest of honour. Curiously he included some rather impertinent remarks in his speech:

> The only flaw in Mr Carnegie's character is that he wants a wife. I attribute that very much to the fact of his having a mother. His mother has taken good care of him, and has

showed that she does not want to hand him over to the tender mercies of some half-cousin, or any of the half-dozen young ladies who are with him today.[22]

John Johnston was there that day and remembered that Margaret Carnegie sat stony-faced at the Provost's remarks while Carnegie himself showed some discomfort. Those in the know saw how Margaret Carnegie stuck to her son, who even composed a squib about the situation which he gave public airing in his book on the tour:

> The good book tells of one
> Who sticks closer than a brother;
> But who will dare to say there's one
> Sticks closer than a mother.

On Friday 27 July the party moved on to Kinross, where Margaret Carnegie had to rest, drained by the emotions of the Dunfermline celebrations. The others viewed the castle set in Loch Leven, from where Mary, Queen of Scots made her famous escape in 1568. Then they moved on to Perth (the Royal George), where on 29 July Carnegie was busy reflecting on the city as the ancient capital of Scotland, and then to Scone, where the coronations of Scottish kings had taken place, while the journey northward next day to Dunkeld had Carnegie comparing the views with Sir John Everett Millais's paintings of the area and poet Thomas Gray's descriptions of the place. A walk in the ruins of Dunkeld Cathedral completed the party's enjoyment of the atmosphere. A relief coachman entertained them with local stories as they passed through the hills around Birnam and Dunsinane – made famous in Shakespeare's *Macbeth*. As they passed through the large estate lands owned by the Duke of Atholl Carnegie's republicanism surfaced: 'Why do not people just meet and resolve that they will no longer have kings, princes, dukes or lords, and declare that all men are born equal, as we have done in America?'[23]

Carnegie declared Pitlochry (Fisher's Hotel) 'a great resort', from where quick visits were made to the famous Pass of Killiecrankie and to the Bruar Water and Falls of Tummel. Poems by Burns and Scott were recited to complement the views as they travelled deep into the Highlands, through Dalwhinnie and Boat of Garten, until at last, on Saturday 3 August 1881, they reached their destination, Inverness. They rested at the Caledonian Hotel. It had taken them seven weeks to travel 831 miles, and they had had, at various times, some thirty-two travelling companions.

The party stayed at Inverness until 5 August, exploring the Highland capital and savouring the Highland air. By canal and boat they made their way to Oban, thence Glasgow, where the party split up to go their various ways. At the Broomielaw Carnegie became nostalgic as he remembered: 'whither father and mother and Tom and I sailed thirty-odd years ago'.[24] While Margaret Carnegie spent some time at Paisley, Carnegie and Harry Phipps left St Enoch's station by train to visit E. Winston Richards, plant manager of the steel mill at Eston, the largest of its type in the world, stopping off en route at the cathedrals of Durham and York to enjoy the organ music.

On 13 August they sailed from Liverpool aboard the *Algeria*, arriving at New York on Wednesday 24 August. The euphoria of the trip having left him, Carnegie spent 'two or three of the most miserable hours' of his life at the St Nicholas Hotel before setting out for Cresson. He was depressed that the party had broken up; he missed the company and felt alone, his mother chiding him for not being content with her company.[25] In the end though, Carnegie looked upon his trip as 'a sacred possession for ever'.[26]

The twopenny jotters were reformed into a book on the tour that appeared as *An American Four-in-Hand in Britain* under Charles Scribner's Sons' imprint in 1883; a first edition of 200 copies sold rapidly and the volume eventually ran to some 18 editions and total sales of some 15,000 copies.[27]

TWELVE

FRIENDSHIPS SWEET AND SOUR

The Republican form of government is the highest form of government; but because of this it requires the highest type of human nature . . .

Herbert Spencer, *The Americans*

While Carnegie was languishing in his 'loneliness' with his ever-present mother, Louise Whitfield and her mother spent the summer of 1881 in the Catskill Mountains on the west side of the Hudson River valley, about 75 miles north-west of New York. She was feeling neglected by Carnegie, who had written only one letter to her on 21 June from the Queen's Hotel, Reading. The sentiment therein saying how he wished she was with the party did nothing to assuage her feeling of being sidelined. Louise had other suitors, but slowly her relationship with Carnegie began to rekindle as each came back into the other's orbit. If she *was* contemplating marriage with Carnegie – although he had not asked her – she was likely to see three main obstacles: his obsessive attention to his mother, the promotion of his place in society, and his business interests. There was also the fact that he was twice her age. Their strange on-off courtship would last for six years.

Carnegie had then one prime subject on his mind: the administration of his steel interests in Pittsburgh. The atmosphere at the Edgar Thomson Steel Co. was not congenial. After the death of chairman David McCandless, general manager William P. Shinn began jockeying for promotion, inflating his own salary and entrenching his position in the company. Soon realising that he was not going to be appointed

114

chairman, Shinn resigned and went to work for a rival, the Vulcan Iron Co. Lawsuits were prepared for Shinn to gain compensation for not advancing in the Carnegie company; Carnegie initially baulked at the figure proposed, but when he realised that the Edgar Thomson Co. books would be examined in court he backed down and Shinn was given a payment of $200,000 to close the unpleasant altercations.[1]

In due course Tom Carnegie was appointed chairman of the company. Carnegie was keen to see off his competitors, a particular rival being the Cambria works at Johnstown, Pennsylvania. Towards this end the year 1881 saw a reorganisation of the various iron and steel businesses into Carnegie Bros & Co. Ltd, which now incorporated the Edgar Thomson and Union Iron Mills, the Lucy Furnaces (named after Tom's wife Lucy Coleman) and the Keystone Bridge Co. Carnegie was the majority shareholder.[2] This portfolio was greatly expanded by 1886, with enhanced profits. By 1886 too, the firm of Carnegie, Phipps & Co. had been organised to run the Homestead mills. Business was further expanded by the purchase of the Hartman Steel Works at Bear Falls.[3] It was a glorious time for Carnegie: 'America had won the steel leadership of the world [from Britain], and Carnegie was at the heart of it.'[4]

For his business to flourish Carnegie needed reliable sources of supplies, especially coke, which brought into Carnegie's orbit one Henry Clay Frick. Born at West Overton, Pennsylvania, of wealthy farming stock, but with little education, Frick was a winner in the ante-bellum race to supply the nation's steel mills with coke, from his Connellsville plant; in 1871 he organised the Henry C. Frick Co. and ten years later Carnegie was a valued customer. By 1883 Carnegie had bought into Frick's company and owned 50 per cent of the stock. Frick became a key player in Carnegie's business life.

What of Carnegie's other interests? Carnegie lived life on various levels, with some facets seemingly less than compatible. A look at some of them offers a flavour of Carnegie's views on British politics, newspapers and literature. Carnegie had been interested in what was happening on the British political scene since the early days of the family's emigration. Back then (1848) the Whig Lord John Russell was Prime Minister, and for forty years the political pendulum had swung left and right, with eleven politicians holding the office of Prime Minister. Carnegie followed the careers of them all. A regular correspondence had been undertaken between Carnegie and his cousin Dod Lauder, exchanging views on the political scenes of their respective countries. On 15 April 1880 Dod wrote a letter in high glee that the second Conservative administration of Benjamin Disraeli had fallen in the general election of that May and that William Ewart Gladstone was to form his second Liberal administration. Queen Victoria, whose contempt for Gladstone dated back to the Roman Catholic troubles of 1845, reluctantly accepted his ministry, and Carnegie hoped that the new administration would bring about the end of the House of Hanover in particular and the monarchy in general. Carnegie's frequent visits to Britain brought him into the world of the country's movers and shakers, but as his republicanism grew, so did his snobbery and his need for the oxygen of high society.

Carnegie followed the progress of Gladstone's government carefully, step by step, from the first budget of 10 June 1880, wherein income tax increased from $5d$ to $6d$ in the pound, through the Irish troubles and the murder of Lord Frederick Cavendish (1882), to the Egyptian and Sudanese troubles (1882–3), the new Representation of the People Bill (1884) and beyond. The death of Disraeli in 1881 caused more delight in the Dod Lauder household, and Carnegie saw that cultivating the Liberals would be to his advantage.

One Liberal in particular would become a close friend. John Morley, later Viscount Morley of Blackburn, was a product of Lincoln College, Oxford, and had entered journalism through the *Saturday Review*, which he developed into the most influential conveyor of liberal opinion. More left wing than Gladstonian Liberals, Morley decided to give up journalism to enter politics and during 1883–95 he served as MP for Newcastle-upon-Tyne, before moving to Montrose Burghs (1896–1908). During 1892–5 he was Chief Secretary for Ireland.

What attracted Carnegie to the agnostic, individualistic Morley – apart from sheer opportunism – was Morley's philosophical and social ideas as well as his books; he had written biographies of Irish statesman and philosopher Edmund Burke (1879), economist and politician Richard Cobden (1881), and Oliver Cromwell (1900). Carnegie believed the latter subject should be left well alone, after all Cromwellian troops had harried the environs of his beloved Dunfermline. Despite such disagreements, their friendship endured, although sometimes Morley found Carnegie's brand of humour and outspokenness hard to take. Importantly too, Morley introduced Carnegie to prominent British political leaders.

There was James Bryce, Viscount Bryce, jurist, historian and statesman, Liberal MP for Tower Hamlets 1880–5, and a member of Gladstone's last cabinet as Chancellor of the Duchy of Lancaster. Joseph Chamberlain, MP for West Birmingham 1885, was another member of Gladstone's (third) cabinet. Henry Hartley Fowler, 1st Viscount Wolverhampton, was MP for divisions of Wolverhampton 1880–1908 and a later cabinet member. Henry Labouchere, 1st Baron Taunton, MP for Michael Borough (1826) and Taunton (1830), served variously under Lord Melbourne, Lord John Russell and Lord Palmerston and was a particular feather in Carnegie's social cap, as was Archibald Philip Primrose, 8th Earl of Rosebery, Prime Minister 1884–5. One of the best known of the Liberal grandees, Rosebery was the son of the Lord Dalmeny who had been verbally assaulted by Carnegie's grandfather at the hustings. In 1883 Rosebery visited Carnegie at Pittsburgh, and Carnegie was to remark that Rosebery was 'handicapped by being born a peer'.[5] Rosebery also introduced Carnegie to Gladstone.[6]

Carnegie gloried in his friendship with his network of Liberal contacts, the highlight being invitations to Gladstone's home at Hawarden Castle, Flint. His snobbery totally masked any disgruntlement he felt at being blatantly used by the Liberals for financial purposes. A letter of 1 July 1887 from Gladstone to Carnegie proves the point:

> Very recently your bountiful disposition gave me an opening which I felt my duty not to pass over, for representing to you the difficulties as to money in which the Liberal party is now placed. . . . Knowing your desire to apply funds to great beneficial public purposes, I hoped you would consider this a fit case for the exercise of your liberality which I know it is your practice to put in action on a truly 'liberal' scale. . . . It is of the utmost public importance to raise at once a considerable fund which will give efficacy to the operations of the party.[7]

Carnegie sent his financial aid directly to Gladstone, and in the future would finance politicians he thought radical enough, like John Elliot Burns, the socialist troublemaker who espoused the Liberals, and of course his friend Morley.

Two other friendships were to be of particular importance to Carnegie, with Herbert Spencer and Matthew Arnold. Carnegie had met Spencer some time before 1882, but was a fellow passenger with him aboard the SS *Servia* bound for New York on 12 August 1882; evidently he did not know Spencer well at that time because he carried aboard a letter of introduction from Morley.[8] Herbert Spencer was a philosopher who by way of schoolmastering had espoused engineering and journalism to produce his *Social Statics* in 1852; by the time Carnegie met him he was well known for his *First Principles* (1862), explaining his synthetic philosophy which Carnegie had devoured years before. Carnegie became a devotee of Spencer's theories and often repeated this mantra: 'Before Spencer, all for me had been darkness, after him all had become light – and right.'[9] Carnegie also was delighted with Spencer's anti-militaristic philosophy. Spencer had expressed an eagerness for things American and was keen to meet his enthusiastic public who had paid his works much attention in America. In the event the naturally reticent Spencer found any public appearances, speeches or visits agonising. Nevertheless when the tours (and a trip to Canada) were finished, he consented to be Carnegie's guest. Carnegie was at his most proud and pompous when he showed Spencer around the steelworks at Pittsburgh.

Carnegie had arranged for Spencer to be put up at a Pittsburgh hotel, but the great man decided to accept Tom Carnegie's invitation to stay at his home. Spencer had taken a particular shine to Tom and his elder brother was greatly put out. However, Carnegie took Spencer to Cresson to rest before his departure back to Britain. The jaded Spencer was dreading his last engagement, a farewell dinner at Delmonico's in New York on 9 November 1882. Carnegie drove Spencer to the banquet,

> and saw the great man there in a funk. He could think of nothing but the address he was to deliver. I believe he had rarely before spoken in public. His great fear was that he should be unable to say anything that would be of advantage to the American people who had been the first to appreciate his works. He may have attended many banquets, but never one comprised of more distinguished people than this one. It was a remarkable gathering.[10]

Spencer was almost in a faint:

> I ought to have been in good condition, bodily and mentally . . . I was in a condition worse than I had been for six and twenty years. 'Wretched night; no sleep at all; kept in my room all day,' says my diary, and I entertained 'great fear I should collapse' . . . I got friends to secrete me in an anteroom until the last moment, so that I might avoid all excitements of introductions and congratulations . . .[11]

Spencer forced himself to speak, but he feared 'though not with much effect'; drained, he sat back and accepted a host of plaudits from such men as historian and Spencerian analyst

John Fiske and clergyman and writer Henry Ward Beecher. Two days later Spencer returned to Britain, having become one of Carnegie's special heroes. The Spencerian philosophy and social Darwinism, as will be seen shortly, became an important part of Carnegie's ideas on wealth.

Matthew Arnold was a very different personality from Spencer, and his friendship with Carnegie was to be one of the most curious of all. Arnold looked upon manufacturers and businessmen of all kinds as 'philistines' – in Victorian Britain this was the most derogatory term one could think of. Further he looked upon America as the home of the most contemptible 'philistines' of all.[12] Yet he instantly liked Carnegie for his 'extraordinary freshness of spirit'[13] and Carnegie described Arnold in his autobiography as 'charming'.

The son of Dr Thomas Arnold, headmaster of Rugby School, Matthew Arnold was a poet and critic and was educated at Rugby, Winchester and Balliol College, Oxford. For a while he was a schoolmaster at Rugby, then he was appointed private secretary to Sir Henry Petty-Fitzmaurice, 3rd Marquis of Lansdowne, who was Prime Minister Lord John Russell's President of the Council, before moving on to become an inspector of schools and Professor of Poetry at Oxford from 1857 to 1867. In June 1883 Carnegie was introduced to Arnold at a London dinner party given by Mrs Henry Yates Thomson, whose book-collecting husband at that time owned the evening paper the *Pall Mall Gazette* (1865), whose contributors included both Arnold and Morley. Arnold was to be a guest on Carnegie's British coach tour of 1884.

Despite his reservations about America, Arnold was mulling over the possibility of a lecture tour – he could certainly do with the fee money; Carnegie solidified the idea with an active proposal.[14] By October 1883 Arnold was on his way to New York with his wife Flu and his daughter Lucy; lectures on 'Numbers' and 'Literature and Science' were already prepared, with another on the American poet and essayist Ralph Waldo Emerson in progress. In all, seventy lectures were contemplated. Carnegie and his secretary met Arnold at the dockside on 22 October and whisked him away to the Windsor Hotel before Arnold could utter any really anti-American remarks to the waiting press. Almost immediately Arnold's inherent prejudices melted as he saw the doors of his suite decorated with flowers and captions of his book titles – Carnegie's favourites *Culture and Anarchy* (1869), *Friendship's Garland* (1871) and *Literature and Dogma* (1873). The 'Scottishness' of Carnegie's apartments (tartan wallpaper and the like) and the Scots burr of Margaret Carnegie's voice delighted Arnold, whose works on 'Burns and the Celtic temperament' had made him a Scotophile.[15]

Drives in Central Park, invitations and receptions to meet the leaders of American art, finance, letters and politics swept Arnold along, preparing him and calming his nerves for the first lecture at Chickering Hall on 30 October on 'Numbers'. It must be said that Matthew Arnold was no orator and the Carnegies sat through the lecture with growing embarrassment. Present among the audience of 2,000 was impresario Major P.B. Pond who reported:

Matthew Arnold came to this country and gave one hundred [*sic*] lectures. Nobody ever heard any of them, not even those sitting in the front row. . . . We had just heard the last few sentences of Mr Depew's introduction when Matthew Arnold stepped forward, opened out his manuscript, laid it on the desk and his lips began to move. There was not the slightest sound audible from where I stood. After a few minutes General Grant said to Mrs Grant, 'Well, wife, we have paid to see the British Lion; we cannot hear him roar, so we had better go home.'[16]

Back at the Windsor Hotel a post-mortem was held on the performance. All present agreed that it was not successful. On being asked for her opinion, Margaret Carnegie, remembering the dirge-like Presbyterian sermons of her girlhood, remarked: 'Too meenesteerial, Mr Arnold, too meenesteerial.'[17]

Arnold was now of the opinion that he should cut his losses, abandon the rest of the lecture tour and make his way home. Carnegie, anxious lest his star guest's quick departure would harm his social reputation, persuaded him otherwise. How about some tutoring in public speaking? Carnegie's suggestion was accepted and he produced the very man to help, one Professor Churchill of Boston. All was arranged and Arnold went to Boston. He reported his progress to his sister:

> I could not half make myself heard at first, but I am improving. A Professor Churchill, said to be the best elocutionist in the United States, came twice from Andover to Boston on purpose to try and be of use to me, because, he said, he had got more pleasure from [Frederick William] Robertson, [John] Ruskin and me than from any other men. He went twice for twenty minutes to the hall with me when it was empty, heard me read, and stopped me when I dropped my voice at the end of sentences, which was the great trouble. I get along all right now and have never failed to draw for a moment.[18]

Arnold was now a success, and his lectures appeared in print as *Discourses in America* (1885); a holiday was enjoyed at Cresson during July 1886, with country walks and visits to the Pittsburgh works. During the trip Arnold suffered heart problems with chest pain which he knew would 'do for me as it did for my father', as he told a concerned Carnegie; he died two years later.[19]

Since the days when his grandfather Tom Morrison had written for William Cobbett's *Political Register*, Carnegie had hankered after owning a newspaper as his 1868 memorandum indicated, wherein he could promoted his own radicalism and republicanism. Already his pro-republican circle of British friends included the jurist Frederick Harrison and royalty-baiter Henry Labouchere, but Carnegie was encouraged to further his political stance by the radical Newcastle MP Samuel Storey – a 6ft tall bully-boy to whom Carnegie gave funds – who published the halfpenny (Sunderland) *Echo* and (Tyneside) *Echo*. Carnegie was fired up by Storey's republicanism and warmed to the MP's denunciation of Queen Victoria, the Prince of Wales and their network of European relatives. Carnegie closely monitored the British press for signs of developing republicanism. As a financier he considered that the theme of royalty draining the public purse like financial leeches was worth promoting. He was particularly interested of late in the financial shenanigans surrounding the marriage of Queen Victoria's youngest son and eighth child Prince Leopold, Duke of Albany, to Princess Helena of Waldeck and Pyrmont in 1882. This was the year that Gladstone, as Chancellor of the Exchequer, produced a particularly stringent budget; the marriage arrangements provoked this comment from the *Reynolds's News*: 'We might usefully inquire how much royal and aristocratic personages take out of the present budget and how much comparatively royalty and aristocracy contribute to taxation.'[20] This was exactly the kind of sentiment Carnegie wished to promote.

Helped by Carnegie's brainwashed childhood, Storey convinced Carnegie that his money and influence, combined with Storey's rhetoric and political influence, could bring about an end to Britain's hereditary privilege. Together they formed a newspaper syndicate to promote the cheap radical press. From its owner and editor, the philanthropist John Passmore Edwards, Carnegie bought two-thirds interest in the daily (London) *Echo* in 1884. The paper was an ardent supporter of all 'progressive movements'. Thus Carnegie and Storey obtained a network of seven daily newspapers and ten weeklies, which covered the areas where the majority of Liberal/radical supporters could be found: from the *Midland Counties Guardian* at Wolverhampton to the *Echo* at Birmingham. At the Wolverhampton-based *Evening Express & Star*, editor (and Scotsman) Thomas Graham – who had met Carnegie during the coach trip of 1881 – turned a Tory paper into a radical one, much to Carnegie's glee.

In the north of England in particular Carnegie and Storey hoped to incite the working classes to whatever local rebellion was necessary, with Queen Victoria, her family, the House of Lords and aristocrats in general, the Tory Party and the

Church of England as the main targets. They supported Liberal candidates at elections and campaigned for the Reform Bill of 1884. Carnegie liked to give his employees pep talks, so he would arrive, for instance, at the offices of the *Evening Express & Star* to pontificate:

> He made no pretence of dictating policy, still less of writing leading articles himself, but he liked to assemble the entire editorial force and give little talks on the great issues then pending in England. The new franchise bill, extending the vote to agricultural labourers, the great popular mass still left outside the breastworks, was the measure on which Carnegie grew most eloquent, though the fierceness with which the Gordon campaign in the Sudan was assailed left a permanent impression.[21]

In everything in which he had a financial stake, Carnegie had a penchant for interfering.

In Queen Victoria's Britain attempts to undermine the Establishment did not sell papers. Carnegie's publishing ventures were soon piling up losses, but his enthusiasm and cash kept things going – Carnegie was never one to give way under adversity and he encouraged his editors to persist. Nevertheless the Tory press was winning the circulation race and Carnegie saw that his cash simply could not buy reader interest or loyalty. As with all his failures, Carnegie blamed others, and the reasons for the newspapers' decline were placed at the doors of such men as Thomas Graham. It must be said too, that Carnegie's dealings with Storey were not all sweetness and light. Storey baulked at Carnegie's efforts to influence his political opinions. In terms of managing newspapers, Carnegie was out of his depth.

'Harmony did not prevail among my British [newspaper] friends and finally I decided to withdraw,' wrote Carnegie.[22] Carnegie and Storey sold back the controlling share in the London *Echo* to John Passmore Edwards at a profit, but Carnegie was unable to pull out entirely from the other papers as Storey and Graham wished to continue; Carnegie accepted 'notes' against his shares as security, a holding he had to retain for many years. He never again backed publications, but used those of others to promote his ideas in articles. In the future too, he would use newspapers as propaganda outlets, and he was not against using his money and influence to have stories against himself and his projects suppressed – using precisely the methods he had openly despised in his younger radical days.

The newspaper interests brought Carnegie negative publicity from some quarters. There were those who were unhappy about Carnegie using his money in the 'task of transforming Great Britain into a republic'.[23] In particular the Tory press was annoyed that 'an American citizen, with a great fortune made in the United States, [was] fanning the flames of English revolution'.[24] The St James's Gazette made its position clear:

. . . the present agitation originated in America, and is an attempt to infuse republican sentiments into English politics. The movement, with all its paraphernalia of banners, processions, monster meetings and other factious machinery which American politicians know so well how to handle, is entirely foreign to English sentiment, and is the result of American influence and paid for by American dollars. Mr Carnegie is at the head of a conspiracy which is more subtle and dangerous than that of the dynamiters and which seeks to destroy both the Crown and the House of Lords.[25]

Carnegie replied that he would, if it were in his power, totally destroy both 'Crown and House of Lords', and any 'vestige of privilege throughout the world', carefully sidestepping the issue that he was using the privilege bought by his wealth and influence to do so. In a letter to Storey, who had suggested that Carnegie's outspokenness was not helping the cause, Carnegie said that he was 'no conspirator' and eschewed violence: 'The first duty of a Republican is to bow to the decision of the ballot box. The weapon of Republicanism is not the sword but the pen.'[26]

Many accused Carnegie of trying to curry favour in order to win himself a seat in the House of Commons; it was even suggested that he intended to replace the Liberal barrister Charles Pelham Villiers as MP for Wolverhampton. Carnegie hotly denied any such thing, although the charge was repeated for several years. Incidentally, in his own cognisance Carnegie was an American, although it could be argued that technically he was not as no naturalisation papers existed; again emigration had not stripped him of his British nationality, so he could have stood for the British parliament . . . certainly his wealth and influence with the Liberals could have brought about such a state of affairs if he had really wanted it.

Carnegie's newspapers failed to provoke a workers' revolution in Britain. Yet the issues they did support, like universal suffrage, payment for MPs and Home Rule for Ireland, did come about. Just as Carnegie's newspaper ventures were failing the Liberals suffered a blip. On 8 June 1885 the Liberal budget was defeated by an alliance of Tories and Irish nationalists, and Gladstone's administration fell at the subsequent general election. Tory Robert Gascoyne-Cecil, 3rd Marquis of Salisbury, became Prime Minister.

While all these opportunities and friendships were being pursued and exploited by Carnegie, another more significant relationship was simmering back home in America.

THIRTEEN

TWO DEATHS AND A WEDDING

Till death, Louise, yours alone.

Andrew Carnegie, November 1886

After years of shilly-shallying on his part, Carnegie and Louise Whitfield became engaged during September 1883. It was an arrangement made in secret, and biographers have speculated that at the moment of betrothal neither party really knew what the other wanted in terms of marriage; and, in the case of Carnegie, whether marriage was what he wanted at all. Louise's mother was delighted that her 26-year-old daughter was to be married; Mrs Whitfield's health was not of the best and she feared that her daughter's concern about her would cause her to remain unmarried. Margaret Carnegie received the news of the engagement in her usual self-centred way when it came to her son's activities. She considered that he was abandoning her. Although Margaret Carnegie was a selfish, rather unpleasant woman, Carnegie's devotion to her need not be overplayed when it came to his possible marriage; he was 48, and although the umbilical cord to his mother was still emotionally attached, it was very long and Carnegie was largely free to go where he liked and do what he wished. Perhaps this was why he wanted the engagement to be a secret outside the respective families. Louise confided in her diary: 'Had a delightful horseback ride with Mr Carnegie. . . . Am so unhappy, so miserable.'[1] She was to slip in and out of happiness with the arrangement, never knowing how secure she was: 'Nothing is certain, nothing is sure. I am striving so hard to do what is right, but I cannot see the light yet. . . .'[2]

During the spring of 1884 Carnegie took another coaching trip. Before he set off, he had a serious talk with Louise and the engagement was broken off. It was clear that Carnegie was unable to accept the commitment of marriage. On 23 April Louise wrote in her diary: 'In the afternoon, took the last sad step [to break the engagement]. Felt it was best. . . .'[3]

Carnegie's coaching trip differed from his tour of 1881 as this time he intended to hobnob with the famous. He assembled a travelling group made up of John Morley; William Black, whose volume *Adventures in a Phaeton* had inspired the 1881 trip; Edwin Austin Abbey, an American artist, who illustrated the works of Shakespeare and Herrick as well as American magazines; (later Sir) Edwin Arnold, author of *The Light of Asia*, a book Carnegie had recently gifted to Louise; Arnold presented to Carnegie the original manuscript of the book; Matthew Arnold, his wife Flu and daughter Lucy, who were picked up en route at Pains Hill Cottage, Cobham; and two of William Ewart Gladstone's eight children. The party was completed by MP Samuel Storey. The prospective route was from Charing Cross in London to Ilfracombe in the south-west; it would take six weeks and encompass stops in Surrey, Hampshire, Dorset and Devon.

Because of his current involvement in radical newspapers and Liberal politics Carnegie was in high political mood. His conversation as they travelled was peppered with his republican and anti-monarchal opinions and he repeatedly engaged the company in his pro-American comparison with all the English things he saw. William Black found this somewhat wearing; having observed Carnegie closely as they travelled in the four-in-hand, he dubbed him 'the Star-Spangled Scotchman'.[4] Carnegie delighted in his new nickname.

Two incidents on the trip, both associated with Matthew Arnold, particularly impressed Carnegie. While in Hampshire a visit was made to All Saints' churchyard, Hursley, to see the two large horizontal tombstones covering the graves of John Keble (1792–1866) and his wife. The poet and divine had been Arnold's godfather and his predecessor as Professor of Poetry at Oxford. The inspirer of the Tractarian Movement (which asserted the claim of the Church to a heavenly origin and a divine prerogative) and a keen promoter of High Church principles, Keble was vicar of Hursley from 1836 until his death and contributed to the famous *Tracts for the Times*. Carnegie watched Arnold's reactions at the grave: 'We walked [in] the quiet churchyard together. Matthew Arnold in silent thought at the grave of Keble made a lasting impression on me.' Later he would say: 'Even his look and serious silence charmed.'[5] At Winchester they visited Arnold's old school, founded by Bishop William Wykeham in 1387. Carnegie bristled at Wykeham's maxim carved as a motto, 'Manners mayketh man', but was mollified when Arnold pointed out that the comment referred not to table manners but to the medieval pursuit of the arts.[6]

During the trip Carnegie thought much about Louise. From Dartmoor, on 11 June, he wrote to her describing the tour and telling her that he would be coming home on the SS *Servia* on 5 July to meet up with his mother at Cresson. As before, Carnegie prepared a private note on the tour for circulation to friends; in due course it too was published by Charles Scribner's Sons.

The Carnegies returned to New York and the relationship with Louise was resumed as if no break had taken place, with horse-rides in Central Park. Louise soon realised, though, that she was no nearer the altar than before. Carnegie advanced and retreated in his ardour each time they met, with Louise assuring him that she was happy with the status quo. At last they were engaged once more on 18 November 1884.

Louise Whitfield, with 'a light and happy heart', was to see little of her peripatetic fiancé, who was at that time deep in the reorganisation of his steel assets. It is clear that Louise loved Carnegie – the antithesis of the ideal man that her girlfriends sought – and found strength in the belief that one day he would be hers. In the spring of 1885 Carnegie announced that, despite some reluctance on his part (to leave his mother . . . and Louise), he was to go to England with Mr and Mrs Henry

Phipps. His radical newspapers needed his attention and he would be away until 22 August.

On this trip Carnegie corresponded regularly with Louise, expressing his loneliness and wishing 'a certain young beautiful lady were only here to brighten [the days] with her smiles and silvery laugh . . .'.[7] Louise spent a forlorn few weeks in a resort hotel at Gilbertsville, Pennsylvania, with her mother. Carnegie's letters to her, in which he complained that hers were not affectionate enough, did not lighten her mood. At length, from her stiff reply describing her own dolefulness, Carnegie understood that he was not the only one feeling lonely and ceased to gripe. In fact Carnegie became more literally demonstrative and Louise began to believe that they would eventually marry . . . but when? Margaret Carnegie still stood in the way, although Carnegie, in trying to hide his mother's selfishness, said that they should hold back for both their mothers' sakes.

In his biography of Carnegie, Joseph Frazier Wall cites a number of cogent reasons why Carnegie, 'who had always aggressively gone after and obtained everything he had ever wanted',[8] was holding back from winning the woman who was more and more in his thoughts:

All of the psychological explanations so dear to the amateur Freudian could be brought forth in way of explanation [of Carnegie's vacillation concerning marriage]: a weak, ineffectual father who had been unable to provide for his sons; a domineering, ambitious mother who HAD provided; an unduly prolonged childhood innocence of sexual knowledge; a sense of competition with a younger brother for his mother's affection; a personal vanity so strong as to indicate latent narcissism.[9]

Whatever the reasons, Louise had the nous to bide her time to get what she wanted: in her copy of Longfellow's poetry, she underlined a line from 'A Palm of Life': 'Learn to labour and to wait.'

As well as his business interests, Carnegie had been allocating time to writing. Magazine articles and travel notes now gave way to a substantial tome entitled *Triumphant Democracy*. Since 1882 the idea for the book had been buzzing around in his imagination, so much so that when Carnegie met Gladstone at Lord Rosebery's he was able to give the Liberal Prime Minister 'some startling figures which I had prepared for it'.[10] These figures proved that, in the English-speaking world at least, republicans outnumbered monarchists and also that America 'could purchase Great Britain and Ireland and all their realized capital and investments and then pay off Britain's debt' without exhausting the national funds. For good measure he added that America was now 'the greatest manufacturing nation in the world'.[11]

This book was Carnegie's 'third literary venture' and he attributed its inspiration to the personal realisation of 'how little the best informed foreigner, or even Briton, knew about America, and how distorted that little was'.[12] He dedicated the book to his 'Beloved Republic' and mocked the 'old nations of the earth' as snails compared with America's speedy economic pace.[13] Lost in a plethora of words, Carnegie damned the monarchy and pontificated on every subject on which he felt strongly, from agriculture to religion. His rose-tinted spectacles, though, did cause him to anger his target audience of radicals with certain statements. For example, ignoring American whore-houses and violent boozers – which he must have seen plenty of in places like Pittsburgh – he made this comment:

As a rule, the American workingman is steadier than his fellow in Britain – much more sober and possessed of higher tastes. Among his amusements is found scarcely a trace of the ruder practices of British manufacturing districts, such as cock-fighting, badger-baiting, dog-fighting, prize-fighting. Wife-beating is scarcely ever heard of, and drunkenness is quite rare.[14]

Like Sir William Wallace driving the English out of Perth, Stirling and Lanark in 1297, the best-loved events of his childhood storybooks, Carnegie cut a swathe through everything he disliked, although in the process he left behind clues as to where his future charitable donations would go:

> Educate man, and his shackles fall. Free education may be trusted to burst every obstruction which stands in the path of the democracy towards its goal, the equality of the citizen, and this it will reach quietly and without violence, as the swelling sapling in its growth breaks its guard.[15]

For the first time in print, too, Carnegie distorted his own family background and his role since emigration. Those who had helped him were sidelined as he gave the impression that all he had achieved had been done entirely by his own unaided efforts. Among those who took offence was T.T. Woodruff – of sleeping-car fame – since Carnegie had portrayed himself as the real promoter of the vehicles. But Carnegie simply brushed aside Woodruff's criticisms: after all, never in his life did he admit mistakes to others.

The 509-page book was published by Charles Scribner's Sons in a number of editions between 1886 and 1888 under its full title *Triumphant Democracy of Fifty Years of the Republic*. Translations into French, German, Italian and other Continental tongues were ordered. Within a few months hardback sales reached some 17,000 in America, with strong sales in Britain; a cheaper edition of 40,000 at a shilling was issued in Britain for the 'working classes'.[16] A revised edition would appear in 1893, in which Carnegie proposed a tariff-free reunion between Britain and America. Carnegie wanted the book to stand out in the bookshops and on library shelves so a bold red was chosen for the binding; on the front cover was Carnegie's own design of two golden pyramids, one firmly based representing the republic, and the other inverted and inscribed 'Monarchy'. Underneath was a broken sceptre. There was a reverse imperial diadem on the back cover, representing

Andrew Carnegie in the upper garden terrace at Skibo Castle, by Dornoch, Sutherland. Carnegie spent large sums developing the gardens. He is seen here with his devoted collie Laddie. *(Carnegie/Constable)*

Margaret Morrison Carnegie (1810–86), Andrew Carnegie's mother. A formidable character, she dominated her sons' lives and her daughter-in-law described her as the most 'unpleasant' woman she had ever met. *(Carnegie/Constable)*

Andrew Carnegie (right) with his only brother Thomas Morrison Carnegie (1843–86). The 1851 studio pose shows the 'protective dominance' the elder brother had for the younger. At the time Andrew Carnegie was serving as a telegraph operator at Pittsburgh. *(Carnegie/Constable)*

Thomas Morrison Carnegie (1843–86). Bullied by his brother Andrew in his youth, Thomas became a partner in Carnegie Brothers & Co. He fathered nine children and was socially more reticent than his brother. Thomas latterly felt marginalised by Andrew and succumbed to alcohol. *(Carnegie/Constable)*

The Misses Selbys' New York studio portrait of Louise Whitfield Carnegie (1857–1946), who married Andrew Carnegie in 1887. She replaced Carnegie's mother as his chief confidante and adviser. *(Carnegie/Constable)*

Margaret Carnegie (1897–1991), Andrew Carnegie's only child, born when her father was sixty-two. She developed as a precocious child and married Roswell Miller in 1919. *(Carnegie/Constable)*

George Lauder (1837–1924). 'Cousin Dod', playmate and associate of Andrew Carnegie's childhood, the two remained friends throughout their lives, and corresponded regularly. Dod became a civil engineer and adviser to Carnegie and was a partner in Carnegie Brothers & Co. *(Carnegie/Constable)*

Dunfermline from the south of the Earl of Elgin's fields, looking north towards the abbey and old medieval town layout that Andrew Carnegie knew so well. Nethertown Broad Street runs along the foreground with Andrew Carnegie's birthplace location of Moodie Street rising up the hill centre right. Pittencrieff estate, which Andrew Carnegie bought in 1902 to present to the burgh, lies to the left. *(Author's Collection)*

Andrew Carnegie's birthplace, *c.* 1914. The eighteenth-century pantiled cottage lies at the junction of Moodie Street (foreground) and Priory Lane. The cottage was developed as the Andrew Carnegie Birthplace Museum and was linked to the Memorial Building, built against the south gable in 1925. *(Author's Collection)*

Andrew Carnegie sits next to his mother on the box of the carriage which took them on their tour of Britain, 17 June–3 August 1881, from the Grand Hotel Brighton to the Caledonian Hotel at Inverness. The distance covered was 831 miles. Joe and Perry the coachmen tend the horses. *(Carnegie/Constable)*

After his marriage in 1887 Andrew Carnegie's house at West 51st Street was inadequate so he had built a new residence of brick and granite at a cost of $1.5m. The address at 90th–91st Street at Fifth Avenue, New York, became one of the best known in the United States. *(Simon/Carnegie Corporation)*

Andrew Carnegie's Scottish residence of Skibo, Dornoch, Sutherland. The western elevation is shown with its gargoyle-bristling towers. Carnegie bought the house and 22,000 acres of grounds for £85,000, and the family spent their first summer there in 1898. Plans for extensions were begun in 1899.
(Simon/Carnegie Corporation)

Thomas A. Scott was superintendent of the Pennsylvania Railroad Co. who employed the 17-year-old Andrew Carnegie as his personal telegraph operator. Scott became Carnegie's early mentor and helped him become a major financial investor. In 1861 as Assistant Secretary of War, Scott chose Carnegie as assistant in charge of military railroads and telegraphs for the Union during the American Civil War. *(Carnegie/Constable)*

John Edgar Thomson, president of the Pennysylvania Railroad Co., became impressed with Carnegie's business skills and supported, albeit with some reservations, Carnegie's advancement in the company. Thomson became an investor in Carnegie's 1872 steel works. *(Carnegie/Constable)*

Right: Powerful private banker John Pierpont Morgan (1837–1913) bought the Carnegie Co.'s assets for $480m in 1901 to make Andrew Carnegie the richest man in the world. *(Carnegie/Constable)*

Below, left: Herbert Spencer (1820–1903) in a studio portrait by Elliott & Fry. He was an English philosopher cum railway engineer and teacher renowned for his volume entitled *System of Synthetic Philosophy* of 1862–93. Carnegie was much attracted by his philosophy and pacifism and hosted him in the USA. *(National Portrait Gallery)*

Below, right: John Morley, 1st Viscount Morley of Blackburn (1838–1928), by artist Walter William Ouless (1848–1933). A radical politician, statesman and prominent biographer, Morley held prominent positions in Liberal administrations. He jocularly gave Carnegie a penny prize for reciting the poems of Robert Burns. Morley joined Carnegie on coaching parties and was a regular correspondent. *(National Portrait Gallery)*

the monarchy which Carnegie really believed was shortly to come to an end. Outer embellishments included pro-American quotes from Gladstone and Lord Salisbury.[17]

In America reviewers were divided in their opinions about the book; some thought that Carnegie was excessively biased in his lauding of the American way of life, while others were happy that their country was so extravagantly complimented. Overall the volume was considered to be an adroit and exhilarating picture of the United States, with the only cavil being that it glossed over the country's imperfections. Few Americans realised that the book was Carnegie's thesis towards a revolution in Britain to bring about the radical society that had so excited his childhood thoughts. Indeed he became something of a defender-spokesman in British radical circles. He loved to accept speaking engagements to tub-thump for republicanism and lambast royalty. He was intoxicated by the applause which greeted some of his provocative pronouncements, such as: 'The Prince of Wales got £105,000 per annum or the gross earnings of 30,000 people and the men who fought their country's battles [in the Crimean War] died in the workhouse.'[18] Consequently left-wing groups and their Liberal bedmates in Parliament received the volume as a justification for their aims. The Tory press saw it as a sinister attack on British society, the *St James's Gazette* leading the pack with the *Saturday Review* promoting an anti-American line.

Carnegie's great friends Arnold, Spencer and Morley also had their say. In a letter about the book to the Liberal statesman and author Sir Mountstuart Duff, Arnold remarked:

You should read Carnegie's book. . . . The facts he has collected as to the material progress of [America] are remarkable. . . . He and most Americans are simply unaware that nothing in the book touches the capital defect of life over [there]; namely that, compared with life in England, it is so uninteresting, so without savour and without depth. Do they think to prove that it has savour and depth by pointing to the number of public libraries, schools and places of worship?[19]

Herbert Spencer put to one side Carnegie's political opinions but hailed the book as 'a record' of 'the triumph of democracy':

> Even recognising in full all you set forth as to the extent of prosperity in the United States, and even admitting that this is all due to the political arrangements, I should still be inclined to make a large discount from the alleged triumph of democracy on the ground that the material activity in America which accompanies it, whether as consequence or simply as concomitant, is a material prosperity by no means favourable to human life. Absorbed by his activities and spurred on by his unrestricted ambitions, the American is, to my thinking, a less happy being than the inhabitant of a country where the possibilities of success are very much smaller; and where, in the immense majority of cases, each has to be content with the hum-drum career in which circumstances have placed him, and, abandoning hopes of any great advance, is led to make the best of what satisfaction in life falls to his share. I believe on the whole that he gets more pleasure out of life than the successful American, and that his children inherit greater capacities for enjoyment. Great as may be hereafter the advantages of the enormous progress America makes, I hold that the existing generations of Americans, and those to come for a long time hence, are and will be essentially sacrificed.[20]

John Morley thought the work 'a substantial, well considered and important book':

> I do not assent to every word in it, and there are some passages where the sentiment is a trifle too republican for a middle-aged monarchist like me: I mean too *aggressively* republican, for there is no difference between us as to the roots of things. . . . The book . . . is a solid contribution on the right side. And it is written in high spirits which give it an attractive literary vivacity.[21]

Carnegie had written the book to his entire satisfaction; the bad reviews washed over him and he was happy with the work as a fine piece of self-propaganda. Having established himself in print as a radical, he wanted now to be seen as a visionary – but there was more to it than that . . . his radical soul wanted a revolution in British society, but his inherent pacifism saw it as a new evolution; he was developing into what modern thinkers would call a revisionist. Several biographers have studied Carnegie's book trying to understand its deeper significance. American writer Robert McCloskey comes close to an answer:

> It seems reasonable to believe that he wrote [the book] because he had an imperious need to explain and justify himself and his environment, because he had to convince both the world and himself that what he was doing was good and that the context within which he operated was just. The book appears to be a defence of democracy; actually, it is a defence of nineteenth-century capitalism – and Carnegie.[22]

Carnegie admitted that writing the book had exhausted him and he felt unwell through the stress of 'statistics'.[23] But there were to be more serious family illnesses. As Carnegie flitted back and forth from New York to Cresson, his brother Tom was dangerously ill with pneumonia back in Pittsburgh. Carnegie combined visits to his brother with business trips to the city but could not bring Tom out of his mental torpor. Now 43, Tom was in a seriously debilitated state; it was as if he did not wish to live, and years of heavy drinking had taken their toll. It is a matter of speculation as to what turned Tom Carnegie into an alcoholic. Some have observed that his life in the shadow of his brother had always made him feel inferior and that in the last few years he felt marginalised because of the structure of the company and Andrew Carnegie's place in it. Certainly his wife Lucy believed that her husband's mental state was entirely due to Carnegie's years of bullying behaviour; being a strong character herself, she had had several spats with her brother-in-law on various subjects. Still they remained in contact. Sadly, Tom Carnegie died on 19 October 1886 three days after taking to his bed, leaving his widow and nine children.

Meanwhile in the house at Cresson 76-year-old Margaret Carnegie was dying; she had been suffering for some while with a weak heart and was now in the throes of pneumonia. She was too ill to be told about her son Tom's death. While with his mother at Cresson Carnegie himself succumbed to a severe chill and his New York physician, Dr Frederick S. Dennis, was called to give the local doctor a second opinion; he confirmed that Carnegie was suffering from typhoid.[24] Carnegie worsened at the news of Tom's death. All the while an anxious Louise was kept informed by daily telegrams from Carnegie's secretary James H. Bridges. On 10 November 1886 the daily telegram informed Louise that Margaret Carnegie had died.

The attendant local physician knew of the intensity of Carnegie's relationship with his mother and did not inform him of her death until 17 November. Carnegie was in such a fragile condition that it was thought best that his mother's coffin should not pass by her son's bedroom door, and it was lowered instead from an upper room window. From the day that he realised she was dead Carnegie never mentioned his mother's name for decades, and all pictures of her and her possessions were removed to storage: 'he could never be reconciled' to her death.[25] Carnegie's grief took a number of odd turns; he became jumpy about death, and suddenly very averse to the books of fellow Scot and fellow mother-obsessive James Matthew Barrie. Carnegie took great offence that Barrie had written about his own mother in the adoringly sentimental *Margaret Ogilvy* (1896) and had made money out of her memory.[26]

On 24 November 1886 Carnegie felt well enough to write to Louise after the news of his mother's death had sunk in: 'Today as I see the great light once more my first word is to you . . . Louise, I am now wholly yours – all gone but you . . . I live in you now. . . . Till death, Louise, yours alone. . . .'[27]

Two Deaths and a Wedding

Although he expressed his feelings of abject loneliness, Carnegie always treasured his blood relations in Dunfermline and elsewhere. For years he husbanded investments on their behalf and bought them necessities as required, such as spectacles for Maria Hogan in 1879; each Christmas too, he sent his relations cash gifts such as the drafts of $300 in 1888.[28]

Carnegie's convalescence was long. From Cresson Dr Dennis took him to his own house at New York for a while and then followed a period of recuperation at Cumberland Island, off the coast of Georgia, a 20,000-acre estate that had belonged to brother Tom. From here a correspondence was conducted with Louise on preparations for their nuptials. Still in a fragile mental state, Carnegie urged Louise to retain secrecy around their plans; for some reason – probably associated with his mother's memory – he wanted no newspaper announcement of the marriage until it had taken place.

A wedding date of 12 April was planned, but Carnegie was called to a court hearing at Pittsburgh so a postponement was necessary. Louise had waited so long for Carnegie that a few more days did not perturb her. She would be given away by her grandfather George Buckmaster Whitfield. Finally at 8pm on 22 April at the Whitfield home at West 48th Street, New York, 51-year-old Andrew Carnegie was married by the Revd Charles Eaton to 30-year-old Louise Whitfield. It was a reasonably quiet affair with around thirty guests, including Aunt Aitken, Cousin Dod and the Phippses. Very shortly after the ceremony the newly-weds were taken to the North Germany Lloyd pier at New York and were waved aboard the SS *Fulda* to honeymoon in England. In true Carnegie fashion the bridegroom wangled the captain's accommodation for their trip.

FOURTEEN

A Honeymoon

Andrew Carnegie may be little but his hoard and heart are
great, and he is a happy bridegroom and rejoiceth as a
bridegroom to have his happiness sure . . .

Mrs James G. Blaine, 1887

As the Carnegies crossed the Atlantic the New York papers
caught up with the news of the wedding and expressed
interest in Carnegie's wedding present to his wife. As well
as a post-nuptial income provision of some $20,000, Carnegie
gave Louise a house at 5 West 51st Street, New York.[1] As
soon as it was convenient, Carnegie sold Braemar Cottage at
Cresson as part of the expunging of Margaret Carnegie's
mortal memories.

The newly-weds spent their honeymoon of a fortnight on the
Isle of Wight, now a flourishing resort island following the
purchase of Old Osborne House in 1845 by Queen Victoria and
Prince Albert. Uncle George Lauder, eager to see his nephew's
bride, visited them on the Isle of Wight and Louise soaked up
Scottish history from him, elaborating on the foundations laid in
her childhood encounters with the Waverley novels of Sir Walter
Scott and Jane Porter's notable novel *The Scottish Chiefs* (1810).[2]
A few days were then spent in London where they received
congratulations on their marriage from William and Catherine
Gladstone. They stopped off at Mentmore, the residence of the
Earl of Rosebery in Buckinghamshire, and then they were off to
Dunfermline and Carnegie's old haunts. En route they paused at
Edinburgh, where Carnegie received the Freedom (Honorary
Burgess) of the City and the foundation stone was laid for the

new Carnegie Library at George IV Bridge, which would open in 1890. Carnegie had contributed a benefaction of $250,000.

For their first summer as man and wife Carnegie leased the Scottish estate of Kilgraston, a mile south-west of Bridge of Earn, Perthshire. By this time the area had developed as a summer resort and there were mineral wells (deemed the oldest in Scotland) nearby at Pitcaithly. Charles Grant (1831–91) had succeeded his father as the owner of Kilgraston in 1873. The red sandstone mansion was badly damaged by fire in 1871 and its rebuilding had sorely depleted the Grant finances; coupled with the agricultural depression of the 1880s, this caused the Grants to move to nearby Drummorie House in order to save money. They let out Kilgraston for profit and thus the Carnegies came to be residents there.[3] From the moment she was greeted at the door of Kilgraston by a Scots piper, Louise, now deeming herself 'more Scotch than her husband', fell in love with the place. She wrote ecstatically to her mother:

I wish I could describe this lovely place. Just now roses are in full bloom around one of my windows with white jessamine around the next one filling the room with the most delicious perfume. The beautiful lawn in front where we play tennis and the Scotch game of bowls, lovely shady walks on one side and in the distance a new mown field with hay cocks. Oh! why aren't you all here to enjoy it too?[4]

At Kilgraston Louise Carnegie saw how energetic her husband could be. He wanted to show her all the haunts of his childhood, and when not afoot or coach riding he was at a desk dealing with mail or writing speeches to be given in answer to the many requests for his thoughts on such subjects as Home Rule (for Ireland).

Involvement in one historical event was considered a must for Carnegie while at Kilgraston. King Alexander III (r. 1249–86), 'The Glorious', is known as the last Celtic King of Scotland. Although a hero in Uncle George Lauder's historic tales for the young Carnegie as a victor over King Haakon IV of Norway at the Battle of Largs in 1263, Alexander was beset with family disaster. He was predeceased by his wife Margaret (daughter of Henry III of England) and his three children; a rapid second marriage to Yolande de Dreux proved childless, and a little over four months after this marriage took place Alexander was riding from Edinburgh to Kinghorn Castle in Fife to join Yolande when he was thrown from his horse to his death over a cliff a mile or so from the castle. The date was 19 March 1286; Alexander was buried at Dunfermline.

From as far back as the 1840s plans had been mooted to erect a new monument to Alexander III (an older marker having fallen into ruin) but nothing positive was achieved until interest was revived for the 600th anniversary of the event. Funds were sought by the monument committee, to which Queen Victoria subscribed £15. In all £270 was collected for a monument of red granite. The unveiling would be assisted by Victor Alexander Bruce, 9th Earl of Elgin, as his first duty as Lord Lieutenant of Fife. In the post came a letter from Carnegie to say that he would attend the unveiling on 19 July 1887 as part of Queen Victoria's ongoing Golden Jubilee celebrations. Carnegie and Louise were part of the procession to the monument site in their carriage, but Carnegie declined to speak although there were calls from the crowd for him to do so. He did express the opinion that 'the monument was built to mark a period of peace and prosperity for all'. In a letter to Queen Victoria, Lord Elgin reported Carnegie's presence at the ceremony and his respectful duty to the royal name; on this occasion Carnegie's republicanism evidently took a back seat.

A bevy of visitors descended upon Kilgraston, from US Senator and Mrs Eugene Hale to Matthew Arnold, who made his last sojourn with Carnegie at Kilgraston, for he died shortly afterwards at Liverpool awaiting the arrival of his daughter Lucy, Mrs Whitridge, who had married an American. One important visitor was the American journalist and statesman James Gillespie Blaine, who was a member of the US House of Representatives from 1863 to 1876; although rising to the post of Secretary of State in Benjamin Harrison's Republican administration in 1889–93, Blaine lost out in the presidential nominations four times, in all of which Carnegie was his staunch supporter. Blaine had explained to Carnegie the differing structures and protocols of the House of Commons and the US House of Representatives, and what if Carnegie decided on a career as a British MP? 'If you take a seat in the House of Commons, you will be a greater man in the US, but, if you enter the House in Washington, you will be a greater man in England' was Blaine's assessment.[5] Carnegie recommended Blaine's book *Thirty Years of Congress* to Gladstone. Writing to her son Emmons, Mrs Blaine left an interesting memory of Kilgraston:

Friday morning and the most beautiful day and Kilgraston a spot worthy of the day. We came to it Monday, not knowing whither Andrew was leading us . . . . Here we are at a country seat such as this island alone I imagine can show – a gillie in tartan to wake us every morning with the pipes, a coach-and-four to take us daily whithersoever we will, two cooks to spread a table before us in this garden of the Lord, and twenty servants to wait upon us at bed and board. Andrew Carnegie may be little but his hoard and heart are great, and he is a happy bridegroom and rejoiceth as a bridegroom to have his happiness sure, so that we are enjoying, as only pilgrims and sojourners at hotels should enjoy, this oasis of home life. Yesterday we returned from an excursion of two days to Dunfermline. As our company was large, half of us stayed with the Provost, a bachelor of sixty and a canny Scotchman. Of course it was a coaching party, twenty-three miles thither, and thirty-two hither yesterday. As we drove in at an opposite direction from that on which we started out, we surprised all the servants dancing at the rear of the house. As English servants are always instructed to keep away from the master and mistress, they scurried to cover like rabbits, and when we drove around to the front door, there was a piper marching up and down imperturbably, playing 'The Campbells Are Coming!' – the butler, the housekeeper, the lady's maid waiting at the entrance, and all the housemaids carrying hot water to the various bedrooms. It was the funniest transformation scene I ever saw. Colonel [John Hay, US Ambassador to Britain, 1897] and Mrs Hay are coming today, to stop over Sunday, a splendid addition to the company. Your father is getting much benefit from the open air, in which he spends the entire day, and think how long the days are in this latitude; it was half past eight when we returned home last night and the sun was just setting, and we were dining at half past nine by its light alone. And your father could read the labels on the champagne bottles without glasses. Also he has danced the Haymarket, which is our Virginia Reel, on the lawn, and has played skittles. We breakfast every morning at nine and as Mr Carnegie will not sit down to the table without him, he gets up in good season . . . . There is nothing comparable to the interest of living people and homes. I would rather dine at Mr Carnegie's old uncle's in Dunfermline than see the Tower of Babel or any other tower.[6]

Carnegie and his party visited many beauty spots nearby and could not resist hob-nobbing with the aristocracy. One notable visit was to the fine wooded estate of Dupplin Castle (1832), then the seat of George Hay-Drummond, 12th Earl of Kinnoul and his Countess Emily, 5 miles south-west of the city of Perth. included in the visit was Colonel John Hay, who later wrote: 'The old Earl . . . is miserably poor – not able to buy a bottle of seltzer – with an estate worth millions in the hands of his creditors, and sure to be sold one of these days to some enterprising Yankee. . . . I wish . . . Carnegie would buy it.'[7] Among the Kilgraston guests were a horde of Carnegie relations from Dunfermline: 'They expressed their surprise to me that [Louise] ever married me, but I told them I was equally surprised.'[8] Although Louise Carnegie was somewhat in awe of the guest list at Kilgraston, and overwhelmed by the cheering of the crowds that had greeted them at the Edinburgh library foundation ceremony which rang in her ears for days, she wrote to her mother that she missed the 'old sweet routine' at home; nevertheless 'the great change' in her life was wonderful and 'Andrew is sweet and lovely'.[9] Louise was much taken with Scots folk, and Mrs Nicholl, the Kilgraston housekeeper hired for the tenancy, was taken back with them to West 51st Street, along with butler George Irvine and servant Maggie Anderson, all of whom would stay in Carnegie service into the twentieth century.

For the whole of June 1887 the Carnegies stayed at the Metropole Hotel, London, and spent time enjoying all the festivals of Queen Victoria's Golden Jubilee, with its main ceremony at Westminster Abbey on 21 June.

Next year the Carnegies were back in Britain with a new summer lease in mind; this time Carnegie selected Cluny Castle in the heart of the Scottish Highlands. For a while he had been promising Louise a coach trip through Britain, and this seemed a good time to do it. In the party for the 700-mile journey from London was James Blaine (absenting himself from the impending presidential election back home), his wife Harriet and their daughters, Henry Phipps and his wife, the Revd Charles Eaton, the pastor who had married them, Lord Rosebery, Walter Damrosch, the Wagnerian conductor at the New York Metropolitan Opera House and author Mary Elizabeth Dodge (who as Gail Hamilton later wrote a biography of James Blaine). Why did Carnegie choose to drag his guests to such a remote part of Scotland? The piper who had entertained them at Kilgraston was a native of Speyside, and this influenced the decision.[10]

Whenever Carnegie entered Britain the daily newspapers took an interest, one of them offering its readers a glimpse of Carnegie's latest touring party:

Mr Blaine, a gentleman of some sixty years, with whitey grey hair and sallow face, wearing a white hat and blue coat, jumped up to his seat by the whip with the alertness of youth.

[Louise Carnegie] in a blue serge travelling costume, carrying a detective camera and a lovely bouquet of Marechal Neils, was assisted to her place at the back by Lord

Rosebery, who, with his close-shaven face and spruce attire, his bell-shaped hat and the humorous smile which plays about his mouth, is the very ideal of a prosperous comedian. Carnegie looked the picture of health and happiness, and as chirpy as a cricket, with a little serge suit, a white hat fixed on his head, a red rose in his buttonhole. Up he climbed to his seat by the side of his charming pretty wife, who, like all American ladies, was not in the least ashamed of showing her keen enjoyment of the lively scene.[11]

The journey would last six weeks. Mary Dodge remembered:

We coached with Mr Carnegie weeks through the cathedral towns of eastern England [Ely, Lincoln, York and so on] and Scotland to Cluny tracking the Roman roads, sleeping in the rooms of Tudor kings, lunching under yew trees which might have been the ones that bothered Caesar, under the oaks of Burleigh House by Stamford town, on the hills of the great White Horse, on the Lammermoors, on the battlefields of York and Lancaster, on the banks of the Tweed, and a little coldly in the damp of Delnaspidal [*sic*].[12]

From Blair Atholl, Carnegie's carriage – a wedding gift from his sister-in-law Lucy Carnegie – clattered through Glen Garry across the Perthshire–Inverness border and into Glen Truim. At Dalwhinnie they left the old military road to the north and made for Laggan Bridge and thence the short distance to the white granite Cluny Castle in the birch- and fir-wooded valley of the Upper Spey. This was Louise Carnegie's first real taste of the Jacobite Highlands. It is a wild place. To the north rise the lonely Monadhliath mountains, and not far from the 11,000-acre Cluny estate is the stone with arrow markings denoting 'the geographical centre' of Scotland.

They had entered the clan lands of the Cluny Macphersons, and near the castle lie buried many clan ancestors in a little churchyard beside the road. Over the centuries there were several families of Macphersons – *Mac a Phearsoin* in Gaelic, meaning 'Son of the Parson' – but the Cluny line evolved as the most important. From the seventeenth century when Donald Macpherson of Cluny was a faithful Royalist the Macphersons supported the House of Stuart, and during the rising of 1745 Ewan Macpherson of Cluny took 600 clansmen to join Prince Charles Edward Stuart. Although his men arrived too late to take an active part in the Battle of Culloden (1746), Macpherson actively helped Prince Charles to escape capture. Almost 150 years later Carnegie eagerly located the cave on Craig Dhu where the prince had sought shelter before his escape to exile. After the disaster at Culloden Cluny Castle was burned down and the clan chief went into hiding from the Hanoverian authorities before escaping to France in 1755. The Cluny estates were forfeit to the Crown, but were restored in 1784 to Duncan Macpherson of Cluny. The castle was rebuilt but on the death of the seventeenth chief it was sold. The castle was full of Jacobite memorabilia, with Charles Edward Stuart's own targe (shield) proudly displayed. For the duration of their stay Carnegie became a Highland laird and Robert Louis Stevenson's recently published (1886) *Kidnapped* – with its tales of notorious Highland Jacobites – was the talk of the dinner table.

Both Carnegie and Louise lapped up the local history, Louise recording the locality with her camera. Carnegie enjoyed the hunting and fishing with the estate gillies and wrote enthusiastically to the erstwhile president of his steelworks William L. Abbott:

> 60 trout caught yesterday by one rod in our own Burn – We have splendid grouse shooting also, everything there is Lochs – Burns, Moors and the Spey River all round us. Two trout streams run past the Castle one on each side. Waterfalls, Rustic Bridges over them. This is indeed a gem – I will have you all over in pairs year after year if you are good boys. . . .[13]

The Carnegies filled the house with American and English guests, Carnegie relations and a clutch of Liberal Party stalwarts. All dined lavishly and enjoyed musical evenings under the direction of Walter Damrosch. The conductor even taught Cluny Macpherson – the castle's current owner – how to play 'Yankee Doodle' on the bagpipes.[14] Independence Day, 4 July 1888, was especially celebrated with cannon fire and fireworks, and for the first time the Stars and Stripes fluttered over the castle turrets.

The British press were not alone in taking an interest in Carnegie's Scottish activities. The American papers also followed his peregrinations, several even criticising him for having an unseemly allegiance to a 'foreign power'. Thinking about what was being said about him, Carnegie made this public pronouncement:

> The exile may be excused if his fondness for his native land knows no bounds. Scotland was to me the land of childhood, the fairyland. Here I have never known labour nor struggle, nor any of the trials – the invigorating trials – of life; nor sorrow, nor pain; and across the Atlantic, amid the early struggles – the fierce struggles of success – amid all my cares and throughout every weary hour, there shone upon my path, shedding its beams of poetry and romance, the resplendent star of Scotland. Return to Scotland was ever to me the prize of life. . . . In the exquisitely beautiful life which Mrs Carnegie and I are privileged to live among you in the Highlands, I reap my reward. The exile has returned. . . .[15]

He went on to pay tribute to the republic in which he had made his wealth with the comment that he would defend it if he had to. 'I am a Celt,' he proclaimed, but one who was loyal to the republic too.

While Carnegie strutted the paths of Cluny Castle like a proud ptarmigan, enjoying the position of tenant-laird, Louise was happy too:

> We are all in love with Cluny. . . . Such walks, such drives, such romantic little nooks! Imagine the most beautiful mountain brooks on each side of the park with rustic bridges,

beautiful waterfalls, plenty of shade trees and shrubs all surrounded by high rocky mountains. . . . It looks in places like the scenery in Die Walkurë. . . .[16]

A pattern of travel was now emerging. From the closing days of October until early May the Carnegies were based in New York, while the summer months were spent in Britain. As summer came slowly up to Cluny Castle, which they were to rent annually for ten years, the first weeks of May–June each year were spent in southern England.[17] For instance, in 1892 and 1894 they rented Coworth Park estate from Lord William Farmer at Sunningdale in Berkshire, and Buckhurst in Hampshire from Lord Canteloupe.

Wherever they went Carnegie delighted in showing off his wife; as an American female she had a certain cachet in British society. Had not Jennie Jerome from Brooklyn, New York, married Lord Randolph Spencer Churchill, the younger son of the Duke of Marlborough, in 1874? (Their eldest son was Sir Winston Churchill.) The Marlboroughs were a fine example of how many aristocrats found themselves in a parlous financial state; the 9th duke married the American heiress Consuelo Vanderbilt to help recoup the family fortunes. And here was Andrew Carnegie, once an impoverished urchin from Dunfermline, now sporting on his arm a beauty from 'Colonial Connecticut' stock.[18] Just as the British landed gentry were being eroded and overwhelmed, Carnegie as a 'Transatlantic Midas' was on the up, enjoying all the trappings the English aristocracy were obliged to rent out.

During 1885–9 the Democrat President Grover Cleveland held office in the White House. A lawyer of limited initial formal education who rose to the highest position in American life, Cleveland was adept at making political enemies: Carnegie was one. In office Cleveland pursued a policy of civil service reforms and stood firmly against a high protection tariff – moves that were to contribute to his defeat for he made the Democrats appear an anti-business party. This was certainly what Carnegie thought and he gave his enthusiastic support to the Republican candidate Benjamin Harrison. To Carnegie's delight, his money having influenced the election, Harrison was returned and remained President until 1893. For the first time in US politics 'big business' interests had played a leading role in winning an election. Carnegie was now one of those men who could influence American politics from Maine to Texas and all along the west coast. In due time he would reap his rewards from the Harrison presidency.

Carnegie was also taking on another role that he did not like; he had become one of America's media 'robber barons', those industrialists who were considered to exploit working practices and land deals. The poor boy from Dunfermline, the hater of royalty and aristocrats, with a personal fortune at that date of $15 million, was now being lampooned in the press. It caused him to think seriously about his public persona and his future position in American society, and he actively set about formulating a personal philosophy of philanthropy.

So far Carnegie had funded libraries at Dunfermline and Edinburgh, and his money had gone into public baths and church organs. But he was a philanthropic pygmy compared with the British-educated John Jacob Astor, whose $350,000 legacy founded New York's public library, or Ezra Cornell, who co-founded and heavily endowed Cornell University at Ithaca, New York, in 1868. Carnegie began an intense study of how the philosophy of philanthropy had been achieved and worked out by others. In particular on the desk in his study were papers on the activities of Peter Cooper, the American manufacturer and inventor of such things as the washing machine, who provided the working classes with educational advantages through his Cooper Union (1854–9) at New York. What Cooper had said about the use of accumulated wealth for the public good impressed Carnegie, who began to formulate his own interpretation of Cooper's thoughts.

Carnegie was keen to parry press and academic criticisms about his own accumulated assets. He found the answer by setting out his thinking in an article, which would appear in the June 1889 number of Lloyd Stephens Bryce's *North American Review* under the bold title 'Wealth'. Based on a defence of wealth and its accumulation, the article developed a theme of giving, identifying three principal methods of donation: family legacies, public donations at death and active lifetime philanthropy. He dismissed the first two as self-memorialising, favouring the latter. He also set out, mirroring his list of 1868, a new set of targets:

1. Found a university.
2. Establish a free library.
3. Found at least one hospital, medical school, laboratory or other institution devoted to alleviating human suffering.
4. Establish a public park.
5. Build halls suitable for musical concerts and meetings of all kinds.
6. Build public swimming pools.
7. Provide permanent structures for churches.

A core statement was to be relevant in understanding Carnegie's thinking about wealth, the substance of which decades of Carnegie students would deem idiosyncratic and totally against what his childhood deprivations had taught him. He said: 'Wealth, passing through the hands of the few, can be made a much more potent force for the elevation of our race than if distributed in small sums [i.e. wages] to the people themselves.' Thus he promoted the low wages that his grandfather and uncle had railed against, and with which his father and mother had struggled. He thought that any surplus wealth or profits should not be spent on enhanced wages but in benefits for the whole community – Carnegie, then, could spend the money more wisely than by simply paying out substantial wages. Another theme of the article was to help those who would help themselves and close the mind to beggars. Carnegie was not interested in giving generous wages to promote a better personal standard of living, but in offering public donations to promote the public good in such things as education and art. He ended his article with perhaps his most famous quote: 'The man who dies thus rich dies disgraced.'[19]

'Wealth' was hailed by the editor Allan Thorndike Rice as 'the finest article I have ever published'.[20] In those days the *North American Review* had a wide international circulation among those interested in American current affairs, and the article gave Carnegie a wider public presence. Gladstone was one who lauded it, asking that it be reproduced in the *Pall Mall Gazette*; it duly appeared therein as 'The Gospel of Wealth', a revised title of which Carnegie approved, and thereafter the work was known by this name. It was soon also available in a penny pamphlet in the United States and Britain. In November 1890 Gladstone wrote his own essay on wealth for the *Nineteenth Century* magazine in which he echoed Carnegie's thoughts in large part.

Thousands of readers pored over what Carnegie meant by his sentence: 'The man who dies thus rich dies disgraced.' How could it be wrong for people to leave money to support their families after their death? Carnegie's postbag was full of letters in such vein. What he meant, he said, was that *misers* descending to the tomb wealthy were the disgraced ones. He further explained his stance in a letter:

When I wrote the article upon wealth, it is true that I had in mind chiefly the 'Millionaire Class'; men like Vanderbilt, Stanford, the two Pratts, Mr Sage, patron of Cornell, and such men as had by close application and rare ability amassed large sums. Mr Astor dies, in my opinion, disgraced by leaving $150,000,000 to one person, while the Astor Library suffers for want of enough money to make purchases of modern books necessary to hold its position as a first-class library. . . . I think that a man forty years old, with $50,000 actively engaged in business, has not a surplus which can properly be devoted to public uses. Private cases of misfortune within his knowledge may, however, be to some extent relieved by him. At sixty, with $300,000 or

$400,000, the case is changed. Men should retire from active business certainly, at or before sixty. After arranging his family expenditures, according to the dictates of his own conscience, he can consider that he has a surplus for which he is only the trustee.[21]

Carnegie received thousands of requests for handouts and as the article circulated more widely the brickbats came. Some dubbed the article the 'Gospel According to St Andrew'.[22] A sticking point for many detractors was the fact that Carnegie appeared to disregard the issue of low wages in favour of charity handouts to public bodies. One vociferous detractor was Professor William Jewett Tucker, later President of Dartmouth College in Hanover, New Hampshire, which was founded in 1769 and developed as a liberal-arts educational foundation. Tucker scorned Carnegie's basic assumption of the inevitability of great wealth accumulating around entrepreneurs, and disputed that such a magnate sitting on the top of a mountain of money was inevitably the 'best administrator of its redistribution'. 'I can conceive of no greater mistake,' thundered Tucker, 'than that of trying to make charity do the work of justice.'[23] Carnegie's article, as well as others past and future from such sources as the *Century Magazine* and *Scottish Leader* of the period 1886–99, appeared in book form as *The Gospel of Wealth* under the New York Century Company's imprint in 1900.[24]

On the other hand Carnegie's article is deemed to have encouraged people like John Davison Rockefeller, the oil magnate, to increase their financial philanthropy; Rockefeller had founded the Standard Oil Co. in 1870 and through it secured control of the US oil trade. Each of the wealthy philanthropists had his own favourite projects; both Rockefeller and J.P. Morgan had churches high on their lists, the former favouring the Baptist Church and the latter the Episcopal. At this time the core of Carnegie's largesse was aimed at books and libraries.

During 1890 it came to Carnegie's notice that Sir John Emmerich Edward Dalberg-Acton, 1st Baron Acton of Aldenham

(1834–1902), a Roman Catholic Whig MP, lord-in-waiting to Queen Victoria in Gladstone's fourth ministry and later Regius Professor of Modern History at Cambridge, had fallen on hard times. It was voiced in the press that Acton's personal library of 80,000 volumes at his Shropshire home at Aldenham would have to be sold to pay off serious debts. Soon another press announcement reported that the library had been saved by a mystery benefactor. In fact, the rescue had been engineered by Gladstone with Carnegie's help. The latter, however, for reasons he never revealed, told Gladstone that he wished to remain anonymous in the matter:

> I wish no one to know this, not even my wife shall know. Lord Granville [Granville George Leveson-Gower, 2nd Earl of Granville, Gladstone's Foreign Secretary and Liberal Leader in the Lords, and stepfather of Lord Acton] should understand that such an arrangement, if known, must make it somewhat uncomfortable for Lord Acton.[25]

The library was in effect sold to Carnegie for £10,000, with the Acton family retaining possession for the lifetime of Lord Acton. After Acton's death in 1902 Carnegie passed the library to his friend John Morley as a gift to dispose of as he wished. In turn Morley gave the library to the University of Cambridge.

To further his aim of promoting medical research Carnegie was prompted to make a specific donation by his doctor, Frederick Dennis, who had set up a laboratory for the study of the causes and cure of diseases at Belleview Hospital, New York. Dr Dennis was particularly interested in the study of cholera; at that time the highly infectious disease was rampant in various European ports, and Dennis was anxious to make sure that America was safe from the deadly infections. This was exactly the type of charitable outlet that stirred Carnegie at the time and started him off on a new range of philanthropy.

Another important promotion of books occurred with the opening of the Carnegie Free Library in Allegheny City. Based on a donation of $250,000, the library was nine years in gestation, eventually housing some 75,000 books and a music hall with a $10,000 pipe organ. To Carnegie's delight the formal opening was attended by President Benjamin Harrison, and the library was dedicated on 20 February 1890. As usual Carnegie gave a speech which would become a template for addresses wherever he opened a library in particular:

> The poorest citizen, the poorest man, the poorest woman that toils from morn till night for a livelihood (as, thank heaven, I had to do in my early days), as he walks this hall, as he reads the books from these alcoves, he listens to the organ and admires the works of art in this gallery equally with the millionaires and the foremost citizen; I want him to exclaim in his own heart: 'Behold all this is mine.'[26]

The build-up to the opening ceremony was marred by the last illness and death in January 1890 of Carnegie's mother-in-law Mrs John Whitfield. Louise had cared for her for months and was deeply distressed at the death. Her deep mourning caused her to be absent from the library opening.

Years before, Carnegie had offered Pittsburgh a library, but the city fathers had rejected his generosity because they believed they had not sufficient civil funds to maintain it. Now, spurred on by the Allegheny City project, they asked Carnegie if his proffered $250,000 was still on the table. The negative reply caused dismay. Then in his idiosyncratic way Carnegie offered them $1 million instead. With its additional art gallery, meeting rooms, music facility and branch libraries, the Pittsburgh library was Carnegie's latest public benefaction to date. As he did in business, Carnegie involved himself in every aspect of the project, from choosing paint to the style of the bookshelves.

These two library projects stirred up Carnegie's detractors again, and not just those in the Democratic party. Carnegie's steelworkers were particularly bitter; they had had their wages cut, and here was Carnegie lashing out thousands to fund a project that few of them wanted to use. Why could they not have fair wages to be able to buy things they wanted?

Carnegie was impervious to such carping. With President Harrison as his friend and colleague he was jubilant. He took Harrison on a visit to his steelworks before the president left Allegheny City and introduced him to his team of managers, including Charles Schwab, the young supervisor of the Homestead Mills, and Harrison saw something of Carnegie's employment philosophy at work:

'How is this, Mr Carnegie? You present only boys to me,' remarked the President.
'Yes, Mr President, but do you notice what kind of boys they are?'
'Yes, hustlers [i.e. go-getters]. Every one of them.'[27]

Carnegie had made Schwab a chief engineer and manager by the time he was 20; now aged 28 he had a partnership in the business and would soon be a millionaire. Harrison observed one of Carnegie's employment secrets: INTELLIGENCE + ENERGY + FORESIGHT + ENTHUSIASM = REWARD. And Carnegie was aiming at political rewards for himself. Harrison was somewhat embarrassed to receive from him a keg of whisky to introduce him to Scottish spirits, and his aides were concerned that he would be seen as too close to rapacious capitalists. Yet Harrison enjoyed himself at the sumptuous dinner Carnegie threw for him at the Arlington Hotel, Washington DC, following the library opening. Carnegie had long wished to be a prominent player on the Washington stage. His friendship with Harrison and Secretary of State James Blaine strengthened that; and when Blaine died in 1893, another Carnegie player – his lawyer and fishing companion George Shiras Jr – was appointed to the Supreme Court to help promote business and Carnegie. Before Blaine died, though, Carnegie was to receive his one and only political appointment.[28]

James Blaine was an internationalist with a particular interest in South America. He organised the first Pan-American Conference, gathering together delegates from North, South and Central America to debate commercial issues. Carnegie was one of America's ten delegates, enjoying the role of envoys' host at Pittsburgh when the party set out on a six-week tour of America's manufacturing, commercial and agricultural locations.

Carnegie began to study South American history and politics. Under Spanish rule from the sixteenth century until 1810, when the first autonomous government was established, with full independence following in 1818, Chile suffered further revolution when rebels overthrew the government in 1891. Leading members of the deposed government were granted asylum in America and Carnegie boned up on Chilean current affairs. Diplomatically America became more involved when several naval men were murdered and others attacked after shore leave was granted to the men of the USS *Baltimore* stationed in Chilean waters.

Public indignation was high in America with calls for immediate gunboat retribution. Carnegie the neo-pacifist counselled President Harrison to tread softly, and careful diplomacy calmed the situation. From this time on, whenever America was involved in tension abroad, Carnegie's personal intervention tactic cranked into action with the sending of memos, letters and telegrams and face-to-face confrontations with all concerned. Carnegie was happy; he felt that the government and president he had helped to buy were on his side, and just as he had exacted profit from his business activities he wished to do the same in politics. Nevertheless there were time bombs lurking in his immediate future which would indelibly harm his reputation.

FIFTEEN

THE HOMESTEAD AFFAIR

> Andrew Carnegie sweated the last dollar out of his workers
> and gave them little in return; his gifts to libraries and other
> institutions were stolen from the pockets of his labourers
> and he got all the credit.
>
> Comment by one of Carnegie's workers reminiscing about
> the Homestead Troubles of 1892

There were certain contracts over the years that Carnegie did
not bid for, notably in the field of armaments for the US
Navy. Carnegie's interest in the US Navy dated from the days of
the Civil War, and the exploits of Captain David Glasgow
Farragut (1801–70), a Southerner who fought for the North in
the Federal Navy, and took part in the siege and capture of
Vicksburgh (1863) and the destruction of Confederate vessels in
Mobile Bay. Carnegie had a picture of Farragut in his Civil War
portfolio and he was developing in his mind a plan to reward
such heroes – a plan which would eventually evolve into his
Hero Fund Trust in 1908. Nevertheless at this point his pacifism
deterred him from dealing in the machines of war; that being
said, he also realised that there was little money to be made
from naval armaments.

However, in December 1889 the construction of the battleship
Maine and the cruiser *New York* was delayed by difficulties in the
supply of steel from Carnegie's rival Joseph Wharton's
Bethlehem Steel Co. President Harrison's Naval Secretary
Benjamin Tracy contacted Carnegie to seek his help. Carnegie
was tempted; an order for 6,000 tons of steel was big and
lucrative. But what of his pacifism? Whether he realised it or not

Tracy had managed to reach Carnegie's weak spot: his vanity. His acceptance of the contract would please his Washington friends and advance his status. Thus Carnegie's conceit mollified his principles, the contract was accepted and the management of the manufacture was given to Henry Clay Frick.

From wherever he was Carnegie monitored the contract's progress, and even when he was at Cluny Castle the US Naval attaché W.H. Emery, based at the US embassy in London, kept him supplied with memos from James Blaine to help him keep within the US government's guidelines for the contract. Thus Carnegie was able to telegraph instructions and advice to Frick. He even bought land in Pittsburgh on which to construct a mill for the contract production. The land purchase promoted its own difficulties but when taken to law Carnegie, Phipps & Co. won. After all, Carnegie was a skilled manipulator. And this was just the beginning. Carnegie was to win more orders for steel for armaments, with stockholder Cousin Dod acting as adviser. Carnegie's detractors past and present cite these arms deals as fine examples of the 'pacifist' Carnegie's 'hypocrisy'. More charges of dissembling would pile up.

From the late 1870s many of America's railroad and coal industries had been sorely troubled by labour difficulties, often in the form of serious riots. Carnegie's Pittsburgh works had been largely trouble-free by comparison, and paths had been smoothed by his cooperation with unions. For instance, from the opening of his rail mill in 1875 he had dealt with worker representative groups like the 'Sons of Vulcan', which merged with the Amalgamated Association of Iron and Steel Workers in 1876.[1] Carnegie's diplomatic relationship with the unions helped him to acquire the trouble-hit mills of Homestead (acquired 1883) and Duquesne (annexed 1890) from their owners who lacked his man-management skills.

By the late 1880s American workers were beginning to flex their muscles more and the smaller unions linked up with larger groups like the American Federation of Labor.[2] Workers became more militant, as the great railroad strike of 1886, which paralysed Chicago, was to show. Extremists even resorted to bomb-throwing and radicalism became the vogue on public platforms and in the press. Capital and labour united was fast becoming capital versus labour, and vice versa. As the employer of 15,000 men, Carnegie offered his opinions on the 'labour question' and 'labour struggles' in such reviews as *Forum*.[3] He agreed in principle that workers should get a better return from profits, and wrapped his sentiments in his usual wordy altruism. However, he much preferred face-to-face bargaining with his workforce than talks with representatives of a nationwide union not known to him, and believed that 'a friendly, even a familiar, relationship was the best protection against the worst evils inherent in a large rolling mill'.[4] He felt that when his workers could refer to him as 'the little boss', or even 'Andy', he could negotiate with them better. Further, while being sympathetic to workers wishing to better themselves, he was against violent revolution: 'Rioters assembling in numbers and marching to pillage will be remorselessly shot down,' was his opinion for the future.[5]

Nevertheless, Carnegie believed, employers should not knowingly provoke violence, as had been seen when 'imported labourers' (i.e. 'scabs' to the striking workers) had been brought in to the work areas to replace the strikers. 'Thou shalt not take thy neighbour's job' became one of Carnegie's mantras. The right to strike peaceably was one thing, noted Carnegie, but rioting violently was another – as were employers who repaid agitation with severity. Even so, another Carnegie mantra developed: 'Union leaders who impeded progress had to be stopped.' Always he sought to increase efficiency in his workforce. Both sides in industry, he believed, should act within the law.[6]

This was his attitude when dealing with the strike at his Edgar Thomson Braddock mill during 1887–8. Because of difficult trading conditions wages had been reduced; the men refused to accept this and the mill was closed on 17 December 1887. When conditions improved in February 1888 Carnegie refused to reopen the mill until a new wages structure was agreed for the future. What he wanted was to tie wages to the price of steel rails in the market place, and he also wanted 12-hour shifts to suit the non-stop operation of the blast furnaces. The men refused these proposals, and Carnegie kept the works closed, honouring his principle not to use 'imported labour'. The works only reopened when the men voted to return on Carnegie's terms. Thus his tactics were to meet frontal attack with blockade. His published views on this subject reached a wide audience, but dismayed many of America's industrial leaders.

Carnegie wanted to introduce the same conditions at his Homestead mill as he had at the Braddock. At Homestead, however, the Amalgamated Association had a stronger influence and opposition was more vigorous; a strike issued when news of the implementation circulated on 1 July 1889. Carnegie was in Europe and the deadlock was in the hands of William L. Abbott, chairman of Carnegie, Phipps & Co. Abbott decided to use 'imported (non-union) labourers'. Violence erupted as the men attempted to descend from the trains bringing them to the works. The Sheriff of Allegheny and 120 deputies headed off the strikers and peace was restored. Abbott negotiated with the men, who were prepared to accept Carnegie's sliding-scale wage structure but not any changes to the existing shift patterns. This agreement would last until 1892. The Amalgamated Association saw it as a capitulation on the part of management and thus a triumph for trade unionism at Homestead. Carnegie, although pleased with the outcome, was not impressed that Abbott had tried to use 'imported labourers' instead of following his tactics at Braddock.

During January 1889 Henry Clay Frick became chairman of Carnegie, Bros & Co., Carnegie believing that the promotion would enhance the company. Frick was to prove a strong character in dealing with strikers in the coke fields in February 1890. Since 1882-3 Carnegie had been a substantial investor in the H.C. Frick Coke Co. and Frick had acquired an interest in Carnegie Bros & Co. in 1887. But there was more to his appointment than that; from at least 1883 Carnegie had been contemplating retirement and he believed that Frick was the man to take over his mantle. Yet there was a serious flaw in the arrangement because Frick did not believe in the sentiments Carnegie had expressed in his 1886 *Forum* articles. Fundamentally he believed that a company could employ who it chose, pay what it chose, and sack who it chose. Frick was no friend of the trade unions.

On 1 July 1892 Carnegie Bros & Co. was federalised and the Carnegie Steel Co. Ltd came into being with Frick as chairman. At this point the capital of Carnegie Bros had risen to $25 million, with a profit of around $4.5 million per year; the new company was formed to embrace this larger business. It was the largest steel company in the world. There were twenty-three major stockholders in the new corporation: Carnegie held $13.8 million; Henry Phipps Jr and Henry Clay Frick had $2.75 million each and George Lauder – Cousin Dod – $1 million.[7] Dod was one of the seven company chairmen. In modern values, by way of example, Dod's shares were worth around $4.33 million.

The emergence of the new company coincided with the expiry date of the wage agreement with the Homestead workers. Overall Carnegie wanted to reduce tonnage wage payments to reflect the increased productivity won by the new machinery he had installed; again he wanted a reduction in the minimum wage to reflect the depressed steel market. Although the path to achieving the new agreements would not be smooth, Carnegie believed that the policy he had enacted in 1889 would win the day and Frick was not unduly worried either. Only 325 of the 3,800 employees at Homestead would be directly affected by the new wage structures anyway.[8]

Most of the men affected were highly skilled and of British or German origin, and most were members of the Amalgamated Association. The bulk of the unskilled workforce included Hungarians, Slavs, Poles, Italians and others, many of whom could not speak English. Among them the Hungarians were considered the wildest, and the most prone to violence and disaffection. Their work was brutal and hazardous, dealing with molten metal in a work environment where health and safety came low on the list of priorities. The unskilled were paid in the range of $12.50 per week compared with the $40 of the skilled. Nevertheless Carnegie was in no doubt that Frick would successfully negotiate new rates with the men involved and in the spring of 1892 he set sail for Europe with Louise.

Eight weeks after Carnegie left, Frick met with the leaders of the representative Amalgamated Association union. Their demands were clear: a renewal of the existing Homestead wage agreement to last until 1895. Frick refused. Proposals were exchanged, with the men agreeing to a one dollar a week reduction in the standard wage; Frick required two dollars. There seemed to be room for manoeuvre. As Carnegie's biographer Burton J. Hendrick points out: 'To the unprejudiced observer it would look as though the disputing parties were approaching an agreement.'[9] Yet the main problem was Frick himself. Instead of following Carnegie's lead and meeting the union leaders face-to-face to talk, Frick conducted negotiations through third parties like Homestead superintendent John A. Potter. In fact Frick's last word was an ultimatum. Later a report would note: 'Frick . . . seemed to have been too stern, brusque and somewhat autocratic. . . .'[10]

Frick knew there would be trouble, and gave orders for the Homestead property to be 'secured'. This meant building a 'high board fence' around the mill's perimeter with a barbed wire topping, searchlights and strategic portholes. The workers saw this as a provocative 'offensive and defensive' measure. Frick also hired operatives of the Pinkerton National Detective Agency. Glasgow-born Allan Pinkerton, had emigrated to America in 1842 and became a detective and deputy-sheriff at Chicago in 1850; in 1852 he formed his own detective agency (the first in the USA) which solved a series of train robberies. In 1861 he guarded Abraham Lincoln and was the head of the US Secret Service during the Civil War. By the 1890s Pinkerton's agents were notorious for their brutality, having helped break or control some seventy strikes. It must be said, though, that in employing these agents Frick was not doing anything unusual, as such a move was common practice among industrialists and railroad companies who felt threatened by crime, riots or labour troubles.

The Carnegie Steel Co. had reached a watershed; as far as Frick and the managers were concerned the Amalgamated Association was of no relevance. Homestead was closed down on 30 June 1892. Every employee was disengaged; any worker wishing to return must do so as a non-union man and each applicant would be vetted. Pinkerton's agents secured the works from any attack and protected the workmen employed by the management to replace the strikers. Outside Homestead workers met, listened to union and anti-capitalist speakers and hung effigies of Frick and Potter from lamp posts. Some caricatures were set on fire.

Striker reaction was swift. They seized the city of Allegheny (population 12,000), the roads of the Monogahela River and assorted Carnegie properties. Mayor John McLuckie, another Carnegie employee, sided with the strikers, as did most of the citizens. An advisory committee was set up to oversee their tactics with worker Hugh O'Donnell as chairman. A cordon of pickets sealed the city, and those with no pressing reason to be there were sent away; even the Sheriff of Allegheny County and his deputies were expelled, his calls for law and order being ignored. The whole countryside was staffed with worker-guards, vigilantes and reconnoitring parties. Frick and his managers were barred from the $6 million Homestead property. By early July 1892 the strikers controlled the Carnegie properties, and anger seethed to the point of anarchy; Carnegie's company faced destruction.

Frick still believed that his Pinkerton agents could bring the difficulties to an end. Even though the local sheriff had been given short shrift, Frick did not feel it necessary to ask Governor Robert E. Pattison of Pennsylvania to call in the state militia. Yet with the strikers blockading Homestead territory, how would the Pinkerton agents gain access?

The best point of access, Frick decided, was via the riverbank landings, accessible under the cover of darkness. Two armed barges containing 300 agents were to be towed in by the tugboat *Little Bill*. The small flotilla left its moorings at Bellevue, some 5 miles south of Pittsburgh, at 2am on 6 July 1892; through a welcome bank of fog they reached their destination unimpeded. Yet from the outset their progress was being monitored by the strikers' pickets. When they reached their destination the agents, under their leader Captain Heinde, were met by a vociferous crowd of strikers and their families who rushed to the riverbanks near Homestead. The agents were subjected to a barrage of stones, assorted missiles and even revolver fire. The crowds swelled as the agents reached the Homestead wharves, with estimates of 10,000 striking workers facing the 300 Pinkerton agents.[11] A shot rang out from the crowd and the agents returned fire with a volley from their Winchester rifles. Captain Heinde was hit in the hip. Indiscriminate firing began and continued for five minutes or so, resulting in three agents mortally wounded, five strikers dead and many more wounded. The agents scattered, taking shelter in the barges and behind piles of goods on the wharves. The crowd, angered by the deaths of their comrades, became a murderous mob; they surged forward and a two-hour battle ensued.

The strikers' skills with dynamite, burning oil and an ancient artillery piece were so inept that the intended murder of all the Pinkertons was not achieved. Slowly the engagement quietened and the more reasonable leaders of the strikers calmed the mob and raised a flag of truce. The agents were urged to surrender. A truce was agreed on the proviso that the agents would be given a safe passage to Homestead railway station. Even so many had to run the gauntlet of the enraged strikers' families on the way to the station, while others hid in buildings or made their way to the hospital. In this, the most terrible event of US industrial history, nothing positive was achieved by Frick and the Carnegie property still remained in the hands of the strikers.

With hindsight, commentators agreed that State Governor Pattison could have prevented the riot. By 10 July he had taken action and 8,000 state militiamen under Major-General Snowdon entered Allegheny; without any resistance from the strikers the Homestead mills were handed back to Frick. The House report of the Congressional Committee convened to examine what had happened underlined the great mistake that Frick had made:

> If Mr Frick had gone to Governor Pattison in person and laid the case before him, instead of employing the Pinkertons in the first instance, we believe that the Governor would, as he finally did, in the discharge of his plain duty, have sent a sufficient force to enable the sheriff to have taken possession and delivered to the Carnegie company their property, to the end they might have operated their mills in their own way and have avoided a riot.[12]

An unexpected event would rescue Frick from eternal ignominy. On Saturday 23 July 1892 an appointment was made with Frick for a man who claimed to be an agent for a New York employment agency to discuss supplying a workforce for Homestead to replace the strikers. At 2pm on that day, while Frick and his vice-chairman John G.A. Leishman sat in the office of the Carnegie Steel Co., the man was shown in. Frick sensed danger; he rose from his desk and advanced towards the man – who raised a pistol and shot him in the neck. As Frick fell the man fired again, hitting him in the neck again. Bravely Leishman grappled with the man, knocking his arm as he fired again so that the third bullet hit the ceiling. Frick scrambled to help Leishman, as the man produced a dagger fashioned from a file. He wounded Frick again in the hip, the side and the leg. At length the man was overpowered by clerks from the adjacent offices. After the man had been handed over to the police, and doctors had attended to Frick's wounds, he resolutely returned to his desk. A telegram was prepared for Carnegie:

> Was shot twice but not dangerously.
> There is no necessity for you to come home. I am still in shape to fight the battle out.[13]

And a bulletin was prepared for the press:

> This incident will not change the attitude of the Carnegie Steel Company toward the Amalgamated Association. I do not think I shall die, but, if I do or not, the company will pursue the same policy and it will win.[14]

Frick then collapsed and was stretchered home, but appeared at his desk again three weeks later. As he gave instructions concerning the running of the Carnegie company from his sickbed, the police discovered that his assailant was a 25-year-old Russian national from Vilna called Alexander Berkman. Although he had nothing to do with the Homestead strikers and union men, as a nihilist agitator he had travelled to Pittsburgh to seek out 'the man who . . . most completely embodied the tyranny of capitalism'.[15] Berkman was convicted and received a 21-year penitentiary sentence; he was paroled in 1905 and deported in 1919. For the history books strike-leader Hugh O'Donnell commented: 'The bullet from Berkman's pistol went straight through the heart of the Homestead strike.'[16] New and old workers flocked to the Homestead mills; the union was disregarded and calm reigned. Writing on 21 July 1932, Carnegie's biographer Burton J. Hendrick noted: 'Not a union man has since entered the Carnegie works.'[17]

At the time of the Homestead riots, on 5–6 July 1892, Carnegie had journeyed from London to Aberdeen to dedicate a new library at Rosemount Viaduct, then set off to holiday at Rannoch Lodge at Kilnoch Rannoch in Perthshire, which he had rented from Sir Robert Menzies because Cluny Castle was being refurbished. Carnegie had planned a restful sojourn exploring the environs of the Black Wood of Rannoch, a relic of the ancient Caledonian Forest, but his peace was regularly interrupted. By letter and telegram he was fed news of the strike and the erupting violence. Greatly disturbed (to the point that Louise worried about his health), Carnegie cabled that he would return on the next available liner. Frick replied in various cables strongly requesting him not to return.

Carnegie's presence would have compromised Frick, as their handling of strikes was different; moreover it would have been likely that Carnegie would have needed to demote or dismiss Frick. In a cable Carnegie supported Frick's actions:

> Cable received. All anxiety gone since you stand firm. Never employ one these rioters. Let grass grow over the works. Must not fail now. You will win easily next trial only stand firm law and order wish I could support you in any form.[18]

Carnegie had no option but to support Frick. Although Frick had gone against the advice given in Carnegie's *Forum* articles, the strikers had resorted to violence that Carnegie said should never be tolerated.

The bloody battle with Carnegie's workers at Homestead made regular front-page news in the American press, with the picture papers like Frank Leslie's *Illustrated Weekly* offering graphic pictures of striking families stoning the Pinkerton agents. The *St Louis Post-Dispatch* declared Carnegie a figure of 'contempt', adding for good measure: 'Say what you will of Carnegie he is a coward.' The British press also had a field day, with Tory editors relishing the criticism of Carnegie who, they perceived, had cockily boasted of American superiority in all things in his *Triumphant Democracy*. The *London Financial Observer* kicked off:

> Here we have this Scotch-Yankee plutocrat meandering through Scotland in a four-in-hand, opening public libraries and receiving the freedom of cities [Aberdeen was the latest], while the wretched workmen who sweat themselves in order to supply him with the ways and means of his self-glorification are starving in Pittsburgh.[19]

The Times also joined the chorus:

> Mr Carnegie's position is singular. The avowed champion of trades-unions now finds himself in almost ruinous conflict

with the representatives of his own views. He has probably by this time seen cause to modify his praise of unionism and the sweet reasonableness of its leaders. Or, are we to assume that the doctrine is true in Glasgow but not in the United States, or that it ceases to be applicable the moment Mr Carnegie's interests are touched?[20]

Hundreds of articles and volumes have covered the Homestead riots, giving varying opinions on the cause and inevitable outcome. A consensus shows that it was a hollow victory of sorts for the workers, but perhaps more importantly historically was the fact that Carnegie's reputation as an enlightened employer was destroyed. Homestead cast a shadow over the rest of his life. He was devastated by the events and thereafter endeavoured to create a new image for himself. Going to Scotland during the Homestead difficulties was the most shameful act of his life; indeed, his choice of Rannoch Lodge – arranged through his London agent J. Watson Lyall – was so remote, with Rannoch railway station some 10 miles away and with no other public transport, this left Carnegie open to the accusation that he was hiding. Perhaps the most hurtful outcome was that he was vilified in his homeland. The left-wing Glasgow Trades Council compared him to Judas Iscariot; the Scots socialist MP Keir Hardy was so incensed that he remitted the funds Carnegie had given him to the Homestead strikers; and some of the leftist Liberal Party denizens slammed shut their doors on him. To many Carnegie's philanthropy was now tainted.

There was political fall-out too. The defeat of Benjamin Harrison's Republican administration was blamed in part on the Homestead affair. Carnegie was already closely identified with the Republican party. Certainly the Democrats made some effective propaganda out of Homestead, but the economic times were growing worse for America. Harrison had allowed the country's gold reserves to be severely depleted and depression escalated. The country turned once more to Democrat Grover Cleveland, who had been President in 1885–9.

Homestead became a slum of desperate men and women living in squalor. The conditions were even worse than those of

Carnegie's childhood home at Dunfermline, and he had contributed to the suffering. Carnegie still provided work, but to make a living wage 12-hour shifts were the norm, with only two days' holiday a year at Christmas and 4 July. The lowest wage rates started at 14 cents per hour for the unskilled, with an average of $12.50 per week for skilled workers.[21] Conditions at Homestead made a mockery of Carnegie's notion of 'fair distribution' advocated in *The Gospel of Wealth*.

Despite all this Carnegie received support from his friends. Most prominent in their sympathy were Lord Rosebery and John Morley; W.E. Gladstone also chipped in, saying: 'I am sure that no one who knows you will be prompted by the unfortunate occurrences across the water . . . to qualify in the slightest degree either his confidence in your generous views or his admiration for the good and great works you have already done.'[22] Perhaps the most curious understanding of all came from Carnegie's uncle George Lauder. In a letter of 25 March 1853 he wrote: 'I am glad your troubles are now all over at Pittsburgh and will remain so for a long time. This working man question is the question of the day. The more you give them the more they will take. I see this every day in little things as well as big.' Where was the radical scorn and bile Lauder would have heaped on the heads of other capitalists in similar circumstances?

In January 1893 Carnegie returned to New York to be welcomed warmly by many of his colleagues as if nothing had happened at Homestead. Certainly manufacturers believed that Carnegie had stood up for property rights. Others made sure that Carnegie's philanthropic purse remained open, importuning him for grants of various kinds and adding his name to memorial ventures.

Slowly Carnegie began to put clear water between himself and Homestead. Just as when a little boy he had cleared himself of blame for wrongdoing with the Scots whine 'It wisna me', so in speech and writing Carnegie now absolved himself of censure for what had happened at Homestead. In his study at 51st Street, New York, he carefully scoured the press for comments attacking him. Should he try to buy off certain editors? He concluded that this was not a practical policy but with John Leishman he did his best to put in place rules that would lead to the sacking of employees who wrote to or spoke to journalists about Carnegie's affairs.[23] He could not stop the Homestead men talking about or remembering what had happened and among their ranks he had made enemies for life. Nevertheless while in Pittsburgh he was all smiles and bonhomie. In a statement he said:

> I have come not to rake up but to bury the past, of which I knew nothing. I am not an officer of the company but only a shareholder. Four years ago I retired from active business. I am selling portions of my interests to such young men in our service as my partners find possessed of exceptional ability.[24]

While blatantly lying about his role in the Homestead débâcle, Carnegie was telling the truth about the 'young men'; one such on the scene was Charles Michael Schwab.

SIXTEEN

FRAUD AND FRACTION

Carnegie was the most cruel task-master American industry has ever known.

John K. Winkler, Biographer, 1931

Charles Michael Schwab was born at Williamsburg in Pennsylvania of North American–German stock. After working in his father's livery stables and in a grocery store, he was employed by Captain William Jones at Carnegie's Braddock mill as a $1-a-day stake driver. His promotion as a steel man was rapid; his enthusiasm for any job he undertook saw him promoted to assistant engineer in the Edgar Thomson Steel Works after only six months; by the time he was 20 Schwab was chief engineer and assistant supervisor to Jones. More importantly, he became Jones's 'messenger' link with Carnegie.[1] Carnegie soon marked him out as a devotee, a role in which Schwab shone, playing to Carnegie's weaknesses of vanity and a need for attention. Then there was humour. More than any other person Schwab could make Carnegie laugh until the tears flowed.

In 1887 Schwab became superintendent at Homestead; when Jones died after an industrial accident in 1889 Schwab returned to Braddock, but after the Homestead difficulties in 1892 Carnegie moved him back to Homestead to sort out the unrest. Schwab was part of the management team that helped to keep the Amalgamated Association at bay in their attempts to win a foothold once more at Homestead. Schwab's success in this made him even more popular with Carnegie, who promoted him to general superintendent of Braddock and

Homestead, with money and stocks and shares rewards. Schwab was to be tested, though, in what one Carnegie biographer described as Carnegie's 'shifty business standards'.[2]

Six months after Democrat Grover Cleveland assumed office as President for the second time in 1893, Secretary of the Navy Hilary A. Herbert was approached by Pittsburgh lawyer James H. Smith with a serious charge. 'Squealers' at Homestead had reported that the US government was being defrauded by the Carnegie Steel Company. The malfeasance was in the manufacture of armour plate for the US Navy. After hearing the accusations Herbert agreed to pay the informants – all subordinate colleagues of Schwab – a percentage of the penalties the government would extract from Carnegie Steel. Herbert's report to Congress showed how the fraud had been carried out:

> The allegations were that the company's employees had failed to temper armour evenly and properly, had plugged and concealed blow-holes, which would probably have caused a rejection of plates by the government inspectors, and had re-treated, without the knowledge of the inspectors, plates which had been selected for ballistic test, so as to make these plates better and tougher than the group of plates represented by them.[3]

The informants showed too, that documentation for the armour plates was falsified and identified Schwab, William Corey and another superintendent called Cline as the perpetrators of the fraud.

Herbert assigned the Chief of the Bureau of Ordnance, Captain William Thomas Sampson, and his staff to investigate. After weeks of examinations the charges were sustained and damages of $288,000 were fixed.[4] Consequently the Carnegie Steel Co. chairman Henry Clay Frick was summoned to Washington and he took with him his aide Millard Hunsicker. A few days after the initial meeting Frick returned with statements on the company's actions, including one from Schwab. This time Carnegie joined the group with his lawyer Philander Knox in tow.

In a report dated 16 December 1893 Captain Sampson noted that Schwab admitted the plates had been tampered with but denied deliberate fraud. To this Sampson added his own opinion that the fraud *was* deliberate. Carnegie now took a hand.

Carnegie was back at the White House on 20 December 1893. He let it be known publicly that he was discussing tariff measures with the President. In reality Carnegie was endeavouring to get his company off the hook, or at least to reduce the damages. He seems to have done it in this way. At the time America was suffering economic difficulties and President Cleveland had a personal measure he wished to bring to fruition, which would be called the Wilson-Gorman Tariff Bill. Carnegie now made a public appeal to his Republican cronies, and to manufacturers all over America, asking them to support Cleveland's proposals which would reverse the high protectionism that they supported. On 10 January 1894 Cleveland wrote to Secretary Herbert. He spoke of the 'alleged irregularities' by Carnegie Steel as a 'default' rather than fraud. He reduced the company fine from 15 to 10 per cent. This amounted to a 'placid disposal of the scandal' and a 'mild rebuke' for Carnegie Steel.[5] In reality, no politician could ignore Carnegie's influence. His Edgar Thomson Steel Works was now worth $25 million, with earnings of $4 million per annum. Carnegie and his colleagues owned the largest and most lucrative steelworks in the world, and ran four major steel plants, two iron mills, a handful of blast furnaces all with private railway networks, and the best coke company in America. Soon they would also be iron-ore producers. Nevertheless Cleveland's actions aroused indignation among naval officers, the press and the public alike. Back in Pittsburgh Frick, Schwab and the managers continued their work and the company did its best through the Carnegie-friendly *Pittsburgh Times* to boost its image. The armour scandal dented Carnegie's reputation further; many thought that once again he had prostituted his principles (as a high market protectionist) to get off the hook. As the controversy bubbled away Carnegie went abroad once more.

On 4 January Carnegie left depression-torn New York and travelled to Egypt, leaving his managers under media siege at Pittsburgh. Then the Carnegies went to Buckhurst Park for three months; when the weather warmed up they were back at Cluny Castle. Interestingly, while he was at Buckland Park Carnegie contacted Andrew D. White, whom he had first met all those years back at Madame Botta's soirées. White was now the US ambassador to the Imperial Court of Emperor Nicholas II of Russia, who had just succeeded his father Alexander III. What were the possibilities of selling armour plating to Russia? Carnegie's pacifist principles were being subsumed once more for profit.

More trouble was brewing for Carnegie. After the armour scandal the Carnegie managers were jumpy and steadily losing confidence in one another. Frick was becoming disenchanted with Schwab, whom he considered guilty of mismanaging the armour affair. Carnegie ignored Frick's opinions, but on 1 January 1895 he received Frick's resignation underlining his wish to retire. There was more to it than this; Frick was tired of Carnegie's management style and his undermining of the chain of command by interfering when he felt like it in company policy. Trust had broken down. Frick was not happy that Carnegie was also meddling in the negotiations for the Russian armour contract; in the event it went to Bethlehem Steel, to Carnegie's annoyance.

Carnegie mulled over Frick's resignation, offering the incentive of him staying on to enable Carnegie to sell out to him and the other partners in due course to make them sole owners of the company. But Frick was not to be bought with blandishments. Partner Harry Phipps was also unwilling to fill Frick's place so Carnegie thought of offering the presidency of the company to Vice-President John Leishman. Alas, Leishman had a reputation for speculative share-dealing that made him unsound. So Carnegie went back to building bridges with Frick. For a while, though, he had been publicly implying that Frick was a sick man, and had even put this in a letter to Phipps exaggerating the extent of the supposed illness. Phipps showed the letter to Frick, who was furious and sent off a blistering reply to Carnegie:

> I desired to quietly withdraw, doing as little harm as possible to the interests of others, because I had become tired of your business methods, your absurd newspaper interviews and personal remarks and unwarranted interference in matters you knew nothing about.
>
> It has been your custom for years when any of your partners disagreed with you to say they were unwell, needed a change, etc.
>
> I warn you to carry this no farther with me but come forward like a man and purchase my interest, and let us part before it becomes impossible to continue as friends.[6]

In his usual persuasive manner Carnegie mollified Frick in some part. Phipps, too, had made it plain that unless Carnegie made up with Frick he would sell his shares in the company and withdraw. The company continued as before, with Frick now as chairman, but the tensions remained obvious. Meanwhile Carnegie continued with his philanthropic plans. Schwab was instructed to prepare plans for a library at Homestead, which detractors interpreted as guilt money over the past difficulties. Carnegie also continued with gifts to friends and family.

During 1895–6 Carnegie was once again, under his own auspices, plunged into politics. For some five decades the United Kingdom and Venezuela had been squabbling over the boundary between the colony of British Guiana (since 1970 the Cooperative Republic of Guyana) and Venezuela. From time to time Venezuela had appealed to the US to mediate over the British 'aggression' but diplomatic negotiations between successive US Secretaries of State and Her Majesty's government in London had proved fruitless. When President Grover Cleveland entered his second administration he took up the Venezuela case with renewed vigour. When W.E. Gladstone had been British Prime Minister friendly cooperation had been on the cards, but on 25 June 1895 the Tory Lord Salisbury was returned as Prime Minister and was also acting as his own Foreign Secretary. The Venezuela dispute broke out again. No Anglophile, Cleveland accused the British of using a fluid boundary to acquire new territory – with mineral and strategic advantages; this was in violation of the US foreign policy statement of 2 December 1823 by President James Monroe (the 'Monroe Doctrine'), which stated simply that any European power attempting to control any nation in the western hemisphere would be viewed as engaging in a hostile act against the United States.

The American newspapers talked of war. Any bad feeling between the US and the UK upset Carnegie, who still dreamed of a quadruple alliance of eternal peace and prosperity between Canada, Britain, the United States and the British Commonwealth. More than that, since he had been a delegate at the Pan-American Conference in 1889 Carnegie considered South American affairs to be his special project. When Cleveland announced his firm line against Britain, the stock exchanges in both countries panicked. Although Carnegie thought that Cleveland and his Secretary of State Richard Olney had provoked Britain, he broadly supported the President's plan to fix a firm boundary. Carnegie endeavoured to sway British opinion towards this plan by jockeying his old friends in England.

He wrote to Salisbury's Lord President of the Council, Spencer Compton Cavendish, 8th Duke of Devonshire, asking him to use 'your great influence in the councils of your country on behalf of a conciliatory policy'.[7] To anyone who would listen Carnegie expounded his thoughts, which he brought to a wider world in the February 1896 issue of *North American Review*. The theme of the pacifist piece was the hope that the whole matter could be settled by arbitration, as he feared that non-cooperation would inevitably lead to war.

Salisbury was listening, not to Carnegie but to Kaiser Wilhelm II's slowly beating war drums, and he put forward the idea of some form of arbitration. He insisted 'though' that 'disputed territory that had been settled by Englishmen "would be retained"'.[8] Carnegie considered this 'inadequate' and wrote to W.E. Gladstone from Cluny Castle on 25 July 1896. The ailing, almost blind Gladstone received Louise and Andrew Carnegie at Hawarden Castle to discuss the matter, remarking that the situation needed 'younger men' to deal with it. In the event, public opinion on both sides of the Atlantic led to the needed arbitration. Although unable to attend the International Tribunal of Arbitration, Carnegie endeavoured to play a role by helping fund it to the tune of $1,000.[9] Ironically, as he was doing his best to promote peace between his beloved countries, his company was busy exploiting armaments contracts to which he gave his full backing.

During the summer of 1896 the Carnegies set off on a grand tour of Europe, and this time the party included Louise's sister Estelle ('Stella') Whitfield who was increasingly acting as extra comforter. For some time Louise had been unwell, Carnegie taking her to Palm Beach spa for her health. This time the tour took in Italy and Austria. According to family tradition the Homestead conflict had affected Louise's health, and the continuing agitation of the armour scandal and the Venezuelan dispute all further debilitated her. There was added duress during 1895–6 when Carnegie had several disputes with the Pennsylvania Railroad over freight charges (after much haggling and threats he won sizeable rebates) and engaged in a new jockeying with John D. Rockefeller.

The depression years had been kind to Rockefeller. He was the foremost leader in oil refinery and was now intent on securing domination of the iron ore industry. This dismayed Carnegie. Going against the advice of Frick and his other colleagues, he entered the fray. He not only wanted a piece of the action, he also wanted to thwart Rockefeller's intended dominance. To counter Rockefeller's purchases of ore interests like those in the Mesabi mountains of north Minnesota, Carnegie sought ore deposits in West Virginia. Nothing in Carnegie's business transactions was now simple and he was further dismayed to hear that Rockefeller wished to enter the steel industry to challenge Carnegie Steel. Realising that he could not compete with Rockefeller in the race for ore, and determined to keep Rockefeller out of steel, Carnegie agreed to buy the ore for Carnegie Steel from Rockefeller. It gave Rockefeller another interest to cool the steel idea.

All these matters produced a great deal of worry in the Carnegie household. Monitoring her fragile health, Louise's doctor believed that she needed a renewed family focus. He felt that Louise would benefit both physically and mentally if she had a child. Carnegie was not sure. He was now 61 and he feared that he might lose Louise in childbirth. Louise herself had no such fears. Her health had improved during their European trip and while in Austria she conceived. So 1897 was to be a year like no other for Carnegie. Carnegie Steel and all his subsidiary companies were prospering, although his colleagues were bearing the brunt of the work, and Carnegie was free to look forward to fatherhood with eagerness.

SEVENTEEN

A DAUGHTER AND A DWELLING

Mr Carnegie, I want to congratulate you on being the richest man in the world.

J.P. Morgan to Andrew Carnegie, February 1901

On 30 March 1897 at 51st Street, New York, 40-year-old Louise Carnegie gave birth to a girl; the infant was named Margaret after her deceased paternal grandmother. Back in Scotland, Cluny Macpherson gave orders that the birth of the daughter of his old friends the Carnegies should be celebrated in true 'Badenoch style' – Badenoch being the name of the wild district of the Scottish Highlands in which Cluny Castle was situated. Carnegie was delighted: 'There were nine bonfires upon as many Cluny hills, to celebrate the advent of little Saint Margaret, and such rejoicing! Such evidences of attachment tell!'[1] Even if conventional fashion had allowed it, Carnegie was not at the birth of his child; he was languishing with pleurisy at his sister-in-law Lucy Coleman Carnegie's house at Greenwich, Connecticut, in the care of Louise's sister Stella.

There was never a more devoted father; he was captivated by every syllable uttered by his 'wonderful wean' (i.e. child).[2] He spent hours with her, following every aspect of her development with delight. When she got older he entertained her with stories 'of ghosts, burglars and other engaging characters, most of which he invented himself'.[3] He interlarded his storytelling with titbits from Scots history and poesy – just as Uncle George Lauder had for him in his Dunfermline childhood. Carnegie's love of games was enhanced with a new playmate to share them with, and whenever her father was away Margaret received letters and notes from him full of fun and information, read to her before she could read herself by devoted Nannie Lockerbie.

Margaret's every cough and snuffle greatly agitated Carnegie. Her most serious illness occurred when she was 8; a sprained ankle did not right itself naturally and the Edinburgh physician Carnegie called in suspected a bone infection. Professor (later Sir) Harold Jalland Stiles, consultant at the Royal Edinburgh Hospital for Sick Children, suspected a bone deterioration, and Margaret was in a plaster cast and then a splint for some three years. At length a condition associated with articular gout was diagnosed and a steady recovery was made. Carnegie wrote to his friend John Morley on 14 January 1906 that 'a heavy weight is lifted from our hearts'.[4] Margaret lived in a household that made her almost a miniature adult from babyhood, and the attention her father had once lavished on her gradually lessened as he became more deeply involved with his philanthropy.

The birth of baby Margaret coincided with another need for change. In 1897 laird Cluny Macpherson, now a 61-year-old bachelor, married Mary Stacey and wished to live in his ancestral home. Over the years the Carnegies had endeavoured to buy Cluny Castle from Macpherson but he would never sell. The Carnegies as tenants must now seek a new refuge. But where? Louise Carnegie was adamant that after the arrival of their child they should cease to be tenants 'obliged to go in and out at a certain date. It should be *our* home . . . I make only one condition. It must be in the Highlands of Scotland.'[5]

The summer of 1897 was the last the Carnegies spent at Cluny. In Britain and the territories abroad it was a great royal year. At Windsor Castle on 20 June 1897 Queen Victoria attended a 'touching service' at St George's Chapel, and the whole nation embarked on a series of commemorations and celebrations to mark the day sixty years before – 20 June 1837 – when 19-year-old Princess Victoria, sixth monarch of the House of Hanover, succeeded as queen of what was to be the largest family of nations the world has ever known; she was crowned at Westminster Abbey on 28 June 1839. On 22 June

1897 the Carnegies joined the crowds along the 6-mile route for the royal procession from Buckingham Palace to St Paul's Cathedral to pay their respects. Carnegie, who as a youngster would have executed every monarch in sight, shared his feelings about the occasion with an American audience:

The principal figure of the Jubilee, Queen Victoria herself, and the position she has gained and will hold to the end of her days, is worthy of study. It is not possible for any American, however well informed of British affairs, to quite understand the feelings with which this human being is now regarded. If he can imagine Old Glory [the American flag] and Old Ironsides, Washington and Lincoln, Bunker Hill and 'My Country, 'Tis of Thee' rolled into one force, and personified in a woman, he may form some conception of the feelings of the average Briton for 'The Queen', for she in her own person symbolizes today the might and majesty of the land, and its long, varied and glorious history from the beginning. 'The Queen' means everything that touches and thrills the patriotic chord. That both as a woman and a sovereign, she has deserved the unique tribute paid her goes without saying; the wildest radical, or even republican, will concur in this. Sixty years of unremitting work – she still signs every state paper herself, including lieutenants' commissions in the militia – prudence, patience and rare judgement have made of this good, able, energetic, managing, and very wise woman a saint, whom her subjects are as little capable and as little disposed to estimate critically as the American schoolboy can imagine or is disposed to imagine, Washington as possessed of human frailties. Washington, [William] Tell, Wallace, Bruce, Lincoln, Queen Victoria or [Queen] Margaret are the stuff of which heroes or saints are made, and well it is for the race that the capacity for hero worship and for saint worship remains with both Briton and American wholly unimpaired.

When a nation ceases to create ideals its glorious days are past. Fortunately for the world, both the republic and the monarchy have the future before them.[6]

A Daughter and a Dwelling

Then in this Diamond Jubilee year Carnegie set out to secure a palace for his own financial kingdom. To help in his search for a permanent home Carnegie recruited the help of Hew Morrison, the librarian at Carnegie's new library foundation at Edinburgh. Morrison had a special interest in Scotland's ancient castles and mansions, and to assist him Carnegie wrote a memo of essential requirements for his Scottish home: 'It must have plenty of land, trout and salmon fishing, woods and hills, lochs and streams, a location bordering the sea, and, even more important, a beautiful waterfall.'[7]

At the top of Morrison's research file of potential properties were a few available within the huge estates of Cromartie Sutherland-Leveson-Gower, 4th Duke of Sutherland. Carnegie had already encountered the Sutherlands: Duchess Millicent had extracted money from him for her project to relieve the widows and orphans of the mining disaster at Audley Colliery (1895).[8] Also on Morrison's list was a property called Skibo abutting the Dornoch Firth. Morrison had done his research well and included maps and a deed with his notes. Carnegie was unimpressed; Skibo was run-down, smaller than he was looking for and had no waterfall.

Carnegie organised a two-week coaching trip to look at properties. From Inverness they travelled up the Moray Firth and east across Ross and Cromarty, to enter Sutherland at the village of Bonar Bridge where Thomas Telford's bridge of 1812 (rebuilt after the flood of 1892) spans the channel between Dornoch Firth and the Kyle of Sutherland. From Bonar Bridge the main road runs east through the fine woods of the north shore of the Firth and would pass the estate of Skibo. Why not give it a passing glance, suggested Morrison. Carnegie reluctantly agreed but decided to go alone with Morrison as a separate jaunt. Their hired wagonette would take them the 8 miles or so to Skibo. As they travelled Morrison pointed out various features and then they entered the long tree-lined drive to the white Scottish baronial-style sandstone castle. Dismounting, they walked around the weed-grown terraces and took in the initial ambience of the place, its gables and turrets, woodlands and magnificent views of the 22,000-acre estate. As Carnegie soaked up the hills, pastures and angling potential – with a mooring for his yacht *Sea-breeze* – Morrison reviewed a little of the castle's history.

It is probable that the coastline around Skibo estate was well known to the invading Norsemen who had anchorages here; at Ospisdale House nearby is a monument said to commemorate the death in battle of the Danish chief Ospis. And some etymologists say the Norsemen even contributed to the castle's name, from a root of 'skif', a word describing a 'place of ships'. Certainly by the thirteenth century the extant castle on the site was called Schytherbolle, and was gifted to St Gilbert de Moravia,[9] Bishop of Caithness, in 1225 by William, Earl of Sutherland. A loyal servant of the secular state as well as a distinguished cleric, Bishop Gilbert used the castle on the site of Skibo as his primary episcopal residence; just as Carnegie would lavish time and money on the terraces and flower beds, so the bishop's retainers had planted orchards and vegetable gardens. From here too, Bishop Gilbert oversaw the building of his new cathedral at Dornoch, which was restored in the year of Carnegie's birth by Elizabeth, Dowager Duchess of Sutherland. Carnegie himself paid for the reconditioning of the organ in 1906 and the cathedral's concealed lighting system was funded in 1950 by Margaret Carnegie in memory of her mother.[10]

In 1545 Bishop Robert Reid of Caithness gave Skibo to one John Gray in perpetuity. The Grays held the property until 1745, when Lieutenant Robert Gray surrendered the castle, estate and appurtenances to his importuning creditors (he died in 1776 a major in the Hanoverian 55th Foot Regiment based at Staten Island, New York).[11] The property then passed through the hands of various creditors and owners until in 1882 one Ewen Sutherland-Walker filed for bankruptcy and the castle and estate he had enlarged and restored fell into the hands of trustees.

On that day in June 1897, as he surveyed the woodland planted by Bishop Gilbert, Carnegie knew that despite his initial reservations Skibo was exactly what he was looking for.

In his usual single-minded way, he swamped Louise with his enthusiasm for Skibo. She had not seen it; could she make a home there? She recommended caution, and Carnegie agreed to dampen his enthusiasm until Louise had seen the property. Instead, Carnegie took out a lease of Skibo with an option to purchase.

Soon after he had viewed Skibo, Carnegie embarked on a yacht tour of the coasts of Harris and Lewis, in the Hebrides, but somehow these mountainous islands with their sandy shores did not raise his spirits. The last visit to Cluny had affected him more than he realised and the melancholy moors and lochs of the Western Isles were more in tune with his feelings. Yes, Skibo would be a new adventure but Carnegie was experiencing a weariness that he had never felt before, and then he caught a severe cold. He was advised by London consultants not to go back to New York's wintry chills, so the Carnegies rented Villa Allerton at Cannes. They remained there until February 1898, making plans to return to New York. It was not just the severe cold that debilitated Carnegie at this time; he was unsettled and anxious about the whole role of businessman. Communications from Charles Schwab about steel matters irritated him and he jibbed at proposed additions and renovations to the plants at Homestead and Duquesne. Suffering from overwhelming ennui, he somehow bestirred himself to return to America.

Carnegie was also disturbed by what he read in the papers. American chauvinists were becoming more anti-Hispanic by the week. Since the early sixteenth century the island of Cuba had remained under Spanish rule; now separatist agitation was brewing against the Spain of Hapsburg-Bourbon King Alfonso XIII and his Cuban administration. As dusk fell on 15 February 1898 an explosion ripped apart the US 'good-will mission' battleship *Maine* in Havana harbour; 266 of the 354 men aboard died. The government of Republican President William McKinley, who had been elected on a platform supporting Cuban independence, was split; American investments in sugar plantations and other forms of trade with Cuba were at risk. McKinley's Secretary of the Navy, Senator Long, believed the

Maine incident was an accident, while Assistant Secretary for the Navy Theodore Roosevelt thought otherwise. Many Americans were stirred to retribution by the newspapers of such men as William Randolph Hearst, and McKinley was pushed towards war.

Carnegie monitored the US blockade of Cuba, and as the war swelled his profits from armour plate his pacifism remained dormant. His own research showed Carnegie that both the US army and the navy were short on firepower and he signalled to his board of managers instructions to establish a plant for making guns. It seemed that his patriotism was engulfing his pacifism. Back in America Cousin Dod suggested that there would be more profit in bullets and shells than would follow from a huge investment in arms founding. Carnegie agreed. Soon US troops landed on Cuba and by 26 July 1898 the Spanish were negotiating for peace. For the Carnegies Skibo beckoned.

From Cannes the Carnegies and Louise's sister Stella, who now lived with them almost permanently, travelled through France and England to arrive at Skibo in June 1898. Louise liked what she saw. Carnegie contacted his Dunfermline lawyer John Ross and negotiations were set in motion to buy Skibo and its 22,000 acres for £85,000.

Almost immediately Carnegie set about expanding his new Scottish fiefdom, engaging the prominent Inverness firm of architects Ross & Macbeth to prepare plans to transform the delapidated mansion into the castle he had in mind. A new list of employees and tenants was drawn up and local contractors were hired to refurbish the estate grounds, roads, bridges and ancillary buildings. Louise took a leading role in planning the contracted work. Within the new wings and reconstructed rooms would be two focal points, a pipe organ in the front hall and a library to house 70,000 volumes – some of which were selected for him by Lord Acton; the bookcases were carved with the coats-of-arms of the cities that had awarded Carnegie their freedoms. Carnegie liked carved mottoes and his large golden oak mantelpiece would display the dictum he copied from Colonel Niles A. Stokes's library mantel back in Greensburg:

> He that cannot reason is a fool
> He that will not is a bigot
> He that dare not is a slave.[12]

As well as a flurry of decorations – Carnegie was as fussy about these as Queen Victoria had been at Balmoral – he added portraits of his heroes from poet Robert Burns to Scottish engineer and inventor James Watt. Whimsy also took over with the naming of the new suites and bedrooms after regional place names, with others named after Carnegie-selected heroes from Gilbert de Moravia to Sigurd the Viking whose ships had entered the Dornoch Firth and whose cadaver Carnegie believed was buried somewhere in the grounds of Skibo.

Before they returned to New York in October 1898 Louise wrote to her friend and pastor the Revd Charles Eaton:

We are all very pleased with our new home. The surroundings are more of the English type than Scotch. The sweet pastoral scenery is perfect of its kind. A beautiful undulating park with cattle grazing, a stately avenue of fine old beeches, glimpses of the Dornoch Firth, about a mile away, all seen through the picturesque cluster of lime and beech trees. All make such a peaceful picture that already a restful home feeling has come. The Highland features to which our hearts turn longingly are not wanting, but are more distant.

To show you the unique range of attractions, yesterday Mr Carnegie was trout fishing on a wild moorland loch surrounded by heather while I took Margaret to the *Sea* and she had her first experience of rolling upon white sand and digging her little hands in it to her heart's content, while the blue waters of the ocean came rolling in at her feet and the salt breeze brought the roses to her cheeks. She is strong and hearty and so full of mischief – a perfect little sunbeam.

With all our fullness of life before we have never really lived till now. . . .[13]

·In all, the period 1900–3 saw Carnegie spend another £100,000 transforming his purchase. Near the mansion a large marble and glass swimming pool was constructed; its facilities included the latest pumps and heaters for the seawater which filled it.[14] The swimming pool also doubled as a ballroom:

Huge electric arc lamps and chandeliers glittered overhead. . . . Tubs of evergreens were spread along the walls, and festoons of coloured paper chains and bunting hung overhead . . . Mrs Logan's dance band from Inverness played in the balcony, varied by bagpipe music for Scottish reels and so forth, Highland Scottische . . . played so harmoniously by the castle piper.[15]

Historically Skibo was one of the last prominent Scottish baronial houses ever built.

On his return to New York Carnegie was eager to play a role in the aftermath of the Spanish–American War. Spanish colonial rule in the New World was coming to an end following two major defeats. Commodore George Dewey, commander of the US Asiatic Squadron, had destroyed the Spanish fleet in the Philippines at the Battle of Manila Bay on 1 May 1898, thus establishing the US as a major naval power. Then General William Shafter led an army of regulars and volunteers (including Theodore Roosevelt and his 'Rough Riders') to destroy Spain's Caribbean Fleet near Santiago, Cuba, on 17 July 1898. By the Treaty of Paris, signed on 10 December 1898, Spain renounced her claims to Cuba and ceded Guam, Puerto Rico and the Philippines to America, thus helping the US to emerge as a world power.

What was all this to do with Carnegie? He was unhappy with America's new international stance, and as a member of the New England Anti-Imperialist League believed that America should repeal the Treaty of Paris; he decided to use his wealth and his pen in what he saw as the saving of 'American democracy'. With the help of his secretary James Bertram he put together a piece for the *North American Review* decrying the US policy of 'Triumphant Despotism' in the Philippines. Carnegie's rhetoric left President McKinley unmoved and America did not withdraw from her new territories. Carnegie, though, contemplated withdrawing from his.

At 63 Carnegie knew that he was coming to an important intersection in his business life. A crucial decision would have to be made. His steel company, for example, needed to encompass new markets. The great epoch of railway construction was ending, and steel was entering the domestic construction industry more and more as the buildings dubbed 'skyscrapers' began to dominate the horizons from Chicago to St Louis. Carnegie Steel would need to diversify into a whole new range of products from tubes to wires. But Carnegie had no stomach for vigorous new enterprises. Was it time to sell out?

Carnegie owned 58 per cent of the total capital value of Carnegie Steel, his partners holding the rest. Among the partners too, there was a sense of unease. By the standards of the age Carnegie was an old man and the partnership agreement – the Iron Clad Agreement – hung over them menacingly. Should Carnegie die, for instance, then according to the terms of the agreement his partners would have to buy his share – it could not be sold outwith their ranks. And realistically they could not afford to buy him out. So pressure was gradually building up on Carnegie to agree to selling the whole company, perhaps to one of the syndicated steel trusts.

Up to now Carnegie had baulked at such an idea, but recently he was paying it more attention. It is a matter of speculation as to why he changed his mind. Was he now ready to be the bountiful philanthropist unfettered by commercial cares? Was he wishing to enter completely into his 'heaven on earth' at Skibo? Whatever the reason, during the cold winter of 1898–9 Carnegie instructed Henry Clay Frick and Henry Phipps to look into the sale of the company. At first they found a group of financiers – who wished to remain anonymous in the initial stage – willing to pay $250 million for the company on a 90-day option. Just as he would have loathed shareholders of a floated company, Carnegie did not trust 'nameless' financiers and insisted on a 'deposit in trust' of $2 million with 58 per cent in his name. The deposit would be forfeit if the option was not taken up in the 90 days. The nameless men agreed and so the matter rested.

Meanwhile Carnegie and Louise were involved in a new housing project. Their residence at West 51st Street was now inadequate. Through a broker, and with careful timing to give him maximum advantage, Carnegie bought options on pieces of land at 5th Avenue, at 90th and 91st Streets. Here he constructed a Scottish-Georgian mansion to the designs of architects Babb, Cook and Willard for $1.5 million. It was full of what might be called Carnegie embellishments – an Aeolian organ, a his-and-hers gymnasium, an Otis lift (the first private residence to install one), oak panelling, sixty-four rooms on six levels, an extensive secure garden (the Carnegies were targets for peeping toms and the deranged) and a study-library.[16] The address was logged as No. 2, East 91st Street, New York, and very soon it 'became one of the most famous addresses in America'.[17]

During late April 1899 the Carnegies left New York for Britain for a sojourn in London and southern England, and then they were off to Skibo. By this time the estate tenants and workers were fully conversant with the identities of their new laird and his lady and gave them a rousing welcome. After the oldest tenant, a nonagenarian, offered a welcoming address at Skibo's gates, Carnegie turned and pointed to his wife, saying: 'Here is an American who loves Scotland.' Then he pointed to himself and said: 'And here is a Scotchman [sic] who loves America.' Finally he pointed to little Margaret: 'And here is a little Scottish-American who is born of both and will love both; she has come to enter the fairyland of childhood among you.'[18] Despite his Americanisation Carnegie could still offer a touch of Victorian sentimentality when he wished.

A Daughter and a Dwelling

From the early days at Skibo Carnegie developed a special rapport with his staff and tenants and treated them with generosity. Not for him the traditional Scottish laird's patriarchal spirit; he was more the beneficent employer. Every time the Carnegies returned to Skibo after significant jaunts away they would visit each tenant's cottage, and would say goodbye to everyone before every departure. After all, Queen Victoria did the same at Balmoral. On such occasions each tenant's child would be given a golden sovereign (since 1817 this had represented a golden £ in British currency).[19] Although not religious, Carnegie also appeared at the local church on the first and last Sundays of residence at Skibo and recognised the 'Presbyterian Sunday' of only necessary husbandry and estate routine. From time to time family, friends and staff would gather for Sunday evening prayers at Skibo with Carnegie supervising the proceedings and choice of hymns; every one of the latter was a Carnegie favourite often introduced by a soliloquy from him on its history and meaning. Highlights of any Carnegie Skibo residence were the 'fêtes', with a prominent one being held near or on 4 July.

By now work at Skibo was so advanced that the cornerstone for the new south elevation was ready for the official laying. At Carnegie's behest 2-year-old Margaret did the honours, giving the traditional tap with a silver trowel. The cornerstone inscription reads:

FOUNDATION STONE OF THE NEW PART OF SKIBO CASTLE
BUILT BY ANDREW AND LOUISE W. CARNEGIE
LAID BY MARGARET CARNEGIE 23 JUNE 1899

As the months passed the guest-book at Skibo was steadily filled with signatures representing the good and the great from both sides of the Atlantic. Rudyard Kipling signed his name, as did prime ministers like H.H. Asquith, together with a whole host of bishops, diplomats, scientists and musicians. Many prominent Liberals visited Skibo; since the resignation of Conservative Prime Minister A.J. Balfour, the Liberals had come to power and would retain it for the rest of Carnegie's life. They were now in charge of the glittering prizes of office; ever the opportunist, Carnegie made sure that he was on nodding terms at least with those who held the reins of government.

Among the guests were particular favourites whom Andrew and Louise Carnegie referred to as 'Old Shoes': 'They came when they chose, stayed as long as they wished, went when they pleased and did precisely as they liked. Year after year they occupied the same rooms, which in time seemed to take on the aura of their presence.'[20] Such folk included Uncle George Lauder ('Dean of the Family Old Shoes') and assorted relations from Dunfermline, a few 'locals' like the Revd Robert L. Ritchie, the Gaelic-speaking minister at Bonar Bridge, and a clutch of peers from Sir Henry Hartley Fowler, Viscount Wolverhampton (a Liberal cabinet minister) to the poet and antiquary James Carnegie, 9th Earl of Southesk, all under the 'Old Shoe in Chief' John Morley.

Two of the castle's first guests were Henry Clay Frick and Henry Phipps, bearing a request from the nameless financiers for an extension of the 90-day option on Carnegie Steel. Carnegie said no, and pocketed his share of the option deposit when the option expiry date passed. The deposit almost covered what he had spent to date on Skibo. Later Carnegie would boast that his Scots home was 'just a nice little present from Frick'.[21]

Although often lampooned in the press as a truculent, greedy Highland poseur with his hands in the pockets of the working class, with kilt and glengarry, and dressed in a mixture of tartan and stars and stripes, only once did Carnegie appear in (borrowed) Highland dress. Usually he greeted his guests, golfed, fished, yachted or walked his acres in 'a light grey Norfolk jacket and knickerbockers . . . with a corresponding peaked cap'.[22] Carnegie was easy to lampoon as his Skibo routine was as predictable as Queen Victoria's 'Balmorality'. Like the monarch, he began his day with a piper to waken him, and resounding organ music to carry him to breakfast. While his guests took to the hills to slaughter the wildlife, Carnegie would retire to his study or take solitary walks in the hills. 'The Sunset Walk' was an especial favourite.[23] Even before the initial euphoria over Skibo had worn off, Carnegie was plunged into a disagreeable situation. During his business life Carnegie proved himself a very good judge of men – except in his assessment of Henry Clay Frick. Although Frick had become chairman of Carnegie Steel in 1893, it is important to realise that in no sense was he one of Carnegie's 'boys' – as were Henry Phipps or Charles Schwab – although Carnegie considered him an employee more than a partner. Frick, as the founder of a separate company which always had his first loyalty, considered himself an independent associate of Carnegie.

Frick and Carnegie were very different characters, with totally dissimilar interests. Frick was not concerned with dabbling in politics, and had little interest in intellectual pursuits or in being a social animal, but was a keen collector of rare medieval and Renaissance art; even so, these took third place to his family and business. Ever since Frick had joined the Carnegie board of managers there had been growing friction between them; Frick considered Carnegie's public pronouncements on labour relations, politics and philosophy, and his enmity towards such entities as the Pennsylvania Railroad, to be ludicrous at best and hypocritical at worst. Further he was quickly irritated by Carnegie's 'meddling' memos from abroad. Initial resentment had been sparked off by Carnegie's behaviour during the Frick Coke Co. strike of 1887, wherein Carnegie countermanded Frick's labour policies, and the Homestead strike of 1892, when Carnegie continued to make snide comments in public and private saying that the violence was all Frick's fault. So by 1899–1900 a serious confrontation between them was inevitable, and Carnegie now regarded Frick as a 'malignant force'[24] within the company, who wanted to deconstruct what Carnegie had set up and pollute his business philosophy.

That Frick and Carnegie had been able to serve the same company for so long was due to two main factors: Carnegie admired Frick's managerial skills and Frick respected Carnegie's important financial role in the company. The fact that Carnegie Steel brought in good returns helped keep the peace, for by 1899 the company led the world in steel production. Carnegie's vacillation over whether or not he would sell his share in the business and retire heightened the tension for Frick. As well as the nameless financier's idea, there was also a proposal – thrashed out at Carnegie's New York home between Frick, Phipps, Dod Lauder, Schwab and others, on 5 January 1899 – that the steel company would be 'reorganised and consolidated' with the HC Frick Coke Co. to form a new company (Carnegie Co.) which would buy out Carnegie who would then retire. Carnegie would get $75 million for his interests and Frick $35 million for his Coke Co. Carnegie discussed the matter with cousin Dod, who felt that this way meant Carnegie (and he, Dod) did not get the best deal.

The board accepted the deal, but Carnegie (with Dod's agreement) wanted to wait for a better return. By this time too, Carnegie had found out that the nameless ones included the Moores brothers, William and John, who were ex-bankrupts, and others of public notoriety whom Carnegie abhorred. This added another layer of disaffection between Carnegie and Frick. The ongoing discussion on the deal of 'reorganisation and consolidation' was brought to crisis point by the price that Carnegie Steel was paying Frick's Coke Co. for fuel. In Carnegie's mind he had agreed with Frick that coke would be bought for $1.35 per ton, but by June 1899 Carnegie Steel was being invoiced for as much as $1.75 per ton. At a meeting of the board on 25 October 1899 the matter of the increase was raised. Dod Lauder emphasised the $1.35 deal. Frick denied any such deal done with Carnegie. The matter rested for a while, and then another deal emerged for Carnegie Steel to buy coke acreage from Frick. The board agreed to the deal, but Carnegie made imprudent remarks suggesting that Frick was deliberately making profit from his partners. Frick was outraged.

Carnegie tried to pour oil on the troubled waters by letter but Frick did not respond. Carnegie then raised the $1.35 coke deal again by letter, remarking how 'touchy' Frick was on coke matters and emphasising that in all his dealings with Frick there was no personal animosity. Frick disagreed. The unpleasantness over the coke and coke acreage deals bubbled away and Frick explained his feelings in a memo to the board of managers on 20 November 1899, stating his case succinctly. The board accepted Frick's version, and Carnegie knew he would have to act. Frick had to go. Carnegie approached Frick asking him to resign; he did so on 5 December 1899, his resignation being accepted by the board. However, unpleasant disagreements went on. Tempers flared and legal proceedings were undertaken to disengage partnership agreements. The press and New York financial cadres were agog. An agreement was made for the 'reorganisation and consolidation' deal. This made the new Carnegie Co. into a $350 million consolidation with Carnegie's interest set at $174.5 million and Frick's at $31.284 million. At the final parting of the ways Frick could be declared a nominal victor.[25]

Frick and Carnegie would never meet again, although they lived but a stroll away from each other in New York, and Frick is given scant mention in Carnegie's autobiography. The estranged pair died within months of each other. A part of the Carnegie-Frick legend tells that as Carnegie was reaching his last years he endeavoured to put the past behind him and seek a reconciliation with Frick. To this end he sent a messenger with his sentiments to Frick, whose terse reply was: 'Tell Mr Carnegie I'll meet him in Hell, where we are both going.'[26]

* * *

As the twentieth century dawned the world was on the brink of another explosion of scientific discoveries; the telephone was expanding, with 1,336,000 in the United States, railroads had transformed mass transportation, and the private traveller would be further encouraged to hit the open road by the Old Company of Detroit beginning the first mass production of automobiles. On 5 February 1900 the United States and Great Britain signed the first Hay–Pauncefote Treaty, giving America the right to construct a canal across the Isthmus of Panama. On 14 March

1900 US Congress passed the Currency Act, placing US dollars on a parity with gold, and on 6 November President McKinley and his Vice-President Theodore Roosevelt defeated Democrat William Jennings Bryan in the elections. With their return to the White House big business seemed secure. (In the event, six months after the inauguration McKinley was fatally shot by an anarchist at the Pan-American Exposition at Buffalo.)

All these 'explosions' of inventiveness would have thrilled the younger Carnegie; but although he would never tire of reviewing Anglo-American affairs and the international situation, he was now convinced that he wanted to escape the everyday cut and thrust of business. A life of philanthropy beckoned for Carnegie, but two obstacles remained in his path. Apart from men like the nameless financiers of a few months previously, who would buy his interests? Furthermore, although his reason was ready to quit, his emotions would not be as easy to salve. On 12 December 1900 Charles Schwab, president of Carnegie Steel, was honoured by a special dinner for some eighty leading businessmen and financiers at the New York University Club. Beside Schwab at the dinner sat J. Pierpont Morgan. In due course Schwab rose and addressed the diners with a discourse on how the steel industry could be run in the future as a 'supertrust', with each steelmaker carrying out interlocking processes. What he had to say was nothing original and it is obvious with hindsight that Schwab was aiming his words at the financier; Morgan duly took the bait and a meeting was arranged to discuss how to proceed.

Consensus of opinion agrees that Schwab and Morgan met without Carnegie's knowledge, and Morgan indicated that he would be willing to buy out Carnegie. How could Schwab arrange such a deal? He consulted Louise Carnegie, who was keen for her husband to retire from business so that he could give all his energies to his family and his philanthropy. She suggested that Schwab should play golf with Carnegie and broach the subject then.

The golf match took place at St Andrews Club, by Yonkers, New York, and Schwab was diplomatic enough to let Carnegie win. Over lunch Schwab told Carnegie of his meeting with Morgan. It was clear, noted Schwab, that Morgan would pay any figure Carnegie cared to put on his holding in Carnegie Steel, but Carnegie showed no real enthusiasm for a deal. His reason, bolstered by his age and his wish to pursue philanthropy, wanted him to sell up, yet his emotions, linked to his childhood of poverty, made him reluctant to loosen his grip on what he had achieved. He needed 24 hours to think. The following morning he took a sheet of paper and set out in pencil the figure he was willing to sell out for. He detailed it carefully:

Capitalisation for Carnegie Company;
$160m bonds to be exchanged at par
for bonds in new company. $160,000,000
$160m stock to be exchanged at rate of
$1000 share of stock in Carnegie Co.
exchanged for $1500 share of new
stock in new company: $240,000,000
Profit of past year and estimated
profit for coming year: $80,000,000

TOTAL PRICE FOR CARNEGIE COMPANY AND ITS HOLDINGS:
$480,000,000.[27]

This represented £260 million in sterling, and around £5–6 billion in modern currency.

These figures he handed to Charles Schwab for transmission to J. Pierpont Morgan. At his office at 23 Wall Street, Morgan quickly reviewed Carnegie's figures and said: 'I accept the price.' It was the most remarkable sale ever in the history of US finance; figures on a scrap of paper, no haggling, no browbeating. To clinch the deal Morgan invited Carnegie to visit him at his house; but no, Carnegie would see Morgan at *his* home. They met and conversed for about fifteen minutes and as they shook hands on the deal Morgan is reported to have said to Carnegie: 'Mr Carnegie, I want to congratulate you on being the richest man in the world.'[28]

EIGHTEEN

A RICH RECTOR OF ST ANDREWS

Thine own reproach alone dost fear.
Inscription for an Altar of Independence, Robert Burns,
1795

Soon after his retirement from 'active business', Andrew Carnegie turned his thoughts to writing his autobiography. For some time his friends and family had been encouraging him to do so and thus commit his reflections to print. Other matters pressing on his time meant that he could only address his autobiographical writing when at leisure at the bungalow at Auchnagar. The writing proceeded, off and on, until Germany's violation of Belgian neutrality caused the First World War to break out on 4 August 1914. Thereafter all writing ceased; as Louise Carnegie noted: 'Henceforth he was never able to interest himself in private affairs.'[1] But back in 1901 there was much to do.

This was the year Carnegie set up the Home Trust Company at Hoboken, New Jersey, to house $300 million of bonds which he realised from the sale of his company. This private bank would handle his financial interests and become executors of his estate, all in the day-to-day care, since 1883, of his financial secretary Robert Franks. The bank also supervised his major future endowments.

One of his first financial provisions was the setting up of a fund worth $4 million, to pay out retirement, injury and destitute family pensions for Carnegie Steel workers; this was called the Carnegie Relief Fund.[2] Another $4.25 million was allocated for pensions and annuities for many of Carnegie's one-time associates and subordinates, including several who had been with him from the early days when he was Superintendent of the Western Division of the Pennsylvania Railroad. His list of worthies included relations and friends as well as Dunfermline acquaintances. Carnegie anecdotes also reveal that he once paid the mortgage of a Dunfermline woman, because she looked like his mother. As time passed a list of 409 recipients was drawn up, who received sums ranging from $300 to $10,000 a year. The Home Trust Company also administered a fund of $6.78 million to pay annuities to forty-five parties designated in his will. Carnegie's aim was to help those who faced daily anxiety about cash flow, just as his own family had suffered in his Dunfermline childhood and in the early days at Allegheny.

Public announcements about the opening of Carnegie's purse brought mailbags full of begging letters for disbursements of all kinds. His friend, writer Samuel Langhorne Clemens (better known as Mark Twain), sent him a humorous 'begging letter':

> You seem to be prosperous these days. Could you lend an admirer a dollar and a half to buy a hymn-book with? God will bless you if you do; I feel it, I know it. So will I. If there should be other applications this one not to count. . . . P.S. Don't send the hymn-book, send the money. I want to make the selection myself. [3]

Mark Twain dubbed Carnegie 'Saint Andrew', but Carnegie took seriously the question of just how he was to spend his money. He received suggestions from all quarters. The UK company Mother Seigel's Syrup promoted a competition with the theme 'How Mr Carnegie Should Get Rid of His Wealth'. Each suggestion – if taken up by Carnegie – would win a sovereign (£1); some 45,000 entries were received. By far the majority plumped for money for themselves, while only 237 altruistically suggested that the money should be used to pay off the British National Debt. [4]

Already Carnegie's investment of $2 million was in place for

Carnegie Hall, New York (opened 1891), the Carnegie Institute (Library and Music Hall, 1895) and the Carnegie Library at Pittsburgh (1895). Carnegie Free Public Libraries were to be a cornerstone of his philanthropy and he sponsored over 2,500 in the United States, the United Kingdom and the Commonwealth, at a total cost of $56 million.[5] By 1900 a foundation was set up to sponsor technical schools at Pittsburgh, which would develop into the Carnegie Institute of Technology (1912) and the Carnegie-Mellon University in 1967.[6] But first, before the purse opened wider, there would be a period of rest.

For some time Louise was busy with the new house at No. 2 East 91st Street to the point of exhaustion, interviewing architects, making plans with decorators and assessing furniture catalogues. More than this, she was upset by the press attention following the sale of the Carnegie Company. Personal publicity was anathema to her and gave her much emotional stress. So on 16 March 1901 the Carnegies left the city aboard the German liner *Kaiseren Theresa* to spend six weeks at Antibes on the French Riviera and at the spa of Aix-en-Provence, Bouches-du-Rhône. Importantly too, Carnegie was fleeing from reporters desperate to interview the world's 'richest man'. Slowly Louise began to relax as she realised that her lifelong rivalry with Carnegie's business career was at an end. She had never liked Carnegie's commercial life or his pursuit of wealth. Their childhoods had been very different, but now wealth would bring them together in several joint ventures.

From the summer of 1901 to the summer of 1902 the Carnegies set about alterations at Skibo with a will, damming rivers to make lochs and pools, creating a nine-hole golf course, and building barns, coach houses, a workshop and workers' cottages. By persuading the Duke of Sutherland to sell him some land, Carnegie now had the waterfall he had long wanted, and he diligently set about improving his golf. To this end he later employed John Henry Taylor, the first English golf professional to win the Open (1894), but his plan was thwarted when he developed the golfer's condition known as bad-loser-itis.

Carnegie often mentioned to guests what a delight it was for him to have peaches, apricots and figs from his own walled garden and to have the house full of flowers from the terraced garden (constructed by Thomas Mawson in 1904); he also enjoyed refreshing walks in the woodland gardens which he refurbished with new specimens. The estate's new buildings included the dairy and dairy house, the electricity house, the coach house and the principal gate lodge designed by Ross & Macbeth in 1900. Further from the castle lay the summer house, the ice house, the boatshed and the kennels. At one time Carnegie had his own (now demolished) pier for his yacht *Sea-breeze*.[7]

Each day brought new ideas and ventures inside and out of Skibo which was now firmly stamped with Carnegie's seal. Even the new stained glass for the castle illustrated not only the history of the place but Carnegie's story too, with coloured glass showing the cottage at Moodie Street, Dunfermline, and the ship *Wiscasset* in which they had gone to America. At Skibo Carnegie would charge his batteries for at least five months of the year to find the strength to tackle his new philanthropic ventures.

On 22 January 1901 Queen Victoria died at Osborne House on the Isle of Wight, aged 82; she had given her name, image and values to most of the past century and was now succeeded by her 59-year-old son as Edward VII. Skibo now reflected the style of the new Edwardian society without the decadence of certain aspects of the king's new court. But the pacifist Carnegie was still saddened by the ongoing Second Boer War, which would drag on until the Peace of Vereeniging, signed on 31 May 1902. Carnegie's old friend Herbert Spencer had suggested that Carnegie should give money to assist the 'widows and orphans of [the Boers] who have been killed'. Carnegie for once showed some political maturity and thought it best not to interfere, lest his actions be 'resented' and thought 'impertinent'.[8]

On their way back from their French holiday the Carnegies had called in at London as usual and Carnegie met up with J.

Pierpont Morgan. They dined at Henry C. Boyes's newly designed Grocer's Hall in Princes Street, where the members of the London Chamber of Commerce were honouring their New York counterparts. Carnegie was ebullient, full of his latest philanthropic scheme.

For many decades in the nineteenth century in particular, Scotland's upper-middle class and the aristocracy had looked to England for the best further education for their children and had sent them to university mainly at Oxford and Cambridge. Consequently, as far as recruitment and funding were concerned, the four Scottish universities of St Andrews (1411), Glasgow (1451), Aberdeen (1495) and Edinburgh (1583) were neglected. This problem was not solved by the constitutional reforms of the Universities (Scotland) Act of 1889. In the December 1900 issue of the influential and respected *Fortnightly Review* (1865) was an article on 'The Scotland University Crisis', which pointed out the great need for funds to modernise the campuses and offered this warning: '[The universities] may drag on for many years of inglorious life, giving second-rate degrees to second-rate students. But they will have lost their place in British education and the national life of Scotland.'

A supporter of this point of view, and a strong advocate for better funding, was the lawyer and politician Thomas Shaw (later 1st Baron Craigmyle), erstwhile Solicitor-General for Scotland and Liberal MP for Hawick District. A Dunfermline lad like Carnegie, Shaw had written an essay on the subject of Scottish education in the January 1897 issue of the *Nineteenth Century* magazine, which Carnegie had read with interest. When the subject came up again in 1901 Carnegie acted. 'How much money do you need?' he asked Shaw. 'Five million dollars,' came the prompt reply.[9] Carnegie offered the amount in US Steel Bonds, but an underestimation soon had this offer doubled.

'The way of the philanthropist is hard,' Carnegie would say ruefully in 1913 and so would be the road to his new target of university bequests. Once he had made his intentions clear the critics soon began attacking Carnegie. *Blackwood's Magazine* was among those who voiced dissent. This was more Carnegie interference in the British way of life, they ventured, while others saw Carnegie's apparent generosity as the thin end of the wedge that would lead to Carnegie interfering in the university curricula. They had a point. In the *New York Tribune* of 13 April 1890 Carnegie had sneered at the classical education of the time afforded by the Scots universities; he favoured an education based on science and technology in accordance with his article's focus, 'How to Win Fortune'. The theme of Carnegie as the corrupter of British education was now taken up by his opponents.

Although somewhat startled by the vociferousness of his critics, Carnegie was not put off his basic funding idea. He reflected on how science and the classics could be balanced in education – a proposal discussed with such men as John Morley. To further his aim he consulted Alexander Hugh Bruce, 6th Baron Balfour of Burleigh, the Conservative Secretary of State for Scotland, Victor Alexander Bruce, 9th Earl of Elgin, and soon to be the Conservative Prime Minister, and First Lord of the Treasury Arthur James Balfour. The consensus of their advice was that equal funding for scientific research and student tuition assistance would be best. Balfour in particular emphasised the vital importance of funds for scientific discovery; this would certainly influence Carnegie's later donations.[10]

Towards this end Carnegie founded the Carnegie Trust for the Universities of Scotland which would prove the most controversial of his endowments. This Trust, the first to use his name after 1900, had a threefold intent, as laid down in the Trust Deed of 1901:

To improve and expand the Scottish universities.

To help pay tuition for 'deserving and qualified' students of Scottish birth or extraction.

To provide research and allied grants, and extend the opportunities for scientific study.

The initial endowment was $10 million in 5 per cent bonds of the US Steel Corporation, which in the first two years provided around £100,000 of funding.[11] Lord Balfour of Burleigh was the Trust's first chairman. To help mollify his critics, who still believed he was 'interfering' in the British way of education, Carnegie (reluctantly) had written into the Trust Deed that all regulations could be altered by a two-thirds vote of the trustees. From 1901 too, Carnegie invited the principals of the four Scottish univeristies to Skibo, and thereafter the first week of September at Skibo was known as 'Principals Week', to which wives and daughters were also invited.[12] The 'week' provided a forum for the principals to discuss matters of common interest in an informal way, with Carnegie interlarding his ideas.

Carnegie said that one of the most important events of his life was his 'election to the Lord Rectorship of St Andrews [University]'.[13] St Andrews had been a seat of learning since the days of the tenth-century Celtic-speaking clergy known as the Culdees, and teaching (for service within the administration of the medieval church) was continued by the Augustinian Canons whose priory abutted the cathedral of St Andrews from the twelfth century. The need for establishing a base for advanced education was satisfied when diocesan Bishop Henry Wardlaw – supported by King James I of Scotland, then a prisoner in England – established the *Studium Generale Universitatis* at St Andrews on 11 May 1410. The bishop chartered the new 'university' on 28 February 1412, an act formalised within Christendom by the six papal *bullae* of Peter de Luna, Cardinal of St Mary in Cosmedia, who ruled as Antipope Benedict XIII.[14]

In the fifteenth century there was little distinction between professors and students, but the head of the society of academics was called the Rector, being elected to the position by the *Comitia*, the general congregation of university members. The first Rector of St Andrews University was the theologian and philosopher Laurence of Lindores, Inquisitor of Heretical Pravity in Scotland. In the early years the Rector's role was to preside over the university's constituent parts, supervising its order and discipline and assisting students in their commitments to the university, and he was also the vital link between town and gown. The role of the Rector varied little until 1858 when the position no longer represented the 'corporate identity' of the university. By 1862 a certain political flavour had entered the election of Rector and this persisted until 1892. Carnegie followed a long line of distinguished men, some of whom, like John-Patrick Crichton-Stuart, 3rd Marquess of Bute, were generous benefactors to the university. From 1885 the Rector paid heed to the Students' Representative Council.[15] (Today the Rector is a public figure elected for three years by the students; he or she represents them at the University Court and gives a rectorial address at his or her inauguration.)

Carnegie became Rector of St Andrews University by the unanimous decision of the students at University College, Dundee (an adjunct of the University of St Andrews) and St Andrews itself. One year later, according to tradition, in October 1902 the academic body gathered in the Volunteer Hall at St Andrews (the Younger Graduation Hall was not opened until 1929) to install Carnegie as Rector, with Principal James Donaldson presiding; the town was represented by Provost James Welch. Carnegie was euphoric; from the moment when he and Louise had been greeted at St Andrews railway station by students – who themselves pulled his carriage to Donaldson's residence on The Scores – Carnegie was on an emotional high. Here he was the successor of great men like John Stuart Mill and James Anthony Froude, as well as his friend A.J. Balfour, enjoying the torchlight procession, the student mummery and lauded with pomp and ceremony to his greatest honour yet. Not bad for a poor, untutored boy from Dunfermline.

The installation ceremony was redolent with student humour; as with past Rectors, students had researched Carnegie's weaknesses to lampoon and mock him. The classicists made much of his 'hostility to dead languages'. When

Donaldson administered the Rectorial Oath in Latin, a Scots voice rang out: 'Oh, Jamie, why don't ye tell Andra what ye're saying?' Carnegie simply beamed. And when he was required to reply in Latin with the word *Juro* (I swear), the students raised the roof with cheers and laughter. Carnegie's Rectorial Address was likewise interrupted, but he did not rise to angry ripost. He had spent a great deal of time on his address. The first draft was extremely autobiographical; he explained why he had abjured organised religion, particularly the beliefs of Channing and Swedenborg favoured by members of his family, and noted how his father had rejected the Reformed (Presbyterian) Kirk. He proposed an alternative religious philosophy to replace Christianity, which reflected the thoughts of Spencer and Darwin. Science, insisted Carnegie, would explain the secrets of the universe. He prepared to exhort his youthful audience to value and promote their lives and careers on earth and not to be in any way concerned with the possibility of an afterlife.[16] Carnegie submitted his first draft of the address under the title 'A Confession of Religious Faith' to Donaldson, who advised that what he had to say did not fit either with the spirit of the age in Scotland, or with the establishment. Carnegie returned to his desk to pen a more 'modern' text. This time he called his address 'The Industrial Ascendancy of the World'; emphasising the rise of industrial America, he suggested how Europe should respond, and laid particular stress on the relationship between America and Britain. Carnegie still believed that Britain's destiny was tied up with America's fortunes.[17] The address went down well and Carnegie could not resist giving the students a piece of advice from his literary hero Robert Burns; in June 1795 Robert Burns had written these lines to financier Patrick Heron of Heron:

> Thou of an independent mind . . .
> Thine own reproach alone dost fear.

Carnegie was Rector of St Andrews until 1907, as the students re-elected him in 1904. Some of the students, unhappy at the prospect of another unopposed re-election, wrote to Scottish man of letters Andrew Lang, inviting him to stand. A graduate and erstwhile lecturer at the university, Lang agreed but then withdrew his nomination when he realised that he was the candidate of a 'rump' and was likely to lose however sportingly he might enter the fray. Carnegie's thoughts on being opposed are unrecorded.

During his Rectorship Carnegie became the university's last great independent benefactor. In 1904 he presented a park to the university, the same year that a Women's Union was established by Louise Carnegie. The next year Carnegie donated a gymnasium and physical education equipment – until then there had been only a 'makeshift arrangement in the college cloisters'.[18] During 1907–9 an extension of the University Library was funded by Carnegie with a gift of £10,000 (later increased to £12,000). Carnegie's gifts to the university also included an organ for the University Chapel. (During 1912–14 Carnegie was elected Rector of the University of Aberdeen, but he bequeathed very little to that university.)

Principal Donaldson held his position throughout the whole of Carnegie's Rectorship – indeed, his Principalship actually lasted 29 years – and there were those who voiced the opinion that Donaldson had 'conned' money out of Carnegie. One such was Douglas Young, polymath and poet, erstwhile lecturer at Dundee and St Andrews, and Professor of Greek at McMaster University, in Hamilton, Ontario, and in North Carolina.

Referring to the 'fine sports park' that Carnegie donated to St Andrews University in 1904, Young asserts that Donaldson 'pulled a fast one'. The land which was 'bought' for the university by Carnegie, the university itself had owned since before 1747.[19] Carnegie had jibbed at the price he had to pay for the land, and Donaldson pointed out that rich jute barons from Dundee were buying land around St Andrews for villas, forcing up the price of land. Carnegie also wrote a cheque for the construction of a modern 'indoor swimming-pool for students'. However, Sir Peter Scott-Lang, Regius Professor of Maths, 'insisted on spending the money on an armoury for the cadet corps'.[20] In due course Carnegie wanted to see the swimming pool he had paid for, and Donaldson took him to the armoury door; fortunately for Donaldson, said Young, Coutts the janitor had 'mislaid' the key and Carnegie was guided 'off to tea at the University Hall'.[21] In their volume on past Rectors of the university, students Greg Twiss and Paul Chennell doubted the whole truth of such playing fields and swimming pool stories.[22] Nevertheless, Donaldson knew that the land was held in trust and had to be exchanged for money. The university received the money and the students got their park, but Douglas Young was not the only one who considered Donaldson a culprit of 'academic roguery' and the stories still persist that Carnegie was duped.

One academic duty that gave Carnegie particular delight is mentioned in his autobiography, with Professor Donaldson cited as its instigator.[23] The Dean of Radcliff College, Harvard University, was Miss Agnes Irwin, who happened to be the great-granddaughter of American statesman and scientist Benjamin Franklin. Franklin had been awarded the degree of LLD *in absentia* in 1759 from St Andrews and when he visited the town later the same year he was received with great honour. As a part of the university's celebration of Franklin's bi-centenary in 1906 the Senate agreed to confer the degree of LLD on Miss Irwin in recognition of Franklin's connection with the university. As Rector, Carnegie conferred the degree on Miss Irwin at the American Philosophical Society in Philadelphia in April 1906.

Despite the euphoria created for Carnegie by the Rectorship, 1901 brought him a severe blow. At the age of 87 his beloved uncle George Lauder died just before Christmas. Both his mother and Uncle George had been emotional crutches for Carnegie since his childhood. He wrote to John Morley: 'I feel so lonely. . . . The intense interest he took in all my doings gave me satisfaction. . . .'[24] He also conveyed his grief to his bereaved cousin Dod:

I am stunned and somehow protected from severe shocks, except every now and then one comes that seems almost to stop the heart.

What this loss is to you and to me no one knows but ourselves; they cannot know. I don't believe there ever was so sweet, so fond and attachment on earth, as between us three men – the Teacher and his pupils.

But I can't write about it; I must quit.

It is so saddening. What on earth will Scotland be to me now? He was Scotland.

Well, I must bite my lips and say nothing. This life, so delightful to us when it touches the precious relationship, is, apart from these sweet touches of affection, a fearful mockery; but good night. Do write a few lines and tell me how you are. This blow doesn't draw us closer – nothing could do that; but it does send the thoughts more to you.[25]

Carnegie sank his grief into his philanthropic plans. Education was very much uppermost in his mind, but he still had a hankering to support medical research. Towards this end he gave $50,000 to the Polish-born French physicist Marie Curie, who, with her husband Pierre, would be awarded the Nobel Prize for Physics in 1903. To the German physician and pioneer bacteriologist Robert Koch, a former Director of the Berlin Institute for Infectious Diseases, he gave $120,000; Koch was also awarded a Nobel Prize in 1905 for physiology and medicine.

Carnegie had created more millionaires than any other businessman with the sale of Carnegie Steel. But what people like Charles Schwab did with their money both angered and dismayed Carnegie. Palatial mansions, gambling, stupendous largesse – it was all monitored by Carnegie. True, what they did with their money was none of his business, but he took it personally, after all he had made them rich; an inveterate 'interferer', Carnegie would clearly have liked to run their lives for them too.

Charles Schwab's declining health caused his resignation as the President of US Steel in 1903: this was bad enough in Carnegie's eyes, but the fall in US Steel stock angered him in case his bonds were devalued and thus blighted his philanthropic plans. His mind was also troubled by the loss of old friends and mentors; Herbert Spencer died on 8 December 1903. But Skibo regularly refreshed him, as did cruises round the Scottish coast in *Sea-breeze*, motoring trips to various parts of the Highlands and the 'simple, happy family life' at Achinduich, a small shooting lodge on Skibo estate with its views of the River Shin.

Honours were coming to him thick and fast; two examples serve to give a flavour. At a 'great gathering' at the City Hall, Perth, on 8 October 1902 the Freedom of the City and Royal Burgh was conferred on Carnegie. For once the warmth and enthusiasm of the reception proved too much for Carnegie and drove 'everything he intended to say . . . from his head'. His shortened acceptance speech was greeted with much applause and cheers. Carnegie became the nineteenth Freeman of Perth since 1833.[26] In the same year Carnegie was made an 'Honorary Master of the Bonnetmaker Craft of Dundee', one of the famous Nine Incorporated Trades of the City, and whose 'Seal of Cause' dates from 1496. A new seal was designed for the Craft and used for the first time on Carnegie's certificate. He donated to the Bonnetmakers a $1,000 gold bond.[27] All such academic, civic and cultural honours pleased him, but one 'honour' was given pride of place in his mind ever after.

On an afternoon in October 1902 a Dornoch telegram boy hastened up the drive of Skibo with an urgent message from Dunrobin Castle, the home of the Duke of Sutherland, 15 miles away. A guest at Dunrobin, King Edward VII, was now on his way to Skibo for an unscheduled visit. After his delayed coronation on 9 August 1902, King Edward was setting about refurbishing Buckingham Palace, which at the time of Queen Victoria's death was something of a mausoleum dedicated to the memory of the late Queen's husband Prince Albert. The King was keen to brighten up the palace and rid it of its atmosphere of funereal gloom; having heard of Carnegie's work at Skibo he wanted to review the modern embellishments. Awakened from his afternoon nap, Carnegie had hardly time to put on his Norfolk jacket before the King's new Daimler appeared at Skibo's *porte cochère*. Somewhat tousled, Carnegie greeted His Majesty, who was delighted to be piped indoors, to stand in the hallway while a flustered organist (who had just emerged from the swimming pool) played the national anthem.[28]

The King took tea, inspected the house and in the billiard room was attracted by a curious sketch. Carnegie had been intrigued in 1898 by a *New York Journal* report of a dinosaur skeleton recently discovered in Wyoming. He had directed the curator of the Carnegie Museum at Pittsburgh to buy it for $10,000 – the sketch the King saw was of this new exhibit, *diplodocus carnegiei*. This was to lead to a further museum collection of dinosaur bones. Edward VII was so impressed by it that he urged Carnegie to have a reproduction placed in the British Museum. This was done, and further publicity led to reproductions being presented to several European capitals. Other bones were named in honour of Louise Carnegie as *Apatosaurus louisae*.[29]

As the royal visit was coming to a close, the King encountered 5-year-old Margaret Carnegie. Years later she recalled the incident:

I had been naughty, and as usual on such occasions, after Mother had talked to me, I was sitting alone in her upstairs sitting room to think matters over until I was ready to say I was sorry. Mother never hurried me, but this time she had hardly left the room until she was back . . . the next thing I knew, I was in the garden picking roses with Nana [Nannie Lockerbie]. She explained that the King was coming that afternoon and that the roses we were picking were for him to take back to the Queen. Then freshly dressed, I was standing . . . in the drawing room with the flowers. A tall bearded man was bending over and asking if I would give him a kiss. I never liked to kiss bearded faces. They had sloppy wet lips, but this face was very different. This man knew how to kiss little girls. I gave the roses to him for the

Queen, and a rosebud, 'for your ownself', which he put in his buttonhole.[30]

A curious tale about the royal visit to Skibo is recounted by author Anthony Allfrey. Carnegie read to the King a poem that had been written to mark his birthday. The poem commenced with certain addresses to various monarchs and to President Theodore Roosevelt. The invocations included the words 'Hail fat Edward' – 'that's you, Sir' was Carnegie's thoughtful aside.[31] Happily this comment did not have any lasting repercussions on Carnegie's reputation in royal circles. Years later the King, in conversation with John Morley, suggested that Carnegie might be honoured with a British title – but as there was no doubt in the monarch's mind that Carnegie was not British, could Morley broach the subject with him?

Carnegie's reply was succinct: 'I could take no title; but tell His Majesty if he wrote me an autograph note expressing his appreciation of what I had done for my native land I should appreciate it highly, and so should those who came after me.' The reply was pure Carnegie, the independent man who liked to write his own praise. Carnegie said he prized the monarch's subsequent letter 'more than a dukedom'.[32] He savoured every word and punctuation mark:

Windsor Castle, November 1908

DEAR MR CARNEGIE:

I have for some time past been anxious to express to you my sense of your generosity for the great public objects which you have presented to this country, the land of your birth.

Scarcely less admirable than the gifts themselves is the great care and thought you have taken in guarding against their misuse.

I am anxious to tell you how warmly I recognize your most generous benefactions and the great services they are likely to confer upon the country.

As a mark of recognition, I hope you will accept the portrait of myself which I am sending you.

Believe me, dear Mr Carnegie,

Sincerely yours
EDWARD R & I[33]

And so pride of place was given to the autographed photograph of a man the child Carnegie would gladly have assassinated.

Andrew Carnegie was a keen collector of modern gadgets and in her journals daughter Margaret listed some of the family favourites. These included the long-distance telegraph, the new electric car (which went 'fast up the hills in Central Park'), and the 'Victor Talking Machine', an early phonograph which played, *inter alia*, Carnegie's favourite ditties by Scots comical singer Harry Lauder, including his famous 'Roamin' in the Gloamin'. In his own autobiography Lauder recalled an incident concerning Carnegie. During one of Lauder's successful American music hall tours Carnegie had visited him in his dressing room in New York. The conversation got round to their respective heights. Both were of small stature – was Carnegie taller? Carnegie wagered that if he *was* the taller he would give Lauder 'a good tip' for the stock exchange. Lauder accepted the wager and Carnegie was duly found to be a tenth of an inch taller. The tip was for United Steel Co. shares, on which Lauder did make a profit. He added: '[Carnegie] was astonished and delighted to meet a man smaller than himself . . .'[34]

During 1902–7 Carnegie set in place a series of important endowments. In 1902 came a first payment of $10 million to found the Carnegie Institute in Washington. He had originally hoped to found an American National University at Washington, but as this was subsequently proved to be impractical he set up a fund to nurture pioneer research in extant universities with a special emphasis on 'physical and biological sciences'. The year 1903 saw the founding of the Carnegie Dunfermline Trust and 1905 the Carnegie

Foundation for the Advancement of Teaching, bent on supporting the status of teachers in higher education by sponsoring a retirement pension fund.

As his philanthropic endeavours expanded Carnegie became more and more taken up with a new mission. When the Carnegies retreated to their stone cottage, Achinduich, on the huge moorland by the River Shin from 22 July to 10 August – so that Louise had some respite from the hectic social life at Skibo – Carnegie had time to relax and develop his plans. He was disturbed by international events; from Finland to Romania, and from the Philippines to Spain, there was rioting, unrest and disaffection. The hint of war already in the air was brought to fruition when without warning Japanese torpedo boats made a night attack on Russian ships near the naval base at Port Arthur, Manchuria. On 8 February 1904 the Russo–Japanese War began. Carnegie backed Russia to win, but he was wrong; the Russian Fleet of Admiral Rozhdestvensky was soundly defeated by the Imperial Japanese Fleet (of British-built battleships and cruisers) under Admiral Heihachiro Togo at the naval battle of Tsushima on 27 May 1905. The West was alerted to the military strength of Japan, already victorious over the crumbling empire of China in the Sino–Japanese War of 1894–5, and the world was now a less stable place. Carnegie would attempt to use his millions to seek world peace.

NINETEEN

PATHWAY TO PEACE: DESCENT TO WAR

Pity the poor millionaire, for the way of the philanthropist is hard.

Carnegie remark, 1913

On 8 April 1904 Great Britain and France established their *entente cordiale*, and as these traditional enemies moved closer together (and away from Germany) Carnegie began in earnest his grand mission to combine his philanthropy with an endeavour to secure peace between nations. For him nothing was impossible; from China to Canada his endowments had made him the most famous man in the world. His studies were full of the various nations' highest honours; his mother would have wept with pride to see his decoration of Knight Commander of the Legion of Honour of France, the Grand Cross Order of Orange-Nassau from the Netherlands and his Grand Cross Order of Danebrog from Denmark. Now he threw himself into his new mission with an energy described as 'preter-human'. His new road, though, was to be the rockiest he had ever tackled. For, alas, the Second Peace Conference, due to take place in October 1904 at the Hague, at the instigation of Theodore Roosevelt, had to be cancelled because of the outbreak of the Russo–Japanese War. But Carnegie was not deflected from his goal; he considered that everything and everyone had a price and he believed that peace could be bought. He set about its purchase in his own inimitable way, setting himself up as an unofficial 'US Secretary for Peace'. His pursuit of peace would become a mania.

Between 1904 and 1914 Carnegie established five major

international funds under the umbrella of the 'Carnegie Peace Foundations and Buildings'. His first foundation was the Carnegie Hero Fund Commission of 1904 with an endowment of $5 million and a remit 'To honour civilians who risk their lives saving or attempting to save the lives of other persons, and to provide financial assistance to disabled heroes and to the dependants of heroes who lose their lives in the performance of the rescue acts'.[1] In 1908 this was extended to Britain as the Carnegie Hero Fund Trust with an initial endowment of £250,000. The new intent was 'To place those following peaceful vocations, who have been injured in heroic effort to save human life, in somewhat better positions pecuniarily than before, until again able to work; in case of death, the widow and children to be provided for'.[2] In all there would be eleven such funds set up internationally during the period 1904–11 with a total endowment of $10.54 million.

The most curious peace fund came in 1906 within the Simplified Spelling Board. Scholar Brander Matthews of Columbia University interested Carnegie in simplifying English language spelling. He personally contributed $170,000 and the Carnegie Corporation $110,000.[3] This was Carnegie's move towards a 'common language' based on English for the world's major powers to use and thereby pursue peace. The spelling idea (lov–love, violens–violence, for instance) was much ridiculed. Newspaper columnists had great pleasure laughing at Carnegie's 'Karnaghefide' literary pretensions; one writer, Wallace Irwin, lampooned him:

> Grate Scot! I kannot spel the wordz
> That sizzle 'neath my brow
> Sins A. Karnaygy spoyled the rulz
> We ust to hav in gramer skule.

But Carnegie continued to fund the project until 1917, and incorporated the simplified spelling (when he remembered) in his own correspondence and business documents.[4]

By 1910 the Carnegie Endowment for International Peace

was established with a funding of $10 million. It resolved 'To hasten the abolition of international war, the foulest blot upon our civilisation . . . and when war is discarded . . . the Trustees will pleas [*sic*] then consider what is the next most degrading evil or evils whose banishment . . . would most advance the progress, elevation and happiness of man.'[5]

Carnegie gave time too, to setting up 'peace palaces' which would try to encourage a dialogue for international peace and justice. These took the form of the International Court of Justice at the Hague (1903; dedicated 1913, endowment $1.5 million; the Pan American Union Building 1907, dedicated 1910, gifts $850,000); and the Central American Court of Justice (1908 and reconstructed 1910, gifts $200,000). Then in 1914 came what some thought the strangest of all: the Church Peace Union (by 1961 this had become the Council on Religion and International Affairs). Here was the agnostic Carnegie trying to drum up the religious, 'to promote peace, through the rallying of men of all religions to supplant war by justice and international brotherhood'.[6] This sentiment had more to do with inspiration from Carnegie's hero Robert Burns than with a genuine belief in the usefulness of clergymen; after all, in 1795 Burns had sounded the psalmody of radicalism, which became a favourite Carnegie quotation:

> Then let us pray that come it may
> (As come it will for a' that),
> That Sense and Worth o'er a' the earth,
> Shall bear the gree [*have priority*] an a' that.
> For a'that, and a'that
> That man to man, the world o'er
> Shall brithers be for a' that.

In setting up these funds and institutions Carnegie met, interviewed, charmed, annoyed, encouraged, flattered, bored and inspired a whole range of international politicians, clergymen, editors and academics to join his cause. Leaders were bombarded with his letters and telegrams and he targeted people like British Foreign Secretary Sir Edward Grey and US Secretary Elihu Root, yet all the while he also pursued his educational and library endowments. He was continually worried about the international situation. Violence was escalating in the Russia of Tsar Nicholas II; Kaiser Wilhelm II of Germany supported Moroccan independence against France for military advantage; in Japan the young Chinese revolutionary Sun Yat-sen was forming a union of secret societies to try to bring down the creaking Manchu regime in China; and in Crete those dedicated to the island's union with Greece were defying the pro-Ottoman Great Powers who supported the status quo. All this happened within the first months of 1905 and as Carnegie saw it the world was moving inexorably towards international war. He thus strove to make himself a leader of the peace movement and he chose to do it at St Andrews.

On 17 October 1905 he delivered to the students of St Andrews University a Rectorial Address under the title 'A League of Peace'. Although some historians have suggested that Carnegie was the first to make a call for an international League of Peace, such men as the Liberal statesman Sir Henry Campbell-Bannerman, soon to be British Prime Minister, had used the term in recent years. Carnegie faced the students in sermonial mood.

'My young constituents,' he began, 'you are busily preparing to play your parts in the drama of life, resolved, I trust, to oppose and attack what is evil, to defend and strengthen what is good, to leave part of the world a little better than you found it.'[7] He thereafter defined war as the greatest threat to their lives, quoting Jean-Jacques Rousseau's phrase: 'War is the foulest fiend ever vomited forth from the mouth of Hell.'[8] Warming to his theme, his quotes from Euripides to Thucydides tumbled thick and fast. He reviewed the need for more arbitration in international disputes and proposed a 'League of Peace' to ensure that 'no nation should go to war'.[9] And finally he urged the students of St Andrews 'to adopt [President George] Washington's words as your own, "My first wish is to see this plague of mankind, war, banished from the earth"'.[10] And he encouraged 'the women students of St Andrews' to voice their opposition to war too, so that all should 'hit accursed war hard'.[11]

It was an impassioned speech that would reverberate around the world. In the United States the International Union sold thousands of copies at $5 per hundred and the speech was translated into thirteen languages. Carnegie followed it with a multitude of articles on the anti-war theme. There were dissenting voices at Carnegie's latest 'interference'. One was his old friend Theodore Roosevelt; he believed that businessmen like Carnegie should stick to commercial affairs and not push their noses into 'matters of war and peace'.[12] Undeterred, Carnegie never failed to offer Roosevelt his opinions, and in 1907 became president of the New York Peace Society, using its members such as Hamilton Holt, editor of the *Independent*, as intermediaries for his views.

One reader of Carnegie's Rectorial Address was Queen Victoria's mentally unstable grandson Kaiser Wilhelm II of Germany. He wished to meet Carnegie, who refused several invitations to do so. Despite his resentment at Carnegie's meddling on the international scene, Roosevelt's administration was disturbed by current European sabre-rattling, and along with Secretary of State Elihu Root encouraged Carnegie to meet the autocratic Kaiser. Delayed by the Russo–Japanese War, a Peace Conference was due to meet at the Hague during 15 June–18 October 1907 to try to win a general agreement to stop the arms race. Roosevelt was anxious to find out the Kaiser's future intentions and such a person as Carnegie might be able to discern some clues. Carnegie was more than ready to comply if there was any suggestion that he might be acting 'for America', and the US ambassador to the Imperial German Court, Charlemagne Tower, arranged for a meeting at the German port of Kiel where the Kaiser had opened a canal in 1895. The Kaiser would be there for the June 1907 regatta, where he strutted annually as a senior imperial officer.

Andrew and Louise Carnegie journeyed to Kiel and were

escorted to the German emperor's imperial yacht *Hohenzollern*. Ever after Carnegie savoured the dialogue that had taken place between them. Carnegie greeted the Kaiser with this: 'This has happened just as I could have wished, with no ceremony [they had first met on deck in an informal moment], and the Man of Destiny dropped from the clouds. Your Majesty, I have travelled two nights to accept your generous invitation, and never did so before to meet a crowned head.'

Slightly mocking, the smiling Kaiser replied: 'I have read your book. You do not like kings.' Carnegie voiced his agreement, but softened the opinion: 'I do not like kings, but I do like a man behind a king when I find him.' The conversation led on to hero kings and it turned out that Carnegie and the Kaiser shared a mutual respect for Robert, the Bruce, King of Scots, which gave Carnegie a chance to expound on Dunfermline, his birthplace, and how he now owned the actual sites of some of Scotland's great historical events. This first encounter left Carnegie swelling with pride; as he turned away the Kaiser remarked: 'The Scotch are much quicker and cleverer than the Germans. The Germans are too slow.'[13]

Later that evening the Carnegies were present at the Kaiser's dinner for sixty guests. Carnegie's table neighbour was Prince Bernhard Heinrich von Bülow, the German Chancellor, and consequently Carnegie's opinions on war and the future were registered at the highest levels in Germany.

During subsequent meetings, the Kaiser expressed an interest in meeting President Roosevelt. In his autobiography Carnegie recorded his assessment of the German leader which he gave to Roosevelt:

I never met a man who enjoyed stories more keenly than [the Kaiser]. He is fine company, and I believe an earnest man, anxious for the peace and progress of the world. Suffice it to say he insists that he is, and always has been, for peace. He cherishes the fact that he has reigned for twenty-four years and has never shed human blood. He considered that the German navy is too small to affect the British and was never intended to be a rival. Nevertheless, it is my opinion very unwise, because unnecessary, to enlarge it. Prince von Bülow holds these sentiments and I believe the peace of the world has little to fear from Germany. Her interests are all favourable to peace, industrial development being her aim; and in this desirable field she is certainly making great strides.[14]

These words, and those he wrote to the Principal of St Andrews James Donaldson – 'I think [the Kaiser] can be trusted and declares himself for peace'[15] – led Carnegie's enemies to call him a dupe of Germany, but this was not entirely fair. Carnegie did see that Kaiser Wilhelm II had belligerent military intentions, and realised that disarmament was not an option in Wilhelm's mind. For Carnegie arbitration was the key. He followed up his meetings with the Kaiser with letters to Prince von Bülow and to the German ambassador in Washington, Speck von Sternburg, promoting the cause of peace. Alas, the Hague Peace Conference was a failure as Germany resisted cooperation.

As far as America was concerned, Germany was thwarting progress in the deceleration of the arms race. Lacking Carnegie's increasingly pacifist views, Roosevelt worked towards buttressing America's (naval) forces against the developing militarism of both Germany and Japan. With his basic ideas on the need for international arbitration gaining prominence in his mind, Carnegie now believed that separate nations *could* formulate peace treaties one with another. He knew that Roosevelt would not cooperate on such a policy, but he persisted in trying to persuade him to slow down America's contribution to the arms race. He was to fail.

Carnegie was also anxious about the economic downturn in America which produced the financial panic of October 1907. His pen became busy with what he thought should be done, promoting the idea of a government-sponsored central bank to guarantee deposits; out of this would evolve the US Federal Reserve System. This was a reversal, of course, of Carnegie's old attitude to *laissez-faire* capitalism – to him America's entire financial structure would have to change. Now that he no longer 'grubbed for money' himself, Carnegie believed that 'the day of the multi-millionaire [was] over'.[16]

Roosevelt's Republican administration ended in 1909, to be replaced by another Republican government under lawyer William Howard Taft, who had served as US Solicitor General (1890–2) and Secretary of War (1904–8). Described as 'a jovial, warm-hearted mountain of a man', Taft was a mediocre politician despite his keen legal and administrative mind. He would fall foul of Roosevelt in a conflict that later cost the Republicans the White House, but in the interim Carnegie sought to get on with Taft and gave $20,000 to his election fund.

On leaving office Roosevelt went off to Africa on safari, a trip supported by Carnegie's purse. Carnegie in turn toured Europe and met King Victor Emmanuel III of Italy, who did not pursue a pacifist role in the oncoming war. From Skibo and elsewhere Carnegie continued to press Roosevelt to meet with Kaiser Wilhelm II to promote peace – and he also persuaded him to push the peace agenda when he went to Sweden to receive the Nobel Prize for Peace (awarded 1906) for his efforts to end the Russo–Japanese War. With the help of Elihu Root (erstwhile US Secretary of State), Carnegie bombarded Roosevelt with advice on how he should deal with the Kaiser, suggesting that he should flatter him into believing that he alone could bring about world peace. He assured Roosevelt that he trusted the Kaiser and that peace was worthwhile at any price.

As time passed, though, Roosevelt went off the idea of meeting the volatile Kaiser and certainly was not enamoured of Carnegie's peace-at-any-price position – although it was a line supported by others in America. Roosevelt was wary that what he was doing would not be agreed to by Taft's government. Nevertheless, oiled by Carnegie's election donation, Taft spoke out publicly on 22 March 1910 in support of Carnegie's 'Peace and Arbitration' proposal.[17]

While in Europe Roosevelt was busy making speeches, delivering one at the Sorbonne in Paris – before meeting the

Kaiser – on the legitimacy of 'righteous wars'. Carnegie was horrified, and sent him a knuckle-rapping letter. Yet Roosevelt repeated this opinion in his acceptance speech for the Nobel Prize at Christiana (modern Oslo), although he also gave credence to the creation of the League of Peace.

In the event Roosevelt did meet the Kaiser against a background of hostile German opinion against any slackening of German rearmament and interference arbitration in the nation's foreign policy. Although the meetings were cordial enough they achieved nothing. Carnegie was disappointed; what he did not know was that Roosevelt had spoken disparagingly of Carnegie to the Kaiser. The whole field of international diplomacy was thrown into reverse gear on Friday 6 May 1910 when King Edward VII died at Buckingham Palace. What a good idea, thought Carnegie, for Roosevelt to meet up with the Kaiser at his uncle's funeral on 20 May in London. But it was not to be. From Skibo Carnegie reassessed the situation and came to the conclusion that he had more chance now of pursuing his peace programme through Taft; he began his manipulation plans.

During 1910 the US Congress gave President Taft the authority to set up an organisation which would form an international naval fleet to police international waters; it was to be dubbed a Peace Commission. Taft received a cable from Skibo offering support for the Commission; as usual Carnegie could not resist interfering by suggesting candidates to sit on it. When Britain's Liberal Foreign Secretary Sir Edward Grey offered public backing for the scheme Carnegie acted. At a private dinner at the White House he put forward his idea for an endowment for international peace. Taft liked the proposal and suggested that he would promote arbitration treaties between the nations if Carnegie would sponsor an infrastructure to further international peace. This resulted in the $10 million (5 per cent Federal Mortgage Bonds) Carnegie Endowment for International Peace, launched on 10 November 1910. Ever after Carnegie claimed the whole idea was his, but as historians have pointed out the originator was really

Independent editor Hamilton Holt, with input from Elihu Root and college president Nicholas Murray Butler.[18] Taft became the fund's honorary president, with Elihu Root its president supported by twenty-eight trustees. Carnegie received more praise for his benefaction, but the public at large remained puzzled as to exactly how the fund could win peace in such unruly times. Japan had just militarily annexed Korea (27 August 1910), revolution was rife in Mexico (20 November) and Kaiser Wilhelm II was busy forming new spheres of military influence.

On the domestic front the Carnegies were following their usual programme of peregrinations, taking in the 'cure' at Antibes, shopping in Paris, and visiting the drawing rooms of London friends, and holding 'open house' at their suite at the Langholm Hotel. The year 1909 was a special one for 12-year-old Margaret Carnegie as it included her first trip abroad aboard the Red Star Line's SS *Finland* to the Mediterranean. It was also a time for her parents to attend to her education. Carnegie had recently invested in a New York school now opened at West 55th Street and run by Clara B. Spence. To prepare her for formal education, Margaret was tutored by one of Clara B. Spence's teachers, Anne Brinkerhoff. When the Carnegies went to visit the 100-inch telescope on Mount Wilson, above Pasadena in California, in February 1910 Miss Brinkerhoff went too as travelling tutor. In the autumn of 1910 Margaret Carnegie entered the Spence School as a 'fourth preparatory'; she remained at the school for seven years.[19]

The Carnegies were ever in the public eye; the newspapers followed Carnegie's every project, while the more sleazy journalists were ever vigilant for anti-Carnegie gossip. To some people Carnegie was a hypocrite, an arms dealer turned pacifist, but there was never a hint of sexual scandal in his life. So those in search of titillation had to look elsewhere in Carnegie's family tree. They found it in his niece Nancy's marriage to a widowed family coachman, James Hever; this was a secret her mother, Carnegie's sister-in-law Lucy

Coleman, had done her best to hide from the public. Nancy had eloped with father of two James. In an attempt to head off further press speculation, Carnegie gave the couple a wedding present of $20,000 with the blessing that 'the family would rather have such a husband for Nancy than a worthless duke'.[20]

While the new peace endowment handed out money to various peace societies and sponsored studies on the cause and effect of war, Carnegie was in pursuit of another goal: the US–UK arbitration treaty. Although Taft was moving towards such an agreement, Carnegie could not help interfering and plied the press with his opinions on how Taft should act. The President was both annoyed and offended; he began to realise too, that if he gave Carnegie an inch he would be encouraged to speak for America on any subject imaginable without authority, as if he were President, Congress and the Senate all rolled into one. Even so, on 29 June 1911 the US, UK and France were united in an arbitration treaty, despite opposition from such men as Theodore Roosevelt, who felt that the US was being drawn closer to a mutual defence pact. Senate wasn't happy either, dissecting each clause in an effort to postpone ratification beyond the upcoming US election. Alas, the treaty would fail, and Carnegie's disappointment was deepened by the fact that he had contributed $100,000 to Taft's re-election campaign which did not bring him his usual dividend.[21] In the presidential election of 1912 the White House was won by scholar, historian and reformer Democrat Woodrow Wilson, the last US President Carnegie would tackle.

In 1913 Carnegie set off for Europe to attend the dedication of the Palace of Peace at the Hague and to attend ceremonies at Berlin to celebrate the 25th anniversary of the reign of Kaiser Wilhelm II. Carnegie would present a memorial to the Kaiser signed by prominent officers of American corporations, societies and institutions to honour his long, war-free reign. The whole thing was a farce. Germany was in the throes of a huge military build-up, yet blinkered Carnegie still believed that the Kaiser was the true champion of peace in Europe. As Carnegie handed over the casket containing the memorial address, the Kaiser mendaciously commented: 'Remember, Carnegie! Twenty-five years of peace! If I am Emperor for another twenty-five years not a shot will be fired in Europe!'[22]

Then it was off to the Hague to inaugurate the Peace Palace. Four hundred guests, led by Queen Wilhelmina of the Netherlands, viewed the exhibits of gifts given by foreign countries to furnish the palace; Carnegie did his best to merge with the crowd. The following day, when busts of King Edward VII and of peace advocate Sir William Randal Cremer were being unveiled, Carnegie delivered an address of peace between the United Kingdom, the United States and Germany, and again called for a League of Peace. An exhausted Louise recalled the occasion:

> Thus the great day has passed, perhaps the greatest in Andrew's life, when he has been permitted to see inaugurated the permanent building which he has given wherein the great ideal for peace may be wrought – until Peace and good will may be realised upon the earth.[23]

Despite Carnegie's obsession with peace, the international world was falling apart. In Mexico on 18 February 1913 President Francisco Madero was overthrown by the ruthless General Victorio Huerta; in response, US troops massed along the US–Mexican border. In Greece King George I was assassinated (18 March) and on 29 June the Second Balkan War broke out.

The new year of 1914 promised the Carnegies the usual round of travel and Carnegie made up his diary to cover visits to London and the receipt of freedoms of the city ceremonies at Lincoln and Coventry; they would head for Skibo on 6 June and in late July and early August the family would decamp to Auchnagar. Carnegie was in a good mood, seemingly unperturbed by the war clouds that had gathered over Europe. But it wouldn't last. On 28 June at Sarajevo the Archduke Franz Ferdinand, heir to the Austro-Hungarian throne, and his wife were assassinated by the Bosnian revolutionary Gabriel

Princip. Backed by Kaiser Wilhelm II, the Austrian Emperor Franz Joseph considered severe retaliation and his unacceptable ultimatum to Serbia led to the Austro-Hungarian government declaring war on Serbia. With Russia likely to back Serbia (Tsar Nicholas II agreed to a general mobilisation on 30 July), the balance of power in Europe was toppled. At Auchnagar Carnegie was more concerned with the possibility of there being a British civil war over the recent compromise Irish Home Rule Bill.

On 1 August Germany declared war on Russia, France mobilised and the German government demanded a passage for its armies through Belgium to attack France; all-out war with France was declared on 3 August. Early the next day German troops entered Belgium, and Great Britain sent an ultimatum demanding that Germany respect Belgian territory and neutrality. The ultimatum was ignored and at midnight Britain declared war on Germany.

Carnegie heard the news of the outbreak of the First World War from an old family friend, the Revd Robert L. Ritchie, parish minister of Creich, who had received a confidential tip-off from London. Carnegie was stunned: how could the Kaiser, whom he deemed a peacemaker, come to this? 'All my air-castles have fallen about me like a house of cards,' he told Ritchie.[24] Could America do anything to stop the war? On 6 August the US cruiser *Tennessee* sailed from New York with $5 million in gold to help US citizens trapped in Europe, and on 19 August President Woodrow Wilson urged the American people to be 'neutral in fact as well as in name'.

On the day Britain declared war on Germany Carnegie's friend John Morley – then Lord President of the Council – wrote to him to say that he had resigned from the Liberal administration of Prime Minister Herbert Henry Asquith. A few days after the letter was received, Morley joined the guests at Skibo, where Carnegie's tenants and employees were already being called up for war service. Carnegie cooperated fully with the authorities and Skibo's 'horses, wagons, traps . . . and . . . beautiful trees' were surrendered to the war effort.[25]

One more event took place at Skibo on the day war broke out: Carnegie finished his autobiography. It came to an abrupt end with the words:

> I dare not relinquish all hope. In recent days I see another ruler coming forward upon the world stage, who may prove himself the immortal one. The man who vindicated his country's honour in the Panama Canal toll dispute is now President. He has the indomitable will of genius, and true hope which we are told, 'Kings it makes gods, and meaner creatures kings.'
>
> Nothing is impossible to genius! Watch President Wilson! He has Scotch blood in his veins.[26]

During April 1917 the United States Congress accepted President Woodrow Wilson's challenge to 'make the world safe for democracy' and declared entry into the war.

At Skibo the war dominated conversation; Carnegie was sad that Morley's resignation had brought his political career to an end, but he fully agreed with the decision to go to war. He even refused to join pacifist protesters against the war.[27] Before the Carnegies returned to America on the *Mauretania* in mid-September 1914, Carnegie made public his feelings about the Kaiser. In it he sadly misjudged the character and motivation of Queen Victoria's petulant grandson:

> The German Emperor has not yet been proved guilty. I believe he has been more sinned against than sinning. Rulers are not seldom overruled and, at best, are unable to supervise wisely all the varying conditions of international quarrels. History alone will record the truth. Meanwhile the Emperor, who alone of all ruling potentates has preserved his country's peace for twenty-six years, is at least entitled to the benefit of the doubt.[28]

His words were taken as 'pro-German' and earned Carnegie some opprobrium, not least in his home town of Dunfermline.

TWENTY

THE ROAD TO SLEEPY HOLLOW

How hardly shall they that have riches enter into the
kingdom of God.

Luke, 18:24

The voyage to America was not without its tensions. Louise's
recurrent seasickness was not helped by thoughts of
German sea raiders and the possibility of the *Mauretania*
suffering the fate of the British cruiser HMS *Amphion*, sunk just
a few weeks earlier; the loss of the *Titanic* on the night of
14/15 April 1912 only heightened the tension as look-outs
nervously scanned the seas for icebergs. Once back in America
the Carnegies fell into their usual routine, now though age
required more leisurely pursuits – social visits, walks, reading
and a little golf, if only a putt or two on the lawns of the New
York house. In his study Carnegie still carried on sifting
through mailbags full of requests for donations and gifts. Even
so he was finding it difficult to disburse his wealth as he
wished; he asked his secretary how much he had left, and the
sum of $150 million was revealed.[1] Occasionally he ventured a
view on what was happening in Europe's theatre of war, still
supporting Kaiser Wilhelm II as a reluctant pawn in the hands
of the German military cadre. Carnegie also gave thought at
this time to the structure of his will. Back in 1911, when the
Carnegie Corporation was set on course, both Louise and
daughter Margaret had agreed to relinquish all claims to the
vast Carnegie fortune, so his thoughts were on others.

As he grew older – he was 79 in 1914 – Carnegie became
more and more interested in his confidential list of pensioners.

Separate from his great endowments and the Carnegie Corporation, this was composed of a roster of men and women selected by Carnegie to receive annual payments. Carnegie's assistants in this matter were charged with making careful assessments of all pensioners and worthy folk: 'My pension list is my chief joy and I want no bad names on it.'[2] Many folk totally unknown to and not recognised by the public, but who had figured somewhere in the Carnegie story (however vaguely), received small pensions of up to $100 monthly, while many from politics, academe, the arts and museums – who had been stripped of their ability to earn through disability and age – received regular funds.[3] To this list were added the names of Dunfermline folk, from erstwhile schoolfellows, neighbours and those down on their luck (if they remained ostensibly sober!). In this matter of local selection Carnegie depended upon his Dunfermline lawyer Sir John Ross. One recipient brought great joy to Carnegie. Since before the centenary of poet Robert Burns's death in 1896, Carnegie had been a loyal sponsor of Burns events; for years it had been a requirement for Carnegie libraries to display a bust of the poet. Now the list of pensioners included a great-granddaughter of Robert Burns.[4] Jean Armour Burns Brown resided at Dumfries and folk always said she bore an uncanny likeness to her forebear – she often dressed up as him on celebratory occasions. By the time Carnegie's pension list was complete there were about 500 pensioners sharing some $250,000 per annum.[5]

Carnegie's last public 'performance' was his appearance at the Industrial Commission of February 1915. This commission was set up by President Woodrow Wilson to examine the social status of American working folk, their earnings, and their involvement in trade unions, strikes and so on. Carnegie was called to appear on the subject of the distribution of 'charity' funds to workers and the role of trustees; this was really to winkle out any possibility of corruption. Carnegie addressed the commission and assembled public – some none too friendly – with his usual public charm. His theme was 'My chief business is to do as much good as I can in the world; I have retired from all other business.'[6] Whether this was relevant to the commission or not was of no concern to Carnegie.

His skills as a communicator grabbed his audience; although Frank P. Walsh, the chairman and examiner at the commission, repeatedly tried to keep Carnegie to the point, the white-haired septuagenarian presented himself neither as a 'robber baron' (to the assorted grim-faced socialists present) nor as a 'heartless ogre' (to the nascent feminists whose hats bobbed above the crowd), but instead entertained his listeners with a résumé of his life and philosophy. Then came a selection of questions from Walsh. Yes, Carnegie agreed to collective bargaining (he had loved his men to call him 'Andy'); yes, he would be delighted if the public were interested in and took part in his charitable foundations. To him such foundations were a vital part of worker development and happiness. He left the stage exhausted but delighted; he had got his message across, his audience was won over.

As February 1915 came to a close Carnegie succumbed to a heavy cold; when it developed into influenza he was bedbound for a fortnight. When he was well enough to rise, the energetic, keen and vibrant Andrew Carnegie was gone and he was enfeebled to the point that his usual routines were abandoned. He saw only close friends, wrote few letters and seldom went out. Nevertheless, whenever he could Carnegie propounded his views that President Wilson should act as arbitrator in Europe. So he was delighted when Wilson planned to send his personal adviser Colonel Edward M. House on a peace mission. Still convinced of the Kaiser's 'earnest desire for World Peace', he wrote to him emphasising the advantages of American neutrality and encouraging him to support a neutrality treaty. The Kaiser was keen enough to keep the Americans out of the war, but the many American deaths caused when the British liner *Lusitania* was sunk without warning off the Irish coast on 7 May 1915 scuppered Carnegie's dearest hopes for the Senate to ratify any neutrality treaty with Germany.

Despite his advancing age and his depression about the war, Carnegie kept up an interest in what was happening in war-torn Europe. On 7 November 1916 Woodrow Wilson was re-elected President and on 7 December David Lloyd George – who had resigned from Asquith's government because he thought the war was being mishandled – became British Prime Minister of a coalition government.

The war raged on and in April 1917 America entered the war, the sinking of their merchant ships having made it inevitable. US troops were in France by June. The involvement saddened Carnegie, although he accepted the inevitability of it all. By 6 November 1918 the Germans were in general retreat. Carnegie's 'reluctant tool' the Kaiser was stripped of his power, his nation now being ruled by its Reichstag, and on 9 November 1918 he was forced to abdicate. At five in the morning in a railway car in the forest of Compiègne, north of Paris, the armistice was signed on 11 November. Carnegie's 'hero funds' and 'dependants funds' would have plenty of work to do; 10 million were dead and 20 million wounded in battle, while another 5 million were lost to disease and starvation. Peace talks began in Paris in January 1919 with Woodrow Wilson negotiating for America, Lloyd George for Britain, Georges Clemenceau for France and Vittorio Orlando for Italy; on 28 June the Treaty of Versailles was signed with Germany. The treaty was a compromise but did not include one of Wilson's 'Fourteen Points' – that a League of Nations be established to ensure world peace in the future. This clause had particularly pleased Carnegie. Alas, the terms of the treaty, which included the redistribution of lands once held by Germany and exorbitant reparations to be paid to the Allies, were an eventual source of future international conflict.

At noon on 22 April 1919 – the 32nd anniversary of his own wedding – a somewhat frail Carnegie walked down the grand staircase of 2 East 91st Street, to give his daughter's hand in marriage to Ensign Roswell Miller. Margaret had been a friend of Roswell's sister Dorothy at Miss Spence's school, and Carnegie had been acquainted for some years with Roswell's father, a former president of the Chicago, Milwaukee & St Paul's Railroad. Margaret and Roswell had known each other only a short while when he proposed. On their wedding day

Margaret was awakened by Angus MacPherson (from Skibo) playing the pipes. Carnegie's last public appearance saw him waving goodbye to his daughter and new son-in-law as their Stutz automobile swept down the drive to their honeymoon – with Nannie Lockerbie in attendance!

Carnegie's relationship with his daughter has always been a point of discussion for biographers. His involvement with business, philanthropy and travel, and Margaret's attendance at private schools, kept them apart. Although he was an attentive father when at home, as Louise was to say, events prevented Margaret 'from ever knowing your dear Daddy'.[7] Was it this that made her question her father's endowments in the name of peace? Again, was she critical about the source of her father's wealth? Maybe there is a clue to her attitude in a comment she made to Carnegie's biographer Burton J. Hendrick: 'Tell his life like it was. I'm sick of the Santa Claus stuff.'[8]

Carnegie now spent a sedentary life at his home in New York in the company of Louise. Walks in his garden were followed by backgammon in the evening after supper, with his irritation at losing as keen as ever. He thought often of neglected Skibo, but his physician did not advise him to take the long journey; even despite Carnegie's opinion that it did not matter if he did die in Scotland. Summers were spent at such places as Pointe d'Acadie, Bar Harbour, Maine, or Brick House, Norota, Connecticut, but in 1917 Carnegie bought the 900-acre estate and house of Shadowbrook on a summit near Lenox overlooking Lake Mahkeenac in the Berkshire Hills, Massachusetts.[9] At Shadowbrook Carnegie enjoyed the peaceful New England surroundings and when work was concluded he pored over letters and papers on the activities of the Carnegie Corporation with his secretary John A. Poynton, who had succeeded James Bertram in 1912. Carnegie enjoyed the totting up of his donations; by 1918 the figure had risen to $324,657,399.[10] Visitors came and went, although Carnegie's contemporaries were fast predeceasing him, but one – cousin Dod Lauder – brought back family memories and the echoes of their childhood in Dunfermline. They walked, fished, talked and played checkers. Alas, Dod had little interest now in American history and politics so Carnegie did not get the stimulating conversation on these subjects he so enjoyed. One of the younger generation to visit Carnegie was Charles M. Schwab, whose ebullience acted on Carnegie as a fillip; Schwab brought news of his war work – building submarines and manufacturing munitions – and always succeeded in making Carnegie laugh.[11] But soon Carnegie was to be past all such tonics. As Elihu Root was to say, Carnegie was 'fading gently and happily out of life'.[12] On 9 August 1919 Carnegie contracted bronchial pneumonia. His last Sunday was spent resting on a porch overlooking Lake Mahkeenac; Louise was with him and his valet Morrison hovering in attendance. In the next hours Carnegie gently sank into a sleep; he never woke and died a short while after 7am on 11 August 1919.

* * *

Before he died Carnegie had received copies of the two-volume edition of John Morley's autobiography entitled *Recollections*; it was full of memories for Carnegie:

Your wonderful book of recollections has given me rare and unalloyed pleasure. You have dealt with matters of state as no others could in my opinion, especially those of India and Ireland . . . I have read every word and it is as if I were again talking these things over with you face to face on the terrace of Skibo. Your references to me are all too flattering, but I am not altogether displeased, though you know my modest nature.

I feel confident that with America's help, the great war cannot last much longer, and Madam and I are thinking and talking of the time when we will return to Skibo and have you with us once more.[13]

On Carnegie's death hundreds of cables, telegrams and letters were received by Louise Carnegie, but perhaps the one she treasured most came from John Morley:

> I cannot realise that my most steadfast of all friends has gone, nor do I realise that this letter will find you lonely in your home. Though he was far from me in place and sight, in goodbye at the Liverpool Station, could we suppose that we were to meet no more, and that the humane hopes we had lived in, and lived by, were on the very eve of ruin. Our ideas and aims were just the same, but the fire and glow of his spirit was his own, and my debt to him from the year when [Matthew] Arnold made us acquainted, was more than I can find words for. His interest in me and my doings was for all this long span of time active, eager, indulgent, long-sighted, high pitched. My days of survival cannot be far prolonged [Morley died in 1923], but they will be much the more dull now that the beacon across the Atlantic has gone out.[14]

Years before he died Carnegie and Louise had chosen their final resting place; Pittencrief Glen, Dunfermline, had been in the frame, but the final decision said the grave would be in that part of colonial America known as Sleepy Hollow Cemetery near Tarrytown, New York State. Here a Dutch church was built in 1697 and around it are the graves of those who played a role in the American Revolution that led to the Declaration of Independence of 1776. Here too lies the American man of letters Washington Irving, who enlivened Carnegie's childhood reading with his tales of Rip Van Winkle and his immortalisation of this area in 'The Legend of Sleepy Hollow'.

Louise and Margaret were inundated with queries about the funeral. Would Carnegie have a grand American public funeral? Louise was adamant that he would not. In life Carnegie had been a public figure, but in death he was hers and Margaret's. On 14 August 1919 a funeral service was held in the public reception room at Shadowbrook. Only family members and intimate friends were present, amounting to no more than sixty people around the flower-banked coffin. There was no eulogy, and although Carnegie had belonged to no denominational church a twenty-minute Presbyterian funeral service of prayers and Bible readings was conducted by the Revd Dr William P. Merrill of Brick Presbyterian Church, New York, assisted by the Revd Dr Benson N. Wyman of the Lenox Congregational Church. The same afternoon Carnegie's coffin was taken by train and hearse to Sleepy Hollow Cemetery, and while hired guards kept all others away the family watched the coffin being placed in the new vault as Dr Merrill intoned the last commitment.

Although there was no eulogy at Carnegie's funeral, newspapers covering the magnate's demise pursued those who had known him well for suitable obituary quotes. The *New York Globe* and the *Pittsburgh Dispatch*, for instance, quoted Dr Henry S. Pritchett, President of the Massachusetts Institute of Technology: '[Carnegie] made vital, in our country at least, the conception that the owner of great wealth is a trustee for the public, obligated to divide his wealth for the public use.' The sentiment was repeated nationwide, although such men as Herbert N. Casson suggested that there might be those who would remember Carnegie 'as a social menace'.

On 19 November 1920 Louise Carnegie wrote to Hew Morrison concerning a suitable gravestone for her husband – Morrison had given invaluable help during the purchase of Skibo estate. The stone she had chosen was Migdale rock from a Skibo quarry and the design was worked out with the help of the Revd Ritchie of Creich parish; the actual design – a tall Celtic cross – was drawn by Ritchie's brother and the selected sculptors were Buchanan of Glasgow. Morrison was asked to oversee the Scottish end of the project.[15] The wording Louise chose is direct:

ANDREW CARNEGIE
BORN IN DUNFERMLINE, SCOTLAND, 25 NOVEMBER 1835
DIED IN LENOX, MASSACHUSETTS, 11 AUGUST 1919

As an after-dinner joke, Carnegie would lighten the conversation further by asking what form of words the epitaph might take for each of the guests assembled round the table. He would kick off by suggesting for himself: 'Here lies one who knew how to get around him men who were cleverer than himself.' The words ultimately chosen by Louise could have been supplemented by another of Carnegie's favourite quotations from Robert Burns's late 1785 poem 'To a Louse':

> O wad some Power the giftie gie us
> To see oursels as ithers see us!
> It wad frae monie a blunder Free us,
>> An foolish notion . . .

An important part of Carnegie business after his death was the execution of his last will and testament; it was released by probate in late August 1919. Each word of the text is Carnegie's own compilation, incorporating his own idiosyncratic spellings, and a copy may be seen at the Library of Congress in Washington DC. Every sentence is identifiable as pure Carnegie, and a special mention of daughter Margaret is made:

Having years ago made provision for my wife beyond her desires, and ample to enable her to provide for our beloved daughter Margaret; and being unable to judge at present what provision for our daughter will best promote her happiness, I leave to her the duty of providing for her as her mother deems best. A mother's love will be the best guide.[16]

The main legacy clauses included:

Butler: George Irvine
Housekeeper: Mrs Nicholl
Nanny: Miss Lockerbie
Senior Servant: Maggie Anderson
Family: Dunfermline relatives, Annie and Maggie Lauder to receive $10,000 each

Various sums were to be paid out to retainers, gamekeepers, crofters, foresters and gardeners at Skibo, with a further long list of annuitants and heads of foundations. Special funds were allocated to such beneficiaries as:

President William Howard Taft: $10,000 per annum
The widow of President Grover Cleveland: $5,000 per
annum
The widow of Theodore Roosevelt: $5,000 per annum
John, Viscount Morley: $10,000 per annum
Prime Minister David Lloyd George: $10,000 per annum
John Elliot Burns MP, Labour leader: $5,000 per annum
Thomas Burt MP, trade unionist: $5,000 per annum

The public clamoured for news about Carnegie's wealth at his death. The *Literary Digest* gave the total of his main benefactions up to 1919 at $350,695,653.[17] He left the sum of $30 million, of which two-thirds was to pass to the Carnegie Corporation of New York. The remaining $10 million went in various legacies, for instance $200,000 each to Pittsburgh University, the Stevens Institute, and the St Andrews Society (New York), and a provision of $4 million to develop the Carnegie pension fund. The contents of Carnegie's will have retained financial influence to this day, and questions about it are still posed. For instance: why did Carnegie not leave all his money to his wife and daughter? The answer is quite simple. In what was perhaps the world's first prenuptial agreement, Carnegie gave his wife a lifetime provision, a home in New York, and Skibo Castle, with ample funds for daughter Margaret's needs. To give them any more Carnegie thought would be a 'burden'.

EPILOGUE

THE CONUNDRUM OF ANDREW CARNEGIE

Put all your eggs in one basket, and then watch the basket.
Often repeated Carnegie maxim in public speeches

Andrew Carnegie was and remains an enigma. His various international trusts, endowments and foundations keep his name alive today, and he is remembered by most for his philanthropy. Some still vilify him as a 'robber baron', but whenever a wealthy person gives a huge donation these days, for whatever public project, he or she is warmly hailed as the new Carnegie. But Carnegie was more than a Santa Claus dispenser of money; he was a romanticist, a writer, a political opportunist, a traveller, a socialiser, a quicksilver and melancholic Celt, and a lover of life. All of these aspects must be recognised as giving clues as to his character in all its idiosyncrasies. It is to form a misleading assessment to judge Carnegie solely by the mores of the twenty-first century; he was a nineteenth-century man with his roots in eighteenth-century Scotland, where actions often considered repulsive today were deemed acceptable in his era.[1]

Whether or not Andrew Carnegie was indeed 'the richest man in the world' probably had more to do with newspaper interest of his day than with reality, but it is likely that Carnegie had no contemporary rivals when it came to amassing 'liquid assets'.[2] For many one question stands out in the whole Andrew Carnegie story – what were the secrets of his financial success? Was there a formula he stumbled across that had made the poor Dunfermline boy rich?

The basic traits which formed Andrew Carnegie's success were evident long before his family emigrated to America in

1848. From his grandfather Thomas Morrison he said he learned his optimistic nature.[3] From his mother he learned self-reliance and that life is a brutal struggle to be overcome; he considered her 'heroic'.[4] He was brought up among Chartists and republicans, from whom he learned that every man was equal; what each person did with that 'equality' in life would be the key to success or failure. It should be pointed out too, that Carnegie was in the right place at the right time; when he arrived in America the country was awakening economically and industrially; it is also worth remembering that during his life Carnegie did prosper from lucky twists of fate. Carnegie went to America with a grounding in three strengths; hopefulness for a better future than Dunfermline or Scotland could offer, the self-confidence to make that better future, and a feeling that he was the compeer of any.

Andrew Carnegie's philosophy of success was based on the premise that all achievement begins with an idea, a theory that he backed up with French poet and author Victor Marie Hugo's maxim: 'There is one thing stronger than all the armies of the world, and that is an idea whose time has come.' He believed also that there is no such thing as something for nothing, and that the secret of success has nothing to do with formal education. For him self-education tailored to the individual's personal needs was the best enlightenment of all.

Carnegie did not believe that he was 'doomed' to poverty or failure, and considered that negative thinking leads to misfortune. Faith in himself was the great antidote to failure, and he was convinced that the fundamental weakness in anyone's plan for success was a lack of self-confidence. The young Carnegie had self-confidence and self-reliance far beyond his years. These factors, he said, should be combined with that optimism and tenacity to solve personal problems that he had learned from his family background. From his early years Carnegie adopted a definite purpose in life and stood by it until all was completed – even if it was just to earn enough money to get his mother a carriage, or a servant, to make her a 'lady'.[5] Incentive was always a driving force for Carnegie; in going to America the Carnegies had burned their bridges and therefore had the incentive to succeed or perish. Thus Carnegie gave his senior staff incentives to bring themselves and him success.

A great collector of quotations by the world's great writers and thinkers, Carnegie had one in his notebooks that gives a clue to his unceasing drive. It comes from English poet and playwright William Ernest Henley's 'Invictus: In Memory of Robert Louis Stevenson':

> I am the master of my fate
> I am the captain of my soul.

Sometimes Carnegie interpreted this ruthlessly, putting his own needs and career before those of, say, his close colleagues. Thus whatever he did – whether buying steel or playing checkers – Carnegie HAD to win, and to do so he took advantage of every opportunity, even if he had to trample on others to get there. If things went wrong it was never Carnegie's fault in his own mind, and others always took the blame; this was particularly brought out in the Frick–Homestead affair.

Carnegie's notions concerning wealth were based on 'Social Darwinism'. The theory was a misconception of Charles Darwin's *The Origin of Species*, in which Darwin propounded the idea of the survival of the fittest in the animal world. This theory was taken up by Herbert Spencer who applied it to human society, which made it run contrary to anything Darwin had said. Spencer noted that in his opinion great wealth was amassed by people of 'superior ability, foresight and adaptability'.[6] Carnegie absorbed all this but reinterpreted it in his own way and concluded that the wealthy had a responsibility towards society and its needs. He chose capitalism as the best route to his goals. In this he revolutionised philanthropy. Although he had a sense of unease about his own wealth, he did not approve of conventional charity. Giving cash to the poor was not a good policy in Carnegie's eyes; giving them education and the tools for self-success was his aim. Strange as it may seem Carnegie had an aversion to cash. As biographer Burton J. Hendrick pointed out, he rarely carried money around. He was even ejected once from a London bus because he had no coppers for the fare.[7] Carnegie believed that he was put on this earth to do good, and that this was the reason he became rich; because of this he believed his mind was tuned to the secrets of financial success.

A careful trawl through Carnegie biographical material and commercial papers reveals several clues to his enigmatic character. First a look at his negative qualities, the favourite areas for his detractors. Carnegie was an autocrat: from the early days of childhood when he fought mock battles around the ruins of the Meal Mill on Monastery Street, Dunfermline, Carnegie exhibited his need to command, control and dominate every facet of his life; from boyhood days he had a belief in his own superiority which eventually earned him the nickname in the steel corridors of power as 'the Great Egotist'. Was it his egotism, self-regard and vanity – traits in his character that his brother Tom abhorred – that made him think that he could buy world peace with his purse? Often too, Carnegie's 'selfs' got mixed up: his small stature and childhood background of poverty helped to make him self-reliant, but it also made him self-serving, and his conceit and immodesty led to a confident air that was often interpreted as arrogance. Consequently too, Carnegie never admitted that he had ever made a mistake, but always expressed in public – without any hint of self-irony – that he was modest. He always advised his youthful audiences at St Andrews and elsewhere never to bear grudges – but he did not heed his own words, for he could be spiteful and loved to 'rub' his opponents' noses 'in the dirt'. For instance, he never forgot nor forgave Thomas A. Scott for 'stealing' the girl Carnegie was in love with; she was Anna Duke Riddle, daughter of the owner of the *Pittsburgh Journal*. Scott married Anna, and thus Carnegie rejoiced when Scott failed in business.[8]

Although Carnegie worked with a large number of colleagues, ultimately he was unable to share power, as his relationship with Henry Clay Frick, for one, was to show.

Carnegie also suffered from paranoia and if anything went wrong with his business he took it as a personal attack on himself. From time to time he was unable to be discreet; he tended to think out loud and often did not consider the potential consequences of what he said. His detractors considered him a hypocrite, citing the fact that he said he hated the aristocracy but hobnobbed with lords; he proclaimed he was a pacifist, yet he made a fortune out of armaments of one kind or another.

Andrew Carnegie was a great meddler in the work he set for others, and in the businesses he handed over to others. When he became rich he seemed to feel that his wealth gave him the right to interfere in American and British politics. His money backed the Republican cause in America and the Liberals in Britain, but in the long run he was only oiling the party machines rather than making a lasting contribution, although his autobiographical writings would give the contrary view. Undoubtedly his biggest blunder was his belief that he could persuade, or even outwit, such men as Kaiser Wilhelm II and become St Andrew, the Bringer of Peace. Although remembered worldwide as a celebrated rags-to-riches industrialist, Andrew Carnegie is still reviled by many in Pittsburgh. Thus no statue has ever been set up for him in the place he made most of his money, although in 2004 the city fathers installed a statue to local boy the actor and dancer Gene Kelly.

What of Carnegie's strong points? He had a natural charm, enhanced by his Fife-Dunfermline brogue, which he used to persuade people to see his point of view. Employees like Charles Schwab were captivated by his personality, although there were a few exceptions, notably Henry Clay Frick. His charm led to success as a salesman of steel railways and iron bridges, for instance, and in the promotion of sleeping-cars. It made it easy for him to make friends; Carnegie always needed such folk about him, yet his personality drove him to use them for his own ends. He thus manipulated 'the Original Six' as a gauge for his own advancement: were they more popular than him socially? Were they more adroit than him in the workplace, and so on? In a way he also learned this from his mother: 'What's in it for us?' she would ask of his latest ventures. Carnegie found great strength from his family background, with his mother as the pivotal point, yet he was a bully to his young brother and later his wife Louise would feel that she would never in his eyes match up to his mother. Again, although he had youthful respect for his father, and was sympathetic and understanding about the economic problems that William Carnegie faced, in his heart Carnegie really looked upon his father as a failure. No known photograph of William Carnegie ever appeared in the Carnegie archives (nor in Carnegie's autobiography), and the family relics Carnegie locked away after his mother's death in 1886 were all hers. It should be mentioned too, that Carnegie could be fiercely loyal to his friends, sometimes when it was not in his interests to do so. Thus he gave his genuine friendship to the Phipps family – after all, they had employed his mother in their lean weeks at Slabtown – but he backed the wrong horse when giving his loyalty to Thomas Miller in the rival Cyclops iron mill venture. Nevertheless, it is from his strong points that one can see how Carnegie found the road to riches.

Carnegie set out a number of important steps to success in making money and a prominent place for oneself in life. First, he discovered, came a positive appetite to succeed in accumulating money. Then he said one should set out financial goals with a clear idea of the specific sums required. This should be followed by what the individual was going to perform to get this money with the realisation that there was never 'something for nothing'. And, said Carnegie, endeavour should round off these initial thoughts with a specific date when the main targets would be achieved.

'Create a plan of action' was Carnegie's advice for those wishing to accumulate wealth and position. At various times in his life Carnegie reassessed his own plans as seen in his 1868 memorandum to himself written at the St Nicholas Hotel, New York. He believed too, that one should study exactly how the wealthy accumulated their funds. Another key to success in Carnegie's eyes was visualisation of success. This he had learned from his uncle George Lauder, whose verbal pictures of the deeds of such heroes as Sir William Wallace had been so vivid for Carnegie. George Lauder also helped the young Carnegie achieve self-reliance in giving him business tasks to do from the grocer's shop at Dunfermline. From this Carnegie learned the importance of choosing the right mentors – people to help the individual advance – and the need to associate with successful people; he also developed his natural need to be noticed, helped along by his uncle Tom Morrison's example as a public speaker. Another key for the establishment of a good business structure, the Carnegie way, was to put in positions of responsibility people who were more accomplished than oneself. All of these factors and characteristics made Carnegie the man he was and enabled him to achieve. His vanity and self-absorption, his opinionatedness and business practices made him an easy target for detractors, just as his generosity made him a hero in philanthropic circles. Thus Carnegie became an enigma. To find the real Carnegie, then, one has to look at the entirety of his life and place it within the society and era in which he lived; only then will the conundrum that is Carnegie be unravelled.

APPENDIX I

THE DEVELOPMENT OF THE CARNEGIE TRUSTS

In 1901 Andrew Carnegie sold the Carnegie Company for $480 million to US financier John Pierpont Morgan, and retired from business to devote himself to philanthropy. Although he received an average of 400–500 'begging letters' per day, and responded with personal cheques to individual projects which appealed to him, his philosophy was to help people to help themselves. He did not believe that throwing money at the poor helped them at all; he considered that wealthy persons could manage their own money better for the benefit of the poor, rather than the poor trying to juggle donated money on their own.

Today in the UK there are a number of main Carnegie Trusts. Three of them are administered from Abbey Park House, Dunfermline: the Carnegie Dunfermline Trust; the Carnegie Hero Fund Trust; and the Andrew Carnegie Birthplace Memorial Fund.

The Carnegie Dunfermline Trust was founded in 1903. In a letter to the trustees, Carnegie described his thinking behind the promotion of such an establishment: 'To bring into the monotonous lives of the toiling masses of Dunfermline more of sweetness and light . . . The problem you have to solve is – "What can be done in towns for the benefit of the masses by money in the hands of the most public-spirited citizens?"' Slowly from 1903 the trust began to touch many aspects of life within Dunfermline and its environs, from clinics to colleges, and from arts to education. Today technology, art, community projects, music schools, sport and heritage are all among the funding activities of the trust.

The Development of the Carnegie Trusts

The Carnegie Hero Fund Trust was founded in 1908 with this as the stated purpose: 'To place those following peaceful vocations, who have been injured in heroic efforts to save human life, in somewhat better positions pecuniarily than before, until again able to work; in case of death, the widow and children to be provided for.' Today the fund oversees the welfare of some 170 men, women and children with financial assistance apportioned in three categories: the dependants of persons who have died; persons who have been injured; persons who have incurred appreciable financial loss through performing acts of heroism in peaceful pursuits.

The Andrew Carnegie Birthplace Memorial Fund was founded in 1926 with the intent of recounting the life story of Andrew Carnegie. It was endowed by his widow and in 1928 a Memorial Hall was built next to Carnegie's actual birthplace at Moodie Street, Dunfermline. Today the museum has a permanent display of Carnegie artefacts and organises relevant exhibitions, events and educational projects, heritage tourism and guided walks.

During 2002 the Carnegie Dunfermline Trust processed grants totalling £116,173; the Carnegie Hero Fund Trust expended resources of £146,676; and the Birthplace Memorial Fund disbursed £46,772. As well as administrative staff and heritage guides, the trusts are managed by a Board of Trustees.

The Carnegie United Kingdom Trust is administered from Comely Park House, Dunfermline, and was founded in 1913 and incorporated by royal charter in 1917. Its purpose was defined as 'For the improvement of the well-being of the masses of the people of Great Britain and Ireland, by such means as . . . the Trustees may, from time to time, select as best fitted from age to age for securing these purposes, remembering that new needs are constantly arising as the masses advance . . .' In its early days the trustees were busy endowing grants for church organs and libraries; by 1919 some 3,500 organs had been funded and the creation of community-based libraries continued until the implementation of the Public Libraries Act of 1947. Major areas of activity have included the funding of projects ranging from village halls to social services and from youth groups to mental welfare organisations. During 2002 the trust received a total income of £1.44 million and disbursed £968,000 in grants.

The Carnegie Trust for the Universities of Scotland was founded in 1901 and the Trust Deed defined its purpose as 'Providing funds for the improving and extending the opportunities for scientific study and research in the Universities of Scotland, my native land, and by rendering attendance at these Universities and the enjoyment of their advantages more available to the deserving and qualified youth of that country . . .' The trust is administered from The Merchants' Hall, Hanover Street, Edinburgh.

Early Carnegie benefactions were centred on his home town of Dunfermline. In 1873 he allocated $25,000 for swimming baths in the burgh which were opened by him as the Carnegie Free Baths on 12 July 1877. On 29 August 1883 the memorial stone of the Carnegie Free Library was laid by Mrs William Carnegie at Dunfermline; the cost of the building was £8,000. Named after his uncle George Lauder, the Lauder Technical School was opened at Dunfermline on 10 October 1889; it was built and equipped for £10,000. Carnegie himself laid the memorial stone for the New Carnegie Baths on 16 July 1902 and the baths were opened on 31 March 1905. And in 1903, the year of the formation of the Carnegie Dunfermline Trust, Carnegie gifted Pittencrieff Park and Glen to the people of Dunfermline. There followed a multitude of contributions to local amenities and services in Dunfermline, from bowling greens to music benefactions, and from playing fields to the Carnegie Centre in Pilmuir Street (1901–5), the College of Hygiene and Physical Education (1905), Carnegie Clinics in Pilmuir and Inglis Streets (1911–12), and the posthumous Carnegie Hall at East Port (1933–7).

Carnegie saw his trusts as becoming part of the fabric of both his homeland and his adopted country. 'It is built to stand for ages and during those ages it is probable that this hall will intertwine itself with the history of our country, said Carnegie when he opened New York's $200 million grand Renaissance-style Music Hall on 57th Street, New York, in May 1891 (it was renamed the Carnegie Hall in 1894). He was right; 'making it' at Carnegie Hall equated with being a success in the United States; here Antonin Dvořák unveiled his New World Symphony on 15 December 1893, and the Beatles played deafening concerts here in 1964.

A more widespread plan of donations, before Andrew Carnegie finally devoted himself to various aspects of philanthropy, began with the foundation of the Carnegie Institute. This commenced with a gift of money for a library and music hall at Pittsburgh, completed and opened on 5 November 1895; an art gallery and museum were added in 1907. The Carnegie Institute today is sited at 4400 Forbes Avenue, Pittsburgh.

Any summary of the main Carnegie trusts and benefactions from 1901 until his death in 1919 also includes the following:

1901   Carnegie Relief Fund: this was created for the financial relief of, and pensions for, Carnegie Steel workers.

1902   Carnegie Institution of Washington: founded as a research and educational institution.

1904   Carnegie Hero Fund Commission in US.

1905   Carnegie Foundation for the Advancement of Teaching

1906   Simplified Spelling Board; founded to make English easier to read and write for 'the masses throughout the world'. It was intended to be a platform for Carnegie's international peace philosophy.

1909   Foundation Carnegie, France.

1910   Carnegie Endowment for International Peace: intended to promote the abolition of international war.

1911   Carnegie Belonningsfud for Heltemod, Denmark.
             Carnegie Corporation of New York.
             Carnegie Heldenfonds, Netherlands.

Carnegie Heltefond for Norge, Norway.
Foundation Carnegie, Belgium.
Fondazione Carnegie, Italy.
Carnegie Stiftelsens, Sweden.

1912 Carnegie Institute of Technology in Pittsburgh: now Carnegie-Mellon University.

1918 Teachers Insurance and Annuity Association: founded primarily to supply pensions for teachers.

APPENDIX II

ANDREW CARNEGIE BIRTHPLACE MUSEUM

The Andrew Carnegie Birthplace Museum stands at the corner of Moodie Street and Priory Lane, Dunfermline. At 2 Moodie Street, the actual birthplace, is a restored late eighteenth-century pantile cottage with swept wallhead dormer windows. It was once the end of a terrace and a portion of the earlier single-storey building – used as a shop – was demolished in the twentieth century to reveal a north-facing gable pierced with two upper-apartment windows. The south-facing gable was breached to link with the memorial building of 1928 designed by James Shearer, a construction he flavoured with seventeenth-century Scots styles.

The Carnegie Birthplace Memorial Fund and Museum was founded in 1926 with the intent: 'To tell the story of Andrew Carnegie's humble beginnings and his remarkable achievements.' Louise Carnegie's original wish was to establish a 'Memorial Treasure House' for her husband's honours. From her original endowment of £10,000 and a further £2,000 in 1932, this fund has received regular endowments and grants; Mrs Margaret Carnegie Miller (daughter) continued the family endowments during her lifetime.

The first Museums Director was appointed in the late 1960s and during 1983–4 an important renovation programme was undertaken at the museum through a fund supported *inter alia* by the Carnegie Trusts and the then Scottish Tourist Board.

The visitor enters the museum though one of the original front doors of the cottage from Moodie Street whose alignment has greatly changed from Andrew Carnegie's time, with facing buildings demolished. From the reception area the visitor is led through the series of rooms on two levels that Andrew Carnegie would have known as a child. One room exhibits a loom of the style invented by the French silk-weaver from Lyon, Joseph Marie Jacquard. On such a loom Carnegie's father William worked his fine damask cloth. Period furniture, a wall-bed and other artefacts show how the Carnegie family lived in the 1830s; the furniture includes a desk given to Mrs Ailie Henderson, who had lent them £20 towards their passage to America in 1848. Other displays show Carnegie family and local Dunfermline history relevant to the period of Andrew Carnegie's childhood.

Downstairs, from the reception area the visitor enters a spacious hallway with a significant collection of cartoons depicting Andrew Carnegie, both humorous and satirical. (These are sometimes replaced by exhibitions of artworks and paintings which form part of the Carnegie Dunfermline Trust art collection.) From here steps lead off into the Memorial Hall proper. The displays are featured in bays, and cover the whole of Andrew Carnegie's life. His private office at Skibo Castle is recreated and there is a stunning display of the caskets Carnegie received when he was honoured with the freedom of many cities. Overall the museum exhibits a range of Carnegie ephemera, from royal tributes from King Edward VII and Tsar Nicholas II of Russia to his travel albums highlighting aspects of his life little known to the general public. A particularly moving display is based around the centrepiece of the Roll of Honour of the Carnegie Hero Fund Trust.

APPENDIX III

THE CARNEGIES' FAREWELL TO SKIBO

O dear blue mountains of my home firth,
My heart is sad because I must leave you
And it will be long before I see you again.
Margaret Carnegie Miller, *Skibo Guest Book*, 1933.

On the afternoon of the last day of February 1920 Louise
Carnegie, accompanied by her sister Estelle 'Stella'
Whitfield, arrived at Ardgay (Bonar Bridge) railway station,
Sutherland; this was her first visit to Skibo since Andrew
Carnegie's death. Thereafter Louise spent successive summers
at the castle where she was often joined by her daughter
Margaret, son-in-law Roswell and her grandchildren. Slowly,
too, she began to fill the place with guests, old friends and new,
as well as employees and associates of her husband's trusts.
Even so, during the 1920s and 1930s the castle was seldom
used. Louise Carnegie spent her last summer at Skibo in 1939;
she left the castle on 1 September, the day Germany invaded
Poland, and at 11.15am on 3 September Prime Minister
Neville Chamberlain's government declared war on Gemany.
Just like her husband back in 1914, Louise Carnegie's visits to
Skibo were thwarted by war.

After Louise Carnegie's death on 24 June 1946 Skibo
entered a new era. Louise's will confirmed that Skibo belonged
to her daughter Margaret, who returned a few weeks after her
mother's death. She entered the gates – under the familiar
banner WELCOME TO SKIBO – with her daughter Louise (Dede),
her son-in-law Gordon Thomson and their four daughters. She
was now the Lady of Skibo.

Margaret Carnegie Miller set about repairs and maintenance of the castle, and the reviving of the estate after six years of war, with the help of estate factor Whittet and head keeper Harry Blythe. In her father's time there had been a staff of 85, now there were fewer than 30, with 5 gardeners instead of 18. Much work was done to try to make Skibo estate self-sufficient.

In 1947 Margaret's daughter Dede Thomson fell ill, stricken with poliomyelitis; she died on 13 August. The family were greatly affected by the early death. Roswell, her father, in particular was devastated. Margaret and Roswell divorced in 1953. Their American home on 90th Street, New York, was given to the Carnegie Corporation of New York. Thereafter Margaret looked upon Skibo as her spiritual home, although in time she had a residence in Connecticut. After Dede's death, the castle provided a permanent home for the Thomson family. Margaret was particularly delighted when her now-widowed lawyer son-in-law Gordon Thomson, who was appointed a King's Counsel in 1953, was elevated as Senator to HM College of Justice in Scotland as Lord Migdale. Members of the Carnegie-Miller-Thomson family were the most regular visitors to Skibo, along with various trustees and associates of Andrew Carnegie's many philanthropic agencies. Hospitality was very much reduced from Margaret's father's time when Edwardian opulence held sway. Nevertheless in 1964 Skibo made ready to receive a royal guest. This was the year that Queen Elizabeth II (and I of Scotland) and Prince Philip made an official visit to the county of Sutherland. Lord Migdale was Lord Lieutenant of Sutherland from 1962, and it was his responsibility to welcome the royal party to the county, with Skibo as the location for a royal lunch. So on 5 June 1964 Margaret Carnegie Miller received her royal guests; that evening Margaret, Lord Migdale and her daughter Margaret ('Migs') were dinner guests aboard the royal yacht *Britannia* moored in the Cromarty Firth.

By the 1970s Margaret began to suffer debilitating arthritis, which restricted her movements. As she grew older it was suggested that she should make Skibo her regular home. This idea did not wholly appeal as she considered herself American, and the United States as her home country. Skibo was the 'heaven' of her childhood, but as she faced worsening infirmity it was likely that she would be unable to make any regular long journeys from her residence in Connecticut to Scotland. Her family then advised that Skibo be given over to Carnegie Trust projects.

Margaret now had discussions with her New York lawyer John Gray, Stephen Seaman (the representative of her Scottish solicitors) and Fred Mann (executive secretary of the Carnegie Dunfermline Trust). Margaret made her last visit to Skibo in the summer of 1980. She had now formally decided that Skibo Castle and a parcel of 600 acres of property should go to the Carnegie United Kingdom Trust, with the idea that it should be converted to some kind of meeting place for international scholars to carry out research and cross-fertilise their ideas. Alas, the trust turned down the offer; they did not have the funds to convert and maintain the property and the castle's position in the north of Scotland made it an inconvenient place to get to. A whole range of ideas as to what Skibo might become were discussed, but in the end Skibo could always be sold and the money given to the Carnegie United Kingdom Trust. Even so, there were legal and tax mountains to climb as well as the fine detail on such things as the family's retention of fishing and shooting rights.

In May 1982, amid much local and national press speculation, Skibo was put on the market by selling agents Savills and local representatives Renton Finlayson of Bonar Bridge. In all 19,000 acres including the castle were put up for sale, in lots or as a whole, at a guide price of £1.85 million; in the event portions of the estate were sold to family partnerships. The castle remained a separate entity. On 27 July 1982 the castle and remainder of the estate was sold to Derek Holt, of Holt Leisure Parks Ltd, Renfrewshire, for a sum in the region of £2.5 million. Holt carried out various improvements to the castle and gardens and held ownership for eight years. In 1990 the entrepreneur Peter de Savary bought the castle and 7,500 acres for £5.6 million and spent £10 million restoring it and establishing the Carnegie Club for paying guests. The property was sold again by the holding company Westbrook Partners (in which de Savary was a minority shareholder) for a sum in the region of £30.5 million in 2003/4. Today Skibo Castle remains the home of the Carnegie Club, ranked highly as 'one of the world's most exclusive private clubs'.

Should Andrew Carnegie return to Skibo today there is much he would recognise. Much of the furniture, carpets, antiques, pictures and wall hangings remain as they were in his time, and his beloved pipe organ made for him by Brindley & Foster (1902) still fills the hallway with the music he loved. The whole ambience of Carnegie is here in the study, downstairs rooms, corridors, lift and library – although a large proportion of the books were sold during Peter de Savary's ownership. Carnegie's portable writing table, now a little the worse for wear, serves as a reminder of the inspiration Skibo brought to his writings.

In the vicinity of Skibo the farms of Fload, Acharry and Creich that Carnegie knew are still in the ownership of Carnegie descendants and his great-granddaughter Margaret Thomson still farms the 500-acre Ospisdale Farm which her father Lord Migdale bought in 1968.

Today, the Skibo estate is being revived for the twenty-first century with such plans as a regenerating wooded development, the reintroduction of shooting and the purchase of properties like Meikle Ferry House to bring them back into the estate. The dozen cottages and lodges on Skibo estate, including the battlemented 'Mrs Carnegie's Castle', have also been refurbished; many of them once served as the homes of Andrew Carnegie's estate employees. The Carnegie Links Golf Course has been redeveloped and plays an important role in Highland and international golf.

The Carnegie Family Tree

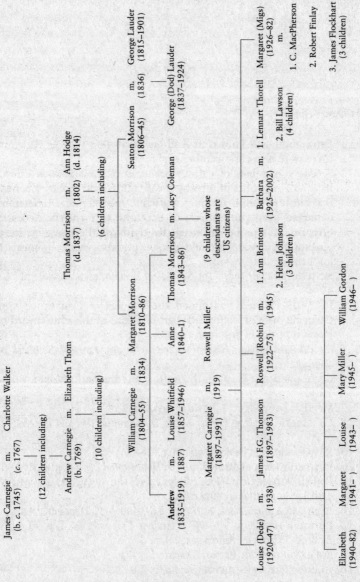

NOTES

Chapter One

1. Pattiesmuir was known in Andrew Carnegie's time as Patiemuir; there were also various other spellings.
2. Seceders: members of various branches of the Secession Church. In 1732 a group of Presbyterian ministers, led by Ebenezer Erskine and Ralph Erskine, erstwhile minister of Dunfermline, departed from the Church of Scotland to form the Secession Church. This group favoured the rights of the congregation to appoint their ministers and pursue a conservative emphasis on faith rather than works.
3. Sir John Sinclair (ed.), *The Statistical Account of Scotland*, vol. X, p. 404.
4. In 1909 Carnegie attended the funeral of Constance Mary Carnegie, wife of Victor, 9th Earl of Elgin, at this churchyard but found no trace of his family graves.
5. Sir William Frazer, *History of the Carnegies, Earls of Southesk and their kindred*.
6. Correspondence between the author and the Earl of Elgin, August 2002.
7. Martha, Lady Elgin, *Household Account Book*.
8. J.B. Mackie, *Andrew Carnegie: His Dunfermline Ties and Benefactions*, p. 7.
9. R. Rait and G.S. Pride, *Scotland*, p. 268.
10. Raymond Lamont-Brown, *Fife in History and Legend*, p. 201.
11. Today Pattiesmuir remains part of the Elgin estate and the 'college' is used as a village hall.
12. *Elgin Estate Cash Book*, entry for 1 January–30 December 1826.
13. Burton J. Hendrick, *The Life of Andrew Carnegie*, vol. I, p. 11.
14. Andrew Carnegie, *Autobiography*, p. 3.
15. Raymond Lamont-Brown, *Discovering Fife*, p. 36.
16. Andrew Carnegie, *Autobiography*, p. 11.
17. *Ibid.*, p. 23.
18. John Pattison, Holograph MS. 1935, Carnegie Museum.

19. Tom Morrison, 'Heddekation and Handication', *Register*, 21 December 1833, pp. 720ff.
20. Andrew Carnegie, *Autobiography*, p. 4.

Chapter Two

 1. To date only two thoroughfares in Dunfermline bear Carnegie's name: Carnegie Drive, at the eastern entrance to the town, and Carnegie Avenue, abutting Pitreavie golf course to the south.
 2. A.H. Millar, *Fife: Pictorial and Historical*; and Raymond Lamont-Brown, *Fife in History and Legend*.
 3. A.H. Millar, *Fife: Pictorial and Historical*, p. 234.
 4. Peter Chalmers, *Historical and Statistical Account of Dunfermline*, pp. 327 and 375.
 5. Edgar Street no longer exists, the site having been redeveloped.
 6. Andrew Carnegie, *Autobiography*, p. 52.
 7. Raymond Lamont-Brown, *Fife in History and Legend*, pp. 175–6.
 8. Strangely Andrew Carnegie makes no mention of his sister in his *Autobiography*.
 9. Used as a proper name, 'Dod' or 'Doddie' is a long-established colloquial form of George in Scotland.
10. Charlie May Simon, *The Andrew Carnegie Story*, p. 15.
11. Andrew Carnegie, *Autobiography*, pp. 15–16.
12. *Ibid.*, p. 16.
13. *Ibid.*, p. 50.
14. *Ibid.*, p. 14.
15. Burton J. Hendrick, *The Life of Andrew Carnegie*, vol. I, p. 21.
16. Andrew Carnegie, *Autobiography*, p. 21.
17. *Ibid.*, p. 26.
18. *Ibid.*, p. 24.
19. *Ibid.*, p. 26.
20. Charlie May Simon, *The Andrew Carnegie Story*, pp. 16–17.
21. Andrew Carnegie, *Autobiography*, p. 10.
22. Arthur Helps (ed.), *Leaves from the Journal of Our Life in the Highlands by Queen Victoria*, p. 6.
23. Burton J. Hendrick, *The Life of Andrew Carnegie*, vol. I, p. 25.
24. Andrew Carnegie, *Autobiography*, p. 13. Carnegie is quoting Robert Burns's 'Man Was Made to Mourn – A Dirge', verse 8, ll. 2–4; the correct quote is:
So abject, mean and vile
Who begs a brother of the earth
To give him leave to toil.

25. *Ibid.*, p. 25.
26. Burton J. Hendrick, *The Life of Andrew Carnegie*, vol. I, pp. 40–1.
27. Andrew Carnegie, p. 25.
28. Burton J. Hendrick, *The Life of Andrew Carnegie*, vol. I, p. 43.

Chapter Three

1. W.A. Carrothers, *Emigration from the British Isles*, p. 305.
2. Andrew Carnegie, *Autobiography*, p. 28.
3. Alvin F. Harlow, *Andrew Carnegie*, p. 14.
4. *Ibid.*, p. 15.
5. *Ibid.*; and Burton J. Hendrick, *The Life of Andrew Carnegie*, vol. I, p. 53.
6. Andrew Carnegie, *Autobiography*, p. 32.
7. *Ibid.*, p. 35.
8. *Ibid.*, p. 35.

Chapter Four

1. Andrew Carnegie, *Autobiography*, p. 37.
2. Burton J. Hendrick, *The Life of Andrew Carnegie*, vol. I, p. 56.
3. Andrew Carnegie, *Autobiography*, p. 38.
4. Burton J. Hendrick, *The Life of Andrew Carnegie*, vol. I, p. 57.
5. *Ibid.*, vol. I, p. 58.
6. Andrew Carnegie, *Autobiography*, p. 41.
7. Peter Krass, *Carnegie*, p. 30.
8. Andrew Carnegie, *Autobiography*, p. 43.
9. *Ibid.*
10. Joseph Frazier Wall, *Andrew Carnegie*, p. 93.
11. Andrew Carnegie, *Autobiography*, p. 42.
12. Burton J. Hendrick, *The Life of Andrew Carnegie*, vol. I, p. 62.
13. Peter Krass, *Carnegie*, p. 39.
14. Joseph Frazier Wall, *Andrew Carnegie*, p. 97.
15. Andrew Carnegie, *Autobiography*, p. 51.
16. Burton J. Hendrick, *The Life of Andrew Carnegie*, vol. I, p. 66.
17. Andrew Carnegie, *Autobiography*, p. 55.
18. *Ibid.*, p. 57.
19. James A. Reid, *The Telegraph in America*.
20. Andrew Carnegie, *Autobiography*, p. 59.
21. John K. Winkler, *Incredible Carnegie*, pp. 54–5.

22. Andrew Carnegie, *Autobiography*, p. 62.
23. Joseph Frazier Wall, *Andrew Carnegie*, pp. 105–6.
24. Andrew Carnegie, *Autobiography*, p. 61.
25. Burton J. Hendrick, *The Life of Andrew Carnegie*, vol. I, p. 70.
26. *Ibid.*, vol. I, p. 71.

Chapter Five

1. Burton J. Hendrick, *The Life of Andrew Carnegie*, vol. I, pp. 83–4.
2. Andrew Carnegie, *Autobiography*, p. 64.
3. *Ibid.*, pp. 67–8.
4. Peter Krass, *Andrew Carnegie*, p. 49.
5. Burton J. Hendrick, *The Life of Andrew Carnegie*, vol. I, p. 11.
6. Andrew Carnegie, *Autobiography*, p. 73.
7. *Ibid.*
8. *Ibid.*
9. *Ibid.*, p. 82.
10. *Ibid.*
11. *Ibid.*, p. 77.
12. *Ibid.*, p. 63.
13. Burton J. Hendrick, *The Life of Andrew Carnegie*, vol. I, p. 93.
14. Joseph Frazier Wall, *Andrew Carnegie*, p. 133.
15. Andrew Carnegie, *Autobiography*, p. 80.
16. *Ibid.*, p. 84.
17. *Ibid.*, p. 85.
18. *Ibid.*, p. 86. Here Andrew Carnegie is quoting from William Wordsworth's 'Lines composed a few miles above Tintern Abbey', l. 33.
19. John K. Winkler, *Incredible Carnegie*, p. 66.
20. Andrew Carnegie, *Autobiography*, p. 88.
21. *Ibid.*, p. 90.
22. Burton J. Hendrick, *The Life of Andrew Carnegie*, vol. I, p. 81.
23. Peter Krass, *Andrew Carnegie*, p. 56, quoting letter of 10 April 1903.

Chapter Six

1. Andrew Carnegie, *Autobiography*, p. 87.
2. *Ibid.*
3. Peter Krass, *Carnegie*, pp. 56–7.
4. Andrew Carnegie, *Autobiography*, p. 88.

5. Burton J. Hendrick, *The Life of Andrew Carnegie*, vol. I, p. 96.
6. Joseph Frazier Wall, *Andrew Carnegie*, pp. 139–41.
7. *Ibid.*, p. 141.
8. Andrew Carnegie, *Autobiography*, p. 91.
9. *Ibid.*
10. *Ibid.*, pp. 93–4.
11. Burton J. Hendrick, *The Life of Andrew Carnegie*, p. 98.
12. Andrew Carnegie, *Autobiography*, p. 97.
13. *Ibid.*
14. Joseph Frazier Wall, *Andrew Carnegie*, p. 151.
15. Andrew Carnegie, *Autobiography*, p. 93.
16. Burton J. Hendrick, *The Life of Andrew Carnegie*, vol. I, p. 103.
17. Viscount Morley, *Recollections*, vol. I, p. 20.
18. Andrew Carnegie, *Autobiography*, p. 89.
19. *Ibid.*, pp. 99–100.
20. *Ibid.*, p. 100.
21. *Ibid.*, p. 109.
22. Letter, 26 July 1861. Burton J. Hendrick, *The Life of Andrew Carnegie*, vol. I, p. 108.
23. Letter, 4 October 1900 to W.T. Stead. Burton J. Hendrick, *The Life of Andrew Carnegie*, vol. I, p. 104.
24. David Bates, *Lincoln in the Telegraph Office*, p. 22.
25. Andrew Carnegie, *Autobiography*, p. 101.
26. *Ibid.*, p. 102.
27. Joseph Frazier Wall, *Andrew Carnegie*, p. 176.

Chapter Seven

1. Burton J. Hendrick, *The Life of Andrew Carnegie*, vol. I, pp. 110–11: Letter, Altoona, 10 p.m., 26 May 1882 to George Lauder Sr.
2. Andrew Carnegie, *Autobiography*, p. 110.
3. Broomhall: Thomas Harrison's edifice of 1796–7, built for the Earls of Elgin; Fordell: a sixteenth-century castle; Donibristle: a sixteenth-century castle rebuilt in 1724, only to be destroyed by fire in 1858.
4. Andrew Carnegie, *Autobiography*, p. 111.
5. *Ibid.*, p. 112.
6. *Ibid.*
7. Burton J. Hendrick, *The Life of Andrew Carnegie*, vol. I, p. 115.
8. Andrew Carnegie, *Triumphant Democracy*, p. 454.

9. Burton J. Hendrick, *The Life of Andrew Carnegie*, vol. I, p. 116.
10. Andrew Carnegie, *Autobiography*, p. 113.
11. Burton J. Hendrick, *The Life of Andrew Carnegie*, vol. I, p. 120.
12. *Ibid.*, vol. I, p. 119. Letter to George Lauder Jr, dated Homewood, Sunday 21 June 1863.
13. *Ibid.*
14. Andrew Carnegie, *Autobiography*, p. 125.
15. Burton J. Hendrick, *The Life of Andrew Carnegie*, vol. I, pp. 123–4.
16. Joseph Frazier Wall, *Andrew Carnegie*, p. 190 and n. 75, p. 1059.
17. *Ibid.*, p. 224.
18. Andrew Carnegie, *Autobiography*, p. 141.
19. *Ibid.*, pp. 141–2.

Chapter Eight

1. Burton J. Hendrick, *The Life of Andrew Carnegie*, vol. I, p. 138.
2. Andrew Carnegie, *Autobiography*, p. 142.
3. Carnegie Travel Letters: *c.* June 1865 to Margaret and Tom Carnegie.
4. Andrew Carnegie, *Autobiography*, p. 142.
5. Burton J. Hendrick, *The Life of Andrew Carnegie*, vol. I, p. 139.
6. *Ibid.*, pp. 138 and 140.
7. *Ibid.*, p. 139.
8. Andrew Carnegie, *Autobiography*, p. 143.
9. Carnegie Travel Letters, 16 October 1865.
10. *Ibid.*, Carnegie to Margaret and Tom Carnegie, 3 December 1865.
11. *Ibid.*, Carnegie to Margaret Carnegie, 2 September 1865.

Chapter Nine

1. Andrew Carnegie, *Autobiography*, p. 149.
2. *Ibid.*, pp. 149–50.
3. *Ibid.*, p. 149.
4. Burton J. Hendrick, *The Life of Andrew Carnegie*, vol. I, p. 143.
5. *Ibid.*, p. 146.
6. *Ibid.*, pp. 146–7.
7. Andrew Carnegie, *Autobiography*, p. 150.
8. *Ibid.*, p. 154.
9. *Ibid.*
10. *Ibid.*, p. 155.
11. Joseph Frazier Wall, *Andrew Carnegie*, p. 172.

12. Andrew Carnegie, *Autobiography*, p. 157.
13. William Power, *The National Wallace Museum*, pp. 1–2.
14. Andrew Carnegie, *Autobiography*, p. 160.
15. *Ibid.*
16. Burton J. Hendrick, *The Life of Andrew Carnegie*, vol. I, pp. 230ff.
17. *Ibid.*, vol. I, p. 224.
18. Peter Krass, *Carnegie*, p. 113.
19. Andrew Carnegie, *Autobiography*, p. 170.
20. *Ibid.*, p. 174.
21. Joseph Frazier Wall, *Andrew Carnegie*, p. 316.
22. Burton J. Hendrick, *The Life of Andrew Carnegie*, vol. I, p. 215.
23. *Ibid.*
24. Andrew Carnegie, *Autobiography*, p. 210.
25. Simon Goodenough, *The Greatest Good Fortune: Andrew Carnegie's Gift for Today*, p. 28.

Chapter Ten

1. Andrew Carnegie, *Round the World*, p. 38.
2. *Ibid.*, p. 47.
3. *Ibid.*, pp. 134–5.
4. *Ibid.*, p. 273.
5. The letter appears in vol. 4 of the Andrew Carnegie papers at the Library of Congress, Washington DC.
6. Andrew Carnegie, *Autobiography*, p. 204.
7. *Ibid.*, p. 206. In fact Carnegie's *An American Four-in-hand in Britain* preceded this work in 1883.
8. Burton J. Hendrick, *The Life of Andrew Carnegie*, vol. I, p. 237.
9. Andrew Carnegie, *Autobiography*, p. 206.
10. *Ibid.*, p. 206.
11. *Ibid.*, p. 207.

Chapter Eleven

1. Burton J. Hendrick, *The Life of Andrew Carnegie*, vol. I, p. 315.
2. Burton J. Hendrick and Donald Henderson, *Louise Whitfield Carnegie*, p. 54.
3. *Ibid.*, p. 57.
4. *Ibid.*, p. 57.
5. Andrew Carnegie, *Autobiography*, p. 253.
6. Andrew Carnegie, *An American Four-in-Hand in Britain*, pp. 2–3.

7. *Ibid.*, p. 31.
8. *Ibid.*, p. 31.
9. Joseph Frazier Wall, *Andrew Carnegie*, p. 405.
10. Andrew Carnegie, *An American Four-in-Hand in Britain*, p. 89.
11. Lilian Gilchrist-Thompson, *Sidney Gilchrist-Thomas*, p. 169.
12. Andrew Carnegie, *An American Four-in-Hand in Britain*, p. 108.
13. *Ibid.*, p. 110.
14. *Ibid.*, p. 150.
15. *Ibid.*, p. 155.
16. *Ibid.*, p. 241.
17. *Ibid.*, p. 243.
18. *Ibid.*, p. 278.
19. *Ibid.*, p. 281.
20. *Ibid.*, p. 282.
21. Burton J. Hendrick, *The Life of Andrew Carnegie*, p. 236.
22. Peter Krass, *Carnegie*, pp. 161–2; he gives his source as a statement recorded by Burton J. Hendrick. John Johnston's comments come from private correspondence with the author.
23. Andrew Carnegie, *An American Four-in-Hand in Britain*, p. 295.
24. *Ibid.*, p. 334.
25. *Ibid.*, p. 337.
26. *Ibid.*, p. 338.
27. Burton J. Hendrick, *The Life of Andrew Carnegie*, p. 237.

Chapter Twelve

1. Peter Krass, *Carnegie*, p. 166.
2. Burton J. Hendrick, *The Life of Andrew Carnegie*, vol. I, p. 286.
3. Andrew Carnegie, *Autobiography*, p. 276.
4. John K. Winkler, *Incredible Carnegie*, p. 167.
5. Andrew Carnegie, *Autobiography*, p. 276.
6. *Ibid.*, p. 309; Burton J. Hendrick, *The Life of Andrew Carnegie*, vol. I, p. 256.
7. Quoted by Burton J. Hendrick, *The Life of Andrew Carnegie*, vol. I, pp. 428–9.
8. Andrew Carnegie, *Autobiography*, p. 332.
9. Joseph Frazier Wall, *Andrew Carnegie*, p. 381.
10. Andrew Carnegie, *Autobiography*, p. 336.
11. Herbert Spencer, *Autobiography*, vol. II, p. 478.
12. Burton J. Hendrick, *The Life of Andrew Carnegie*, vol. I, p. 242.
13. John Morley, Viscount Morley, *Recollections*, vol. II, p. 110.

14. Burton J. Hendrick, *The Life of Andrew Carnegie*, vol. I, p. 243.
15. *Ibid*.
16. J.B. Paul, *Eccentricities of Genius*, pp. 323–4.
17. Burton J. Hendrick, *The Life of Andrew Carnegie*, vol. I, p. 246.
18. *Letters of Matthew Arnold*, vol. II, pp. 269 and 276.
19. Burton J. Hendrick, *The Life of Andrew Carnegie*, vol. I, p. 249.
20. *Reynold's News*, 30 April 1882, p. 1.
21. Burton J. Hendrick, *The Life of Andrew Carnegie*, vol. I, p. 263.
22. Andrew Carnegie, *Autobiography*, p. 330.
23. Burton J. Hendrick, *The Life of Andrew Carnegie*, vol. I, p. 260.
24. *Ibid.*, vol. I, p. 263.
25. *Ibid.*, vol. I, pp. 263–4.
26. *Ibid.*, vol. 1, p. 265. Letter, 18 October 1884, New York.

Chapter Thirteen

1. Burton J. Hendrick and Daniel Henderson, *Louise Whitfield Carnegie*, pp. 64–5.
2. *Ibid*.
3. *Ibid.*, p. 66.
4. Joseph Frazier Wall, *Andrew Carnegie*, pp. 435–6.
5. Andrew Carnegie, *Autobiography*, p. 298.
6. Burton J. Hendrick, *The Life of Andrew Carnegie*, p. 252.
7. Joseph Frazier Wall, *Andrew Carnegie*, p. 415: Letter, 23 July 1885.
8. Joseph Frazier Wall, *Andrew Carnegie*, p. 416.
9. *Ibid.*, pp. 416–17.
10. Andrew Carnegie, *Autobiography*, p. 309.
11. *Ibid.*, p. 331.
12. *Ibid.*, p. 330.
13. Andrew Carnegie, *Triumphant Democracy*, p. 1.
14. *Ibid.*, p. 125.
15. *Ibid.*, p. 135.
16. Burton J. Hendrick, *The Life of Andrew Carnegie*, p. 273.
17. *Ibid.*, pp. 273–4.
18. *Reynold's News*, 14 September 1890, p. 1. Speech at Dundee.
19. *Letters of Matthew Arnold*, vol. II, p. 396.
20. Letter, Herbert Spencer to Andrew Carnegie, London, 18 May 1886, quoted by Burton J. Hendrick, *The Life of Andrew Carnegie*, pp. 277–8.
21. Letter, John Morley to Andrew Carnegie, London, 17 May 1886, quoted in *ibid.*, pp. 278–9.

Notes

22. Robert G. McCloskey, *American Conservatism in the Age of Enterprise*, pp. 157–8.
23. Andrew Carnegie, *Autobiography*, p. 332.
24. *Ibid.*, p. 213.
25. Burton J. Hendrick, *The Life of Andrew Carnegie*, p. 255.
26. *Ibid.*, pp. 254–5.
27. Letter, 24 November 1886.
28. Peter Krass, *Carnegie*, p. 180.

Chapter Fourteen

1. Joseph Frazier Wall, *Andrew Carnegie*, p. 420.
2. Andrew Carnegie, *Autobiography*, p. 215.
3. Margaret McNeill, *Notes on the History of Kilgraston*. The house was sold in 1930 to the Society of the Sacred Heart who developed it as a private school; from the First World War the house served as a MoD military hospital.
4. Burton J. Hendrick and Daniel Henderson, *Louise Whitfield Carnegie*, p. 105.
5. Burton J. Hendrick, *The Life of Andrew Carnegie*, vol. I, p. 266.
6. *Letters of Mrs James G. Blaine*, vol. II, pp. 156–8.
7. J.B. Thayer, *Life and Letters of John Hay*, vol. II, p. 74. Letter to Henry Adams.
8. Andrew Carnegie, *Autobiography*, p. 216.
9. Peter Krass, *Carnegie*, p. 235, quoting Louise Carnegie's letter to her mother Mrs J.W. Whitfield, 17 July 1886.
10. Andrew Carnegie, *Autobiography*, p. 217.
11. Burton J. Hendrick and Daniel Henderson, *Louise Whitfield Carnegie*, pp. 118–19.
12. Burton J. Hendrick, *The Life of Andrew Carnegie*, vol. I, pp. 326–7.
13. Letter, Andrew Carnegie to William L. Abbott, 25 July 1888.
14. Burton J. Hendrick and Daniel Henderson, *Louise Whitfield Carnegie*, pp. 123–4.
15. Burton J. Hendrick, *The Life of Andrew Carnegie*, vol. I, p. 324.
16. Burton J. Hendrick and Daniel Henderson, *Louise Whitfield Carnegie*, p. 123.
17. The Carnegies did not spend 1892 at Cluny Castle as it was being refurbished by the Macphersons. The family sold the property in 1940 and some of the historic relics that had been in the castle in Carnegie's time were donated to the clan museum at nearby Newtonmore.

18. Burton J. Hendrick, *The Life of Andrew Carnegie*, p. 316.
19. *North America Review*, June 1889. Carnegie had, prior to this, published articles and addresses on his ideas in *Macmillan's Magazine* (January 1885), *The Forum* (April 1880), and (New York) *Times* (October 1888).
20. Burton J. Hendrick, *The Life of Andrew Carnegie*, p. 330.
21. Letter, Andrew Carnegie to philanthropist Joseph G. Schmidlapp, dated New York, 30 December 1890.
22. Milton Meltzer, *The Many Lives of Andrew Carnegie*, pp. 121–2.
23. *Ibid.*, p. 121.
24. Andrew Carnegie, *Autobiography*, note on p. 255.
25. Burton J. Hendrick, *The Life of Andrew Carnegie*, vol. I, p. 355.
26. *New York Tribune*, 21 February 1890.
27. Charlie May Simon, *The Andrew Carnegie Story*, p. 190.
28. Andrew Carnegie, *Autobiography*, p. 353.

Chapter Fifteen

1. Burton J. Hendrick, *The Life of Andrew Carnegie*, vol. I, p. 366.
2. *Ibid.*
3. *Forum*: issues for April 1886 and August 1886.
4. Burton J. Hendrick, *The Life of Andrew Carnegie*, vol. I, p. 369.
5. *Ibid.*, vol. I, p. 371.
6. *Ibid.*, vol. I, p. 370.
7. John K. Winkler, *Incredible Carnegie*, p. 189.
8. Burton J. Hendrick, *The Life of Andrew Carnegie*, vol. I, p. 381.
9. *Ibid.*, vol. I, p. 388.
10. Congressional Committee: House reports, 2nd session, 52nd Congress 1892–3, vol. III, Report 2447.
11. Burton J. Hendrick, *The Life of Andrew Carnegie*, pp. 394–5.
12. See Note 10.
13. Burton J. Hendrick, *The Life of Andrew Carnegie*, vol. I, p. 398.
14. *Ibid.*
15. *Ibid.*, vol. I, p. 399.
16. *Ibid.*
17. *Ibid.*
18. John K. Winkler, *Incredible Carnegie*, p. 208.
19. *Ibid.*, cutting quoted p. 213.
20. *Ibid.*
21. John A. Fitch, *The Steel Workers*, p. 104.

Notes

22. Letter from Barmouth, 19 October 1892. Quoted by Burton J. Hendrick, *The Life of Andrew Carnegie*, vol. I, p. 410.
23. Peter Krass, *Carnegie*, p. 301.
24. John K. Winkler, *Incredible Carnegie*, p. 219.

Chapter Sixteen

1. John K. Winkler, *Incredible Carnegie*, p. 224.
2. *Ibid.*, p. 226.
3. *Ibid.*, pp. 227–8.
4. *Ibid.*, p. 229.
5. *Ibid.*, p. 233.
6. Henry Clay Frick to Andrew Carnegie, 24 December 1894. Quoted by Peter Krass, *Carnegie*, p. 317.
7. Burton J. Hendrick, *The Life of Andrew Carnegie*, vol. II, pp. 429–31. Letter, 26 December 1895.
8. *Ibid.*, vol. II, p. 432.
9. Peter Krass, *Carnegie*, p. 333.

Chapter Seventeen

1. Burton J. Hendrick and Daniel Henderson, *Louise Whitfield Carnegie*, pp. 144–5.
2. Burton J. Hendrick, *The Life of Andrew Carnegie*, vol. II, p. 170.
3. *Ibid.*
4. Joseph Frazier Wall, *Andrew Carnegie*, p. 949.
5. Andrew Carnegie, *Autobiography*, p. 217.
6. Andrew Carnegie, 'Some Important Results of the Jubilee', *North American Review*, vol. 165, October 1897, p. 506.
7. Burton J. Hendrick, *The Life of Andrew Carnegie*, p. 147.
8. Denis Stuart, *Dear Duchess: Millicent Duchess of Sutherland 1867–1955*, p. 92.
9. John Dowden, *The Bishops of Scotland*, pp. 234–5.
10. James A. Simpson, *Dornoch Cathedral*, pp. 14, 23.
11. Peter Gray, *Skibo: Its Lairds and History*; family references.
12. Joseph Frazier Wall, *Skibo*, p. 54.
13. Burton J. Hendrick and Daniel Henderson, *Louise Whitfield Carnegie*, p. 152.
14. John Connachan-Holmes, *Country Houses of Scotland*, p. 110.
15. William Calder, *The Last Country Houses*, p. 188.
16. Peter Krass, *Carnegie*, p. 443.

17. The West 51st Street home was kept on at New York for Carnegie's sister-in-law Lucy Coleman Carnegie.
18. Burton J. Hendrick and Daniel Henderson, *Louise Whitfield Carnegie*, p. 151.
19. Burton J. Hendrick, *The Life of Andrew Carnegie*, vol. II, p. 152.
20. *Ibid.*, vol. II, p. 167.
21. *Ibid.*, vol. II, p. 88.
22. *Ibid.*, vol. II, p. 152.
23. *Ibid.*, vol. II, p. 155.
24. Joseph Frazier Wall, *Andrew Carnegie*, p. 715.
25. For the fine detail and legal background of this section the following may be consulted: Joseph Frazier Wall, *Andrew Carnegie*, ch. XIX, pp. 714ff; Burton J. Hendrick, *The Life of Andrew Carnegie*, vol. II, ch. 4, pp. 89ff; Peter Krass, *Carnegie*, ch. 27, pp. 380ff.
26. Peter Krass, *Carnegie*, pp. 395, 571.
27. Simon Goodenough, *The Greatest Good Fortune: Andrew Carnegie's Gift for Today*, p. 35.
28. Burton J. Hendrick, *The Life of Andrew Carnegie*, vol. II, pp. 138–9.

Chapter Eighteen

1. Andrew Carnegie, *Autobiography*, Preface, p. v.
2. Simon Goodenough, *The Greatest Good Fortune: Andrew Carnegie's Gift for Today*, p. 261.
3. Andrew Carnegie, *Autobiography*, p. 295.
4. *Review of Reviews*, London, vol. 23, April 1901, p. 344.
5. Simon Goodenough, *The Greatest Good Fortune: Andrew Carnegie's Gift for Today*, p. 259.
6. *Ibid.*, pp. 67–79.
7. *Sea-breeze* was requisitioned by the MoD during the First World War and was subsequently broken up.
8. Peter Krass, *Carnegie*, p. 403: Letter, 10 October 1900.
9. Burton J. Hendrick, *The Life of Andrew Carnegie*, vol. II, p. 217.
10. *Ibid.*, vol. II, pp. 218–19: Letter, 21 May 1901.
11. Simon Goodenough, *The Greatest Good Fortune: Andrew Carnegie's Gift for Today*, p. 80.
12. Andrew Carnegie, *Autobiography*, p. 272.
13. *Ibid.*, p. 271.
14. Raymond Lamont-Brown, *The Life and Times of St Andrews*, pp. 92–4.

15. *Ibid.*, pp. 96–8.
16. Burton J. Hendrick (ed.), *Miscellaneous Writings of Andrew Carnegie*, vol. II, pp. 291–319.
17. *Ibid.*, vol. I, pp. 78–125.
18. R.G. Cant, *The University of St Andrews*, p. 133.
19. Douglas Young, *St Andrews: Town and Gown, Royal and Ancient*, p. 258.
20. *Ibid.*
21. *Ibid.*
22. Greg P. Twiss and Paul Chennell, *Famous Rectors of St Andrews*, pp. 67–8.
23. Andrew Carnegie, *Autobiography*, pp. 272–3.
24. Burton J. Hendrick, *The Life of Andrew Carnegie*, vol. II, p. 258.
25. *Ibid.*, vol. II, pp. 258–9: Letter, 22 December 1901.
26. *Council Minutes*, Royal Burgh of Perth, 8 October 1902: Files, A.K. Bell Library, Perth, Scotland.
27. Revd T.R.S. Campbell, *A Short History of the Bonnetmaker Craft*, pp. 6, 12.
28. Burton J. Hendrick, *The Life of Andrew Carnegie*, vol. II, p. 172.
29. Simon Goodenough, *The Greatest Good Fortune: Andrew Carnegie's Gift for Today*, p. 53.
30. Linda Thorell Hills (ed.), *Margaret Carnegie Miller: Her Journals*, pp. 2–3.
31. Anthony Allfrey, *Edward VII and his Jewish Court*, p. 94.
32. Burton J. Hendrick, *The Life of Andrew Carnegie*, vol. II, p. 174.
33. Andrew Carnegie, *Autobiography*, pp. 264–5.
34. Sir Harry Lauder, *Roamin' in the Gloamin'*, pp. 264–5.

Chapter Nineteen

1. Simon Goodenough, *The Greatest Good Fortune: Andrew Carnegie's Gift for Today*, p. 215.
2. *Ibid.*, p. 226.
3. *Ibid.*, p. 214.
4. John K. Winkler, *Incredible Carnegie: The Life of Andrew Carnegie 1835–1919*, pp. 281–2.
5. Simon Goodenough, *The Greatest Good Fortune: Andrew Carnegie's Gift for Today*, p. 237.
6. *Ibid.*, p. 253.
7. Andrew Carnegie, *League of Peace*, p. 1.
8. *Ibid.*, p. 2.

9. *Ibid.*, p. 33.
10. *Ibid.*, p. 43.
11. *Ibid.*, p. 47.
12. Peter Krass, *Carnegie*, p. 467.
13. Andrew Carnegie, *Autobiography*, pp. 366–8.
14. *Ibid.*, pp. 369–70.
15. Peter Krass, *Carnegie*, p. 476.
16. *Ibid.*, p. 481.
17. *Ibid.*, 488.
18. *Ibid.*, p. 490.
19. Linda Thorell Hills (ed.), *Margaret Carnegie Miller: Her Journals*, pp. 10–11.
20. Peter Krass, *Carnegie*, pp. 460–1.
21. *Ibid.*, p. 499.
22. *Ibid.*, p. 514.
23. Burton J. Hendrick and Daniel Henderson, *Louise Whitfield Carnegie*, p. 181.
24. Burton J. Hendrick, *The Life of Andrew Carnegie*, vol. II, p. 345.
25. *Ibid.*, vol. II, p. 346.
26. Andrew Carnegie, *Autobiography*, pp. 371–2.
27. Burton J. Hendrick, *The Life of Andrew Carnegie*, vol. II, p. 347.
28. *The Times*, 23 August 1914.

Chapter Twenty

1. Burton J. Hendrick, *The Life of Andrew Carnegie*, vol. II, p. 349.
2. *Ibid.*, vol. II, p. 356.
3. *Ibid.*, vol. II, p. 355.
4. *Ibid.*
5. *Ibid.*, vol. II, p. 359. Jean Armour Burns Brown was the granddaughter of Robert Burns's son Robert.
6. *Ibid.*, vol. II, p. 360.
7. Peter Krass, *Carnegie*, p. 535.
8. *Ibid.*, p. 536.
9. Burton J. Hendrick, *The Life of Andrew Carnegie*, vol. II, pp. 381 and 382.
10. *Ibid.*, vol. II, p. 383.
11. *Ibid.*
12. *Ibid.*, vol. II, p. 384.
13. Joseph Frazier Wall, *Andrew Carnegie*, p. 1035; quoting letter, 21 Janaury 1918.

Notes

14. *Ibid.*, p. 1040; quoting letter, August 1919.
15. Louise Carnegie to Hew Morrison from 2 East 91st Street, New York. Skibo Castle Collection.
16. Quoted by Burton J. Hendrick, *The Life of Andrew Carnegie*, vol. II, p. 385.
17. *Literary Digest*, vol. 32, 30 August 1919, p. 42.

Epilogue

1. It was Andrew Carnegie's daughter Margaret who decried her father's 'Santa Claus' role; when Burton J. Hendrick was commissioned to write Carnegie's biography for publication in 1932 she asked him to write about Carnegie the man not about his philanthropy.
2. J.P. Morgan is considered to have been the first to describe Carnegie as 'the richest man in the world'. Burton J. Hendrick, *The Life of Andrew Carnegie*, vol. II, p. 139.
3. Andrew Carnegie, *Autobiography*, p. 3.
4. *Ibid.*, p. 33.
5. *Ibid.*, pp. 89–90.
6. Herbert Spencer, *Social Statics*.
7. Burton J. Hendrick, *The Life of Andrew Carnegie*, vol. II, p. 270.
8. Peter Krass, *Carnegie*, p. 121.

BIBLIOGRAPHY

Andrew Carnegie Papers and Letters

239 volumes of relevant papers are held at the Library of Congress, Washington DC.

Carnegie Autograph Collection, New York Public Library, New York.

Carnegie Steel Company Records, Historical Society of Western Pennsylvania, Pittsburgh, Pennsylvania.

Annandale Archives, Pennsylvania.

Carnegie Birthplace Museum, Dunfermline, Scotland.

Private archives of the Carnegie-Miller families.

Works by Andrew Carnegie

Andrew Carnegie wrote a dozen main books, several pamphlets and dozens of articles on various subjects. These are the major works referred to in the text:

Our Coaching Trip: Brighton to Inverness, circulated privately, New York, 1882.

An American Four-in-Hand in Britain, Charles Scribner's Sons, New York, 1883.

Round the World, Charles Scribner's Sons, New York, 1884.

Triumphant Democracy, Charles Scribner's Sons, New York, 1886.

The Gospel of Wealth and Other Timely Essays, The Century Co., New York, 1900.

League of Peace: A Rectorial Address Delivered in the University of St Andrews, 17th October 1905, Ginn & Co., Boston, 1906.

Autobiography, Houghton Mifflin Co., Boston/Constable & Co. Ltd, 1920.

Burton J. Hendrick (ed.), *Miscellaneous Writings of Andrew Carnegie*, New York, 1923.

Bibliography

Works on Andrew Carnegie

Andrew Carnegie's first biographer was Burton J. Hendrick, who spent five years compiling his two-volume edition of *The Life of Andrew Carnegie*, published by Doubleday, Doran & Co. Inc., New York, 1932. The whole, including a salary for Hendrick, was funded by Louise Carnegie.

Margaret Carnegie paid for Hendrick to write a biography of her mother, *Louise Whitfield Carnegie*, Hastings House, New York, 1950. The project was completed by Daniel Henderson after Hendrick's death.

Goodenough, Simon, *The Greatest Good Fortune: Andrew Carnegie's Gift for Today*, Macdonald Publishers, Edinburgh, 1985.

Harlow, Alvin F., *Andrew Carnegie*, Kingston House, Chicago, 1959.

Judson, Clara Ingram, *Andrew Carnegie*, Follet Publishing Co., Chicago, 1964.

Krass, Peter, *Carnegie*, John Wiley and Sons Inc, 2002

Livesay, Harold C., *Andrew Carnegie and the Rise of Big Business*, Little, Brown, Boston, 1975.

Mackie, James B., *Andrew Carnegie: His Dunfermline Ties and Benefactions*, Dunfermline, 1916.

Meltzer, Milton, *The Many Lives of Andrew Carnegie*, Franklin Watts/Grolier Publishing, New York, 1997.

Root, Elihu, *Andrew Carnegie 1835–1919*, New York, 1920.

Schwab, Charles M., *Andrew Carnegie, His Methods with His Men*, Pittsburgh, 1919.

Simon, Charlie May, *The Andrew Carnegie Story*, E.P. Dutton & Co. Inc., New York, 1965.

Swetnam, George, *Andrew Carnegie*, Twayne, Boston, 1980.

Wall, Joseph Frazier, *Andrew Carnegie*, University of Pittsburgh Press/Oxford University Press, 1970 and 1989.

——, *Skibo: The Story of the Scottish Estate of Andrew Carnegie, from its Celtic origins to the present day*, Oxford University Press, New York/Oxford 1984.

Winkler, John K., *Incredible Carnegie: The Life of Andrew Carnegie 1835–1919*, The Vanguard Press, New York, 1931.

Other Works

Arnold, Matthew, *Letters of Matthew Arnold*, London and New York, 1900.

Bates, David Homer, *Lincoln in the Telegraph Office*, New York, 1907.

Blaine, Mrs James, *Letters of Mrs James Blaine*, New York, n.d.

Calder, William, *The Last Country Houses*, London, n.d.

Campbell, Revd T.R.S., *A Short History of the Bonnetmaker Craft of Dundee*, Nine Incorporated Trades, Dundee, 1987.

Cant, Ronald G., *The University of St Andrews*, Scottish Academic Press, Edinburgh, 1970.

Carrothers, W.A. *Emigration from the British Isles*, London, 1929.

Chalmers, Peter, *Historical and Statistical Account of Dunfermline*, Edinburgh, 1844.

Connachan-Holmes, J.R.A., *Country Houses in Scotland*, House of Lochar, Argyll, 1995.

Dowden, John, *The Bishops of Scotland*, James Maclehose, Glasgow, 1912.

Elgin Castle Cashbook.

Elgin, Lady Martha, *Household Account Book*, privately printed, n.d.

Fitch, John A., *The Steel Workers*, University of Pittsburgh Press, 1989.

Frazer, Sir William, *History of the Carnegies, Earls of Southesk and their Kindred*, Edinburgh, 1867.

Gilchrist-Thompson, M., *Sidney Gilchrist-Thomas*, London, 1940.

Gray, Peter, *Skibo: Its Lairds and History*, Oliphant, Anderson & Ferrier, Edinburgh, 1906.

Helps, Arthur (ed.), *Leaves from the Journal of Our Life in the Highlands from 1848–1861*, Smith, Elder & Co., 1868.

Hills, Linda Thorell (ed.), *Margaret Carnegie Miller: Her Journals*, privately printed in USA, 2000.

Lamont-Brown, Raymond, *Discovering Fife*, John Donald, Edinburgh 1988.

——, *The Life and Times of St Andrews*, John Donald, Edinburgh, 1989.

——, *Fife in History and Legend*, Birlinn, Edinburgh, 2003.

Lauder, Sir Harry, *Roamin' in the Gloamin'*, Hutchinson, 1928.

McCloskey, Robert G., *American Conservatism in the Age of Enterprise*, New York, n.d.

Miller, A.H., *Fife: Pictorial and Historical*, A. Westwood & Son, Cupar, Fife, 1895.

Morley, Viscount John, *Recollections*, New York and London, 1919.

Paul, J.B., *Eccentrics of Genius*, New York, n.d.

Power, William, *The National Wallace Museum*, Stirling Town Council, n.d. 1867–1955, Victor Gollancz Ltd, 1982.

Rait, R. and Pride, G.S., *Scotland*, Edinburgh, n.d.

Bibliography

Reid, James A., *The Telegraph in America*, New York, 1879.

Simpson, Eric, *The Auld Grey Toun: Dunfermline in the Time of Andrew Carnegie 1835–1919*, Carnegie Dunfermline Trust, 1997.

Simpson, James A., *Dornoch Cathedral*, Dornoch, 1978.

Sinclair, Sir John, *The Statistical Account of Scotland: Counties of Fife & Kinross*, 1845.

Spencer, Herbert, *Principles of Sociology*, London, 1879–96.

Stuart, Dennis, *Dear Duchess: Millicent Duchess of Sutherland*, Gollancz, 1982.

Young, Douglas, *St Andrews Town & Gown Royal & Ancient*, Cassell, 1969.

INDEX

Index